War in the Media Age

The Hampton Press Communication Series
Political Communication
David L. Paletz, Editor

Eastern European Journalism
Jerome Aumente, Peter Gross, Ray Hiebert, Owen Johnson, and Dean Mills

The In/Outsiders: The Mass Media in Israel
Dan Caspi and Yehiel Limor

Eden Online: Re-inventing Humanity in a Technological Universe
Lisa St. Clair Harvey

Media Entrepreneurs and the Media Enterprise in the United States Congress: Influencing Policy in the Washington Community
Karen M. Kedrowski

The Politics of Disenchantment: Bush, Clinton, Perot, and the Press
James Lemert, William R. Elliot, William L. Rosenberg, and James M. Bernstein

Mediated Women: Representations in Popular Culture
Marian Meyers (ed.)

Political Communication in Action: States, Institutions, Movements, Audiences
David L. Paletz (ed.)

Glasnost and After: Media and Change in Central and Eastern Europe
David L. Paletz, Karol Jakubowicz, and Pavao Novosel (eds.)

Germany's "Unity Election": Voters and the Media
Holli A. Semetko and Klaus Schoenbach

Gender, Politics and Communication
Annabelle Sreberny and Liesbet van Zoonen (eds.)

Strategic Failures in the Modern Presidency
Mary E. Stuckey

War in the Media Age
A. Trevor Thrall

forthcoming

Civic Dialogue in the 1996 Presidential Campaign
Lynda Lee Kaid, Mitchell S. McKinney, and John C. Tedesco

Business as Usual: Continuity and Change in Central and Eastern European Media
David L. Paletz and Karol Jakubowicz (eds.)

War in the Media Age

A. Trevor Thrall
Michigan Virtual University

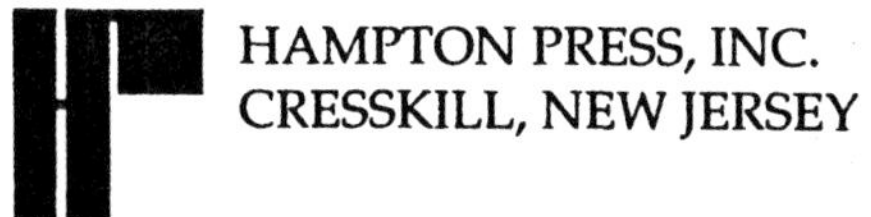

Printed in the United States of America

Library of Congress Cataloging-in-Publication Data

Thrall, Trevor A.
War in the media age / A. Trevor Thrall.
p. cm. -- (The Hampton Press communication series. Political communication)
Includes bibliographic references and indexes.
ISBN 1-57273-246-6 (cloth) -- ISBN 1-57273-247-7 (pbk.)
1. Mass media and war--United States. 2. Government and the press--United States. I. Title. II. Series.

P96.W352 U558 2000
070.4'4935502'0973--dc21

00-024644

Hampton Press, Inc.
23 Broadway
Cresskill, NJ 07626

Contents

1

Introduction

In August 1990 President Bush committed the United States to pushing back Iraq's invasion of Kuwait, eventually sending over 500,000 troops to Saudi Arabia to draw a "line in the sand." Mindful of public opinion, Bush promised repeatedly that the situation in the Persian Gulf would not become "another Vietnam."[1] He was correct on at least two levels. This time, of course, the U.S. military destroyed its opponent in an unprecedented show of mastery on the modern battlefield. In addition, Bush and the military defeated the press, severely limiting journalists' access to the battlefield while providing their own images and reports for public consumption.

A brief comparison reveals that the government's Gulf War press policies were far more aggressive and restrictive than those of the Vietnam era. First, military public affairs policies, those that most directly influence and limit journalists' conduct on and access to the battlefield, did far more to obstruct newsgathering in the Gulf than in Vietnam. During the Vietnam War journalists could move about the countryside at will either by themselves or by military transport. During Desert Storm, however, not only were the numbers of journalists allowed to visit military units sharply limited, the military also dictated when and where they could go. During Vietnam journalists operated without military supervision; in the Gulf the military assigned public affairs officers to accompany journalists wherever they went, a policy that the press felt obstructed its newsgathering efforts. And finally, during Vietnam journalists abided by voluntary guidelines concerning what information could be published. There was no censorship; the military did not see news reports before they appeared in the paper or on television. In the Gulf, however, news stories were subject to "security review;" military officers reviewed all news before it was published.

White House public relations in Vietnam and the Gulf War differed in the same way. White House public relations strategy during Vietnam tended to be reactive; it operated primarily to help the government recover from negative reports and unanticipated events. As a result, the White House often failed to influence the manner in which events were interpreted and reported by the press. Gulf War public relations strategy, however, was extremely proactive. The White House and the military seized the initiative in the battle to determine the images and information the media would relay to the public. The result was that the president and the military framed the debate, set the public agenda, supplied television with many of the defining images of the war, and enjoyed very favorable press coverage throughout the conflict. The success of the government's Gulf War press strategy and policy represented the modern peak of government control of the press in wartime, and perpetuated a trend that began with the U.S .invasion of Grenada in 1983.

This book seeks to explain this dramatic change and its consequences by illustrating how the rising importance of the press in everyday political life has compelled presidents to change their strategies for dealing with the media during war and also encouraged them, as have political and military lessons from Vietnam, to alter their approach to waging war more generally. To do so it traces the evolution and implementation of government press strategy from Vietnam through the Gulf War. In so doing, this book challenges the popular existing explanation for the rise of modern press restrictions and amends the history of recent wartime government/press relations which the conventional wisdom has skewed, relocating the subject of wartime press policy and public relations within the broader arena of government/press relations and American politics where it belongs. This book also aims to provide the reader with a thorough grounding in the history of recent government/press relations during conflict, and in the mechanics of how presidents, the military, and the press do their jobs during war.

THE GROWTH OF PRESS CONTROLS AND THE CONVENTIONAL WISDOM

Despite the fact that government/press relations during war have always stirred debate, especially recently, little scholarly work has focused on understanding the dynamics of their evolution. Folk theory and anecdotal explanations thus dominate the debate. The conventional wisdom for why military press controls have become so restrictive arises primarily from the writings of those journalists and military officers who have been involved in recent conflicts. They have tended to develop their arguments, however, without correcting for their professional biases, often basing them on impressionistic reviews of history or narrow personal experience. In addition, they have focused more often on professional issues surrounding how they go about their tasks than on broader explanations for their actions. Thus, though valuable for understanding the military/media relationship and documenting their interactions, these writings have not provided explanations for the growth of press controls grounded in careful historical research or thorough analysis of the issues. The result of their dominance of the debate is that press controls during war are seen as a consequence purely of military/media tensions, mutual dislike, and mutual misunderstanding. Though these points all have merit, they provide far too narrow a basis for understanding what has been happening.

Academics have not gone much further in analyzing the evolution of government/press relations during war. Scholars have tended to focus either on normative discussions of the proper role of the press during war or on historical descriptions of military and press behavior in particular conflicts. Thus, there exist several accounts of Vietnam military/media relations, such as William Hammond's excellent account of Army public affairs. The U.S. invasions of Grenada and Panama spurred fewer such studies, but are well documented nonetheless. And the Gulf War prompted an avalanche of discussion and opinion about public relations and military press policies. Many insightful analyses of press coverage and its impact have also been done, such as Daniel Hallin's superb study of the media in Vietnam and Peter Braestrup's thorough analysis of press coverage of the Tet Offensive.

No study, however, has attempted to link the government's handling of the press in each conflict with a single theoretical thread. Nor has anyone considered the government's wartime dealings with the press to be influenced by more fundamental themes and forces at work in American politics, particularly by critical changes in the nature and role of the news media in politics over time. Thus, even though the history of individual cases has been thoroughly documented, the result has been a distortion of the broader historical record and an inability to explain satisfactorily the rise of press controls and wartime public relations since Vietnam and their significance.

The most popular explanation for the evolution of wartime press policy revolves around the military's experience in Vietnam. Since then, almost all have argued, policies restricting press freedoms have stemmed from the military's bitter experience with the press in Vietnam. The conventional wisdom argues that military leaders, convinced that the press had turned the public against the war through distorted and sensationalized reporting and by beaming the horrors of war into living rooms each night, planned to ensure that the press would never again roam free on the battlefield. Beginning with the 1983 invasion of Grenada, the explanation continues, the military polished its techniques for restricting the press, finally perfecting them during the Gulf War.[2]

New York Times military reporter Drew Middleton was among the first to popularize this explanation when he wrote after Grenada:

> The majors and commanders of the Vietnam War who believed the media had worked against the American command there had become influential generals and admirals determined not to expose the Grenada operation to what they continue to view as a hostile adversary.[3]

The conventional wisdom remained unchanged in the wake of the invasion of Panama, which many journalists and other observers saw as a rerun of Grenada. *Time* magazine's Stanley Cloud argued that

> But two weeks ago, when U.S. Marines and Rangers led the charge into Panama as part of Operation Just Cause, not a single journalist accompanied them. . . . Responsibility for that failure lies with the military.[4]

And in the wake of the Gulf War it emerged once again, refreshed. Philip Taylor's observation in his book *War and the Media* represents perfectly almost all of the commentary on the issue after the war and illustrates the longevity of the "Vietnam revenge theory":

> Vietnam may be widely regarded as having been the 'first television war'—although strictly speaking the Korean War more accurately deserves that description—but television was widely blamed for having alienated American public sympathy and support for that later conflict. Regardless of the rights and wrongs of this thesis (and there is much to question in it), it dominated military public relations planning—in other countries as well as the United States–in wars fought since the 1960s.[5]

Despite their many flaws such explanations have enjoyed near unanimous support from those who have written and spoken on the problem for almost fifteen years.

WAR IN THE MEDIA AGE: AN ALTERNATIVE EXPLANATION

This book refutes the conventional wisdom. The White House, not the military, is in fact primarily responsible for the growth of press controls. By focusing so heavily on the military and its tensions with the media the conventional wisdom largely ignores the critical changes in the American political system that have in fact driven changes in press policy and thus also obscure the broader issues such changes raise. Changing government strategies for dealing with the press during war are a critical element of the new political-military strategy presidents have adopted to wage war since Vietnam. Presidents of the post-Vietnam period have broken with traditional American political-military strategy for waging war and replaced it with one that reflects widely accepted beliefs about the military inadequacy and political dangers of the previous approach; dangers which, I will argue, have only increased as a result of the rapid growth of press power since Vietnam.

To understand this shift, one need only contrast the Vietnam War with the Gulf war again. During Vietnam the U.S. government followed a course of gradually escalating the conflict, attempted repeatedly to strike deals with the enemy by promising to halt U.S. air strikes if North Vietnam agreed to peace negotiations, suffered over 50,000 dead and many more wounded, and dragged the conflict out until public opinion, which had been supportive for years, finally ensured that a U.S. withdrawal was the only policy a president could follow.[6] During the Gulf War, on the other hand, the U.S. combined a massive bombing campaign with an overwhelming ground strike to destroy the enemy's capability to wage war and force a quick end to the conflict with minimal U.S. and allied casualties on terms dictated by the coalition.[7] The old strategy of gradualism has been replaced by one which emphasizes overwhelming firepower, speed, minimizing U.S. casualties, and minimizing the length of time the public is required to support a conflict. It also stresses that the president and military must have the support of the American people behind them before they consider taking military action, and that a quick victory is the best way to maintain that support. At the core of this new political-military strategy, as noted, is the new, more aggressive news management strategy employed so successfully in the Gulf War.

These new military and media strategies have emerged as presidents have adapted to the rising importance of the press in the American political system since Vietnam. I argue that it is the White House that has in essence learned and acted upon the lessons of Vietnam and presidents who now respond to new dangers and opportunities in the changed political environment. Specifically, presidents and their advisors have responded to two consequences of the fact that the media now play a more central and decisive role in American politics than at any time in the past. On one hand, they are responding to what they perceive to be growing certainty that the media, if left to their own devices, will turn public opinion against even those conflicts that initially draw great support. This fear has led to the first prong of the new media strategy: more aggressive press restrictions to ensure that journalists have as little opportunity to cover combat as possible. On the other hand, presidents have also taken advantage of the fact that just as the press has more power to hurt them, that same power, when turned around, now provides an even greater tool for pursuing their political goals before, during, and after war. Presidents believe that if they dominate the messages reaching the public through the media they will be more likely to win support for both their war policies and themselves. This belief has led to the second prong of the strategy: more intense and more sophisticated public relations efforts to complement the press restrictions.

Implications of the Media Age Argument

Why should we care about whether the White House tries to restrict press access to the battlefield while providing the public with its own version of events? What is at stake? As Chapter Three will discuss in greater detail, many observers agree with presidents that the media pose a serious risk to presidential foreign policies and the success of American military campaigns. Only if presidents are able to keep journalists and hypernegative press coverage in check, they believe, will the public be able to support a military conflict, thereby allowing presidents to pursue the national interest. Others, however, believe quite the opposite, that excess presidential control over the media during war poses risks of its own. Without a truly free press during war, they argue, the president may gain too much control over what the public learns about the causes, character, and consequences of the battles fought in its name. The result will be that the government will report only its successes, giving presidents the power to build and maintain public support for their actions even when they are based on dubious premises.

These concerns highlight the importance of the argument that the White House and civilian officials, rather than the military, are primarily responsible for the growth of recent press restrictions during war. Although the military may itself find many reasons to seek restrictions, from worries over operational security to a desire to gain public approval, the military does not occupy the central position in American political life that the president does. A military that does not like journalists is normal and the consequences of military-driven restrictions are limited to times of war. But a president seeking to restrict the press coverage of war may not only threaten the unique bond between the public and its highest elected official but certainly threatens the everyday working relationship between the White House and the press. This relationship, once poisoned during war, will not be easily repaired; president/press tensions may have long lasting negative consequences for politics and the policy process. Many would agree that the United States still suffers from the breakdown of mutual trust and understanding that resulted from presidential battles with the press during the Vietnam/Watergate era a generation ago.

This work should also prove a resource for those interested in understanding the relationship between political communication and public opinion. This is not a theoretical work on public opinion, but it is a study of government officials acting on their beliefs about public opinion and its relation to war and press coverage of war. It is thus an analysis of institutional responses to the practical dilemmas of building public support and preventing the media from destroying that support. This work in a sense picks up where quantitative analyses such as John Mueller's *War, Presidents, and Public Opinion* leave off. Having identified connections between war and opinion, one begs the question: how does knowledge of their existence change the way people think and act during war? Can anything be done to alter the relationship between war and opinion? Can a president escape disapproval for an unpopular war? By looking at presidential attempts to do something about the situation Mueller's work revealed, this work offers an indirect test of Mueller's work. If presidents can change the connection between casualties and opinion through public relations and press restrictions in spite of Mueller's claims, we have discovered something of both practical and theoretical significance. If they cannot, Mueller's insistence that the media have little to do with the deterioration of public support for war will be bolstered.

In addition to concerns about how the public will react to press coverage of war, we must also consider what such an emphasis on public opinion and news management may have on the nature and quality of presidential actions and decisions. Have presidents become concerned with the potential negative impact of press coverage to the point where their fears have degraded the decision making process during time of crisis? Do presidents now choose policy options in times of armed conflict more on the basis of how they will play in the media than on their moral, legal, and practical consequences?

Finally, the new White House press strategy reflects the nature of the broader government/press relationship today. The state of that relationship has fundamental implications for every branch of politics and policy both in the short and long term. In particular we need to know how well the press fulfills its obligations in a democratic system. Does the press function as a watchdog on government, informing the public about the work of its officials and keeping the government honest, thereby fulfilling its democratic function as foreseen by the framers? Is the press too critical of government, disrupting policy, destroying careers, and endangering U.S. interests with negative and sensational coverage? Or does the press serve to promote official views by relying heavily on government officials for information and news, thereby choking off public debate on important issues and marginalizing political opposition to entrenched power? Unsurprisingly, these competing images of the press are accompanied by competing beliefs about what role the press should play, and what a journalist's relationship with officials should be. Should the press criticize government as much as it does, or should it defer more to the wisdom of officials who have the ultimate responsibility for making policy and running government? Does the press enhance or stifle democracy through its reporting practices?

This work provides ammunition to those involved in this debate through detailed analysis of the government/press struggle. By asking the appropriate questions, we can determine which of the competing views of the press seems to best describe the wartime situation. Did the press provide the public with an independent analysis of crisis and war? Did government pronouncements and views dominate debate and press coverage? Did press coverage marginalize political opposition? Did press coverage disrupt policymaking or threaten the ability of the United States to prosecute war successfully?

METHODS

This book documents the impact of rising media power on government strategy for dealing with the press during war by tracing the interactions among the White House, military, and press from Vietnam through the U.S. invasions of Grenada and Panama and finally to the Gulf War. Each case study relies on three complementary strands of analysis to build the argument. First, each examines how the White House sought to use press restrictions and public relations to control the information reaching the public and thereby manage the relationship between war and public opinion. Among the questions addressed in this vein are: To what extent did the White House determine the shape and implementation of battlefield press restrictions and to what extent did the White House seek to control the information that reached the public through the media? What factors shaped the White House public relations strategy? How did press restrictions aid the White House in its efforts to use public relations effectively? How successful were presidents in using the media to their advantage and why?

Second, each case illustrates the military side of the development and execution of "public affairs policy," the actual guidelines that the military enforces and that journalists must follow to report from the war zone. How has military public affairs policy evolved since Vietnam? Did the military in fact hatch plans ahead of time to ensure that the press would never again roam free on the battlefield? Does the conventional wisdom accurately explain the military's public affairs performance during recent conflicts? A close analysis of the historical record shows that in fact the military has not been responsible for the government's new media strategy. We then ask what exactly the military's role has been as it has implemented press policies during war and carried out the commands of its political leaders.

Third, the case studies analyze both how the government's restrictions on the press and public relations offensives influenced the gathering and reporting of news during these conflicts and how the press responded in the wake of its wartime performances. The two central questions to be asked here are first, did government restrictions seriously hamper news gathering efforts and second, did restrictions substantially alter the nature of press coverage from what it would have been without restrictions? With what consequences?

To build my argument I rely on four principal sources of information. Of greatest value are the firsthand accounts of those journalists, military officers, and civilian officials involved and several secondary historical works that rely heavily on interviews with them. These works help to bring into focus how the government/press relationship looked, especially at the ground level, to those who had to make the White House media strategy work and to those who had to work around it. I should note briefly that I chose not to do additional interviews with the officials who were involved with recent conflicts and press policy. My rationale for this is that I wanted to preserve my independence of judgment. The issues raised by government control of the press as well as the role of press during war more generally are extremely volatile and carry a good deal of political baggage. It is dangerous for any public official to admit publicly that he or she thought that restricting the press was a good idea, even for national security reasons. And it certainly would be suicide to admit that one had sought control over the press during war to advance presidential political goals. It should not be surprising, then, that officials have not said a great deal in public about their roles in creating and imposing restrictions on the press. And were I to have asked questions and received less than fully revealing answers along these lines my analysis would have suffered as a consequence. I have chosen instead to build my case using other resources. I note where the absence of more direct information has limited my analysis. Given the nature of my arguments and other resources, however, I believe the impact to be minimal.

The second main source of information is the scattering of government documents that offer valuable insight into government press policy planning, especially for the Persian Gulf period. Unfortunately many potentially useful documents, such as National Security Council minutes or Joint Staff planning materials, are classified and will remain so for quite some time.

Third, I have plundered the scholarly literature on the government/press relationship and the role of the press in American politics. One of the most important conclusions to emerge from this study is the extent to which the press has permeated all government decision making and shapes every political action taken. Just as the press has changed the face of political life on an everyday basis, so has it begun to change the way America wages war. Tying this study into broader academic debates about the role of the press in politics adds to those debates and strengthens the study itself.

The final resource is the journalistic product itself, along with works that analyzed or described various elements of press coverage of the cases under study here. Although, as I discuss at greater length in Chapter Three, I do not undertake any content analysis of press coverage in this work, I do make some general claims about press coverage of critical aspects of the conflicts. Where I do so I reference enough press coverage and/or academic studies to allow qualitative, though not quantitative conclusions.

Taken together, the case studies provide powerful evidence that the growth of media power has prompted widescale, politically potent, and probably irreversible changes in the way presidents approach war and in the way they deal with the press during war. The cases also raise a host of other issues tangential to the central focus of this work that involve heated debates in other corners of academia.

Outline of the Book

Chapter Two provides an historical baseline for interpreting the evolution of government press strategy through an analysis of the government's press policy and public relations efforts during the Vietnam War. It was in part the dismal failure of these policies, at least in official eyes, that helped point future White Houses in a new direction. Chapter

Three then describes in detail why presidential respect for and fear of media power have increased in the wake of Vietnam and how this has encouraged the White House to seek to impose tighter controls on the press and on information during war since then. Chapter Four begins the historical case against the conventional wisdom with the U.S. invasion of Grenada in 1983. In addition to providing the first post-Vietnam combat test for the military, Grenada marked the beginning of the trend toward growing press restrictions and public relations during war. This chapter challenges the conventional wisdom with a discussion of what really happened in military public affairs planning after 1973 and explains the often overlooked significance of post-Grenada changes in military public affairs. Chapter Five investigates the 1990 U.S. invasion of Panama and the first test of the new public affairs policy featuring the Department of Defense National News Media Pool. This chapter focuses on the failure of the pool to fulfill its intended mission due to civilian pressures and the ineffective attempt by the Joint Chiefs of Staff to ensure its proper functioning in the future. Chapter Six analyzes the Gulf War, the modern peak of government control over the press and the ultimate example to date of the use of public relations to bolster a political-military strategy. Chapter Seven, finally, offers concluding observations and predictions of where government press strategy is headed in the future.

ENDNOTES

1. George Bush's televised speech to the nation, January 16, 1991.
2. The list of authors who have propagated this conventional wisdom is long. I have taken the liberty of condensing their arguments and observations into a more coherent whole than is available in any one source. Although no one has rigorously analyzed this conventional wisdom, many authors accept it as fact, and thus spend little time outlining it in detail. Those who make this argument in at least some form include: James Brown, "Media Access to the Battlefield," *Military Review*, July, 1992; Patricia Axelrod, "Operation Desert Sham," *Penthouse*, 1992; William Boot, "The Press Stands Alone," *Columbia Journalism Review*, March/April 1992; Marie Gottschalk, "Operation Desert Cloud: The Media and the Gulf War," *World Policy Journal*, Vol. 9, No. 3, Summer 1992; Debbie Nathan, "Just the Good News Please," *The Progressive*, February 1991, pp. 25-27; Sydney H. Schanberg, "Censoring for Political Security," *Washington Journalism Review*, March 1991; Walter Cronkite, "What Is There to Hide?" in Micah L. Sifry and Cristopher Cerf, eds., *The Gulf War Reader: History, Documents,*

Opinion (New York: Times Books, 1991); John J. Fialka, *Hotel Warriors: Covering the Gulf War* (Washington: Woodrow Wilson Center, 1992); Donovan and Scherer, *The Unsilent Revolution: Television News and American Public Life* (New York: Cambridge University Press, 1992); Wayne P. Hughes, "Guarding the First Amendment–for and from the Press," *Naval War College Review*, May 1984; Carlyle A. Thayer, "Vietnam: A Critical Analysis," in *Defense and Media in Time of Limited War* (Portland, OR: Frank Cass, 1992); *Sharkey, Under Fire: Military Restrictions on the Press from Grenada to the Gulf* (Washington, D.C.: Center for Public Integrity, 1991).

3. Drew Middleton, "The Military and the Media: Barring the Press from the Battlefield," *New York Times Magazine*, February 5, 1984.
4. Stanley W. Cloud, "How Reporters Missed the War," *Time*, January 8, 1990.
5. Philip Taylor, *War and the Media: Propaganda and Persuasion in the Gulf War* (New York: Manchester University Press, 1992), p. 2.
6. On Vietnam strategy and history, see Herring, *America's Longest War* (New York: Knopf, 1986).
7. On Gulf War strategy see Lawrence Freedman and Efraim Karsh, "How Kuwait Was Won: Strategy in the Gulf War," *International Security*, Vol. 16, No. 2, Fall 1991, pp. 5-41; for the insider's view of the development of Bush's Gulf War strategy, see Bob Woodward, *The Commanders* (New York: Simon & Schuster, 1991). But one need not have inside information, the adminstration's political-military strategy was easily discerned through the media. See, for example, Maureen Dowd, "Bush Moves to Control War's Endgame," *New York Times*, February 23, 1991; Thomas L. Friedman, "The Rout Bush Wants," *New York Times*, February 27, 1991; R. W. Apple, Jr., "A Short, Persuasive Lesson in Warfare," *New York Times*, March 3, 1991.

2

The Seeds of a New Strategy: Press Policy in Vietnam

> It was the first time in history a war had been declared over by an anchorman.
>
> —David Halberstam[1]

> In view of the impact of public opinion on the prosecution of the war, the accuracy and balance of the news coverage has attained an importance almost equal to the actual combat operations.
>
> —General William C. Westmoreland[2]

The Vietnam experience had three powerful consequences with respect to the issue of wartime press policy. First, it showed presidents that the press had more power during wartime than was healthy for occupants of the White House. And second, it convinced many people, especially those who had been involved with Vietnam from the government's side of things, that a relaxed press policy that allowed journalists free run of the countryside and the battle zone was a very good way to make things even worse for the White House. Unfortunately for the Vietnam-era presidents, they did not learn these lessons until it was too late, and the press policies of that war remained problematic for the White House until the very end. Finally, Vietnam created a venomous division between those who believed that press power had hurt the nation and damaged national interests as well as presidential political interests and those who believed that the press had played a noble role by telling the public the truth about the war, thereby helping to end a horrible and unpopular war. This division has echoed throughout the years as a debate about whether or not the press "lost the war" in Vietnam and it has had, I argue, a long-lasting impact on the way the White House approaches the media in times of crisis and war.

This chapter provides the background for these observations as well as a baseline for analysis of recent conflicts by describing and explaining what the government's press policy looked like in Vietnam and why. In great contrast to the Gulf War, the military's public affairs policy in Vietnam—that is, those groundrules that journalists had to follow in order to report from the war zone—were unrestrictive; the government did not attempt to censor press reports or to exert much control over where journalists traveled. This openness, I will argue, resulted primarily from the *political* decisions made by the White House that overt press controls were likely to be counterproductive to the government's cause. Although presidents during Vietnam had nowhere near as sophisticated an approach to the media as their successors and spent far less time engaged in managing the day-to-day implementation of public affairs and war-related public relations, giving far more leeway to the military in country (i.e., the phrase commonly used to refer to military units actually in Vietnam), the White House nonetheless made the key decisions that provided the broad guidelines for press policy throughout the war. Indeed, from this perspective press policy in the post-Vietnam era reflects continuity, not change.

THREE POLITICAL PROBLEMS: PUBLICITY, NEGATIVITY, AND CREDIBILITY

The government's approach to dealing with the press in Vietnam reflected the attempt by civilian and military officials to deal with problems that had plagued the U.S. mission in Saigon and policy makers back in Washington from the early 1960s. The handful of correspondents then in Vietnam covering the small but growing U.S. presence in South Vietnam had caused problems out of proportion to their number. Homer Bigart, Francois Sully, David Halberstam, Neil Sheehan, Malcolm Browne, Peter Arnett, and a handful of others had challenged official versions of events in Vietnam in their reports, casting doubt on the efficacy of the administration's efforts and prospects in Vietnam, and adding to the tensions between the South Vietnamese and American governments.[3]

Officials felt that as the war escalated, bringing many more journalists to Vietnam, the administration's political difficulties would worsen if a more coherent plan to deal with the press were not crafted.[4] By the time officials from Saigon and Washington met in Honolulu in March 1965 to consider such a plan, they were well aware of the three central problems that the Johnson administration and the military faced. Excess publicity, "negative" reporting, and eroding government credibility had been problems since 1961, when John F. Kennedy began to increase the number of U.S .military advisors in South Vietnam.

The first problem confronting Kennedy and later Johnson was simply to keep the public from learning about the extent of U.S. involvement in Southeast Asia. As William Hammond writes, "The claim that South Vietnam was fighting with only US advice and support shaped US relations with newsmen in Saigon from the beginning."[5] Daniel Hallin concurs, noting of the government that "its public information policies were generally designed to keep American involvement in Vietnam out of the news."[6] Too much attention from the press, especially on the fact that U.S. "advisors" were accompanying South Vietnamese troops into combat and suffering casualties, would have brought publicity that in officials' eyes would have made pursuing limited U.S. aims difficult and put the president in a risky political situation.[7]

The Kennedy administration needed to keep South Vietnam as the central figure in the news, in part because to intervene directly in South Vietnam violated the 1954 Geneva Agreements prohibiting such intervention.[8] A second equal or more powerful reason for doing so was that if Vietnam became a visible political issue, domestic political forces on the right might demand escalation, forcing the president into a land war in Asia and thereby raising the stakes dangerously high. Although Kennedy wanted to portray himself as a tough Cold Warrior, he and other Democrats viewed with trepidation any analogy with the deeply unpopular Korean War, which they believed had cost Truman the presidential election in 1952. It was thus widely doubted that the public would have the stomach for another war in Asia.[9]

Among the more blatant efforts to keep Vietnam out of the news were presidential denials of the true role of U.S. forces in Vietnam. Tom Wicker of the New York Times recalled this one:

> After long and solemn deliberations around Reston's desk on January 15, 1962, I was entrusted with a question for President Kennedy that perhaps ten Times reporters had honed to what we thought was a fine point. Kennedy could not entirely evade it, we were sure. So as soon as he recognized me later that day, I arose—feeling the cameras aim flatteringly at me—and demanded in my sternest voice: "Mr. President, are American troops now in combat in Vietnam?"

> Kennedy looked at me—six feet away and slightly beneath his elevated lectern—as if he thought I might be crazy.
>
> "No," he said crisply—not another word—and pointed at someone else for the next question.[10]

U.S. troops were in fact seeing combat and taking casualties, both as advisors accompanying South Vietnamese troops and later as pilots flying missions supposedly being flown by South Vietnamese pilots. But the administration rationalized that because they were not technically "combat troops," such an evasion was not quite an outright lie.[11]

State Department Cable 1006 to the U.S. mission in Saigon epitomized the early approach to public affairs and the attempt to keep Vietnam out of the news. The 1962 cable impressed upon officials in Saigon the need to keep the press focused on the role of the South Vietnamese and to keep the U.S. role out of the news. The cable noted that "it is not . . . in our interest . . . to have stories indicating that Americans are leading and directing combat missions against the Viet Cong."[12] The cable also urged officials to impress upon journalists that "frivolous, thoughtless criticism" of the South Vietnamese government would not aid the American cause. The cable recommended that journalists never be taken on military missions that might create negative press coverage.[13] Although officials at the time denied that the cable was a form of news management, journalists believed that the government was in fact trying to get the press to write more favorable stories.[14]

Although government/press relations were quite poor in the early days of the conflict, both Kennedy and Johnson were initially quite successful in their effort to keep Vietnam under wraps.[15] A 1964 Washington Post poll found that 63 % of the public paid little or no attention to the situation in Vietnam.[16] This ignorance persisted despite the fact that over 16,000 U.S. forces were by that time in South Vietnam, leading and advising South Vietnamese forces and taking casualties of their own. This low profile was due in part to the fact that the presidents had said little in public about direct U.S. involvement in South Vietnam and even less about U.S. casualties and how they had occurred. Up until that point, casualties had been light, but were rising throughout the early 1960s.[17] Another factor helping Kennedy and Johnson allay any public concern was the bipartisan consensus on foreign policy. Both liberals and conservatives felt the need to help South Vietnam as a way to contain China and communist dominance of Asia. And as Daniel Hallin notes, press coverage of the time reflected this consensus, further legitimizing the conventional arguments for intervention in Indochina.[18]

Later, Johnson would try to keep Vietnam off the public agenda not only to avoid public concern over casualties but also to protect his domestic political goals. He feared that once the war had fully gripped the public, keeping the war limited would be impossible. He would have to throw all of America's weight behind the war effort, and thereby risk his Great Society legislation. Johnson thus sought to minimize the perceived scope of the U.S. engagement and to avoid dramatic gestures of escalation. Johnson's efforts to keep things quiet, however, worsened his other two problems—negative coverage and lack of credibility.

Officials in Washington felt that correspondents in Saigon were opposed to the U.S. effort. Certain journalists, like David Halberstam, Neil Sheehan, and Malcom Browne, infuriated officials on a regular basis with their coverage of the crisis in Vietnam. National security adviser W. W. Rostow summed it up succinctly: "It is easy in Washington to underestimate the cumulative effect of Halberston's [sic] New York Times reporting, as well as other recent . . . stories . . . it may be wise to consider whether a low key campaign of public information may, even now, be in order."[19]

In fact, however, reporters initially supported U.S .goals in Vietnam. The problem lay in the fact that the Saigon journalists were reporting that the U.S. policies in place to reach these goals were ineffective. Journalists were becoming impatient with hearing official optimism about South Vietnamese government and military effectiveness when their firsthand experience told them a different story. The difference was not over policy in a broad sense, but over tactics.[20] As David Halberstam has argued, "The pessimism of the press corps was of the most reluctant kind: many of us came to love Vietnam, we saw our friends dying all around us, and we would have liked nothing better than to believe that the war was going well and that it would eventually be won. But it was impossible to believe these things without denying the evidences of our senses."[21]

This distinction had trouble making the Pacific crossing; every president had moments when he was sure the press was out to shoot down his Vietnam policies. U.S. efforts in Vietnam depended heavily on the stability and competence of the government of South Vietnam. Unfortunately for U.S. policy makers, those qualities were both abundant in their absence. The instability and ineffectualness of first Ngo Dinh Diem and later the various generals who tried to run South Vietnam put the United States in a difficult position. The United States could not simply take over and fight the communists themselves—the president did not want the publicity, and South Vietnam was, after all, a sovereign nation, no matter how troubled. The United States could not just step in and run the war. But with the press in Vietnam seeing for itself how badly South Vietnam's army (the Army of the Republic of Vietnam—ARVN) was doing and commenting critically on the ability of the government in Saigon to win the population to its side in the fight against the Viet Cong, the job of U.S. diplomats became very difficult, and in Washington officials worried about the impact on opinion such negative reporting would eventually have.[22] Ambassador Lodge wrote back to Washington in the middle of a period of heightened tensions between correspondents and officials in Saigon to say that, "The US press should be induced to leave the new government alone. . . . They have exerted great influence on events in Vietnam in the past, and can be expected to do so again. Extensive press criticism, at this juncture, could be critical."[23] McNamara had already voiced similar feelings at a Honolulu conference in 1962, arguing that anti-Diem reports hurt "our case with the public, with congress, and with our own officials."[24] Homer Bigart, a Saigon correspondent for the *New York Times*, also noted the tension: "The Kennedy Administration is still rigidly following its sink or swim with Diem line . . . the Administration believes the American correspondents here are giving a distorted picture . . . of American involvement in the shooting war. The Administration feels the reporters are magnifying incidents where American servicemen find themselves in combat situations, and are writing too much about American casualties."[25] Unfortunately for future administrations, the situation never improved much after Diem.

Kennedy and Johnson thus went to great efforts to encourage positive coverage to counter what they believed were overly critical reports from Saigon. Their campaigns included angry calls to newspapers to complain about biased coverage, private policy discussions by Johnson to influence editors of important newspapers, and government sponsorship of trips to Vietnam by local newspaper reporters who were presumed to be more accepting of official views and more likely to do favorable stories on "hometown boys." The president and other administration officials made speeches around the country to put forth the government view.[26] But official statements too frequently did not match what journalists were seeing and reporting on the ground in Vietnam. This resulted in a continuing crisis of credibility.

Since the earliest days of U.S. involvement, the government had established a pattern of publicly avowed optimism coupled with a reluctance to reveal operational details that might be perceived in a poor light or used as propaganda by the communists. These attempts to avoid publicity and negative press coverage, however, led to an even greater problem as the press and public stopped trusting government pronouncements. Reporters had little trouble in South Vietnam getting access both to information and to the battle zone. They readily discovered for themselves that things were not going as well as the U.S. mission or Washington argued.[27] After enough revelations that government and military reports were either inaccurate or misleading, reporters lost faith in them. The daily military briefings in Saigon, for example, were dubbed the "Five O'clock Follies," and few correspondents relied on them for a true picture of the war.[28] This erosion of government credibility with journalists eventually made its way to the public. In 1965 a CBS poll reported that 67% of the public felt that the government's statements about the war were not always truthful.[29]

THE BASIC PUBLIC AFFAIRS PACKAGE EMERGES, 1965

In 1965 Lyndon Johnson introduced the first U.S. ground troops into Vietnam, thereby deepening the US commitment and making U.S. actions in Vietnam far more newsworthy. By the end of the year Johnson had sent over 180,000 U.S. forces to South Vietnam. Along with ground forces came journalists. The Saigon press corps, only seven in 1962, grew by August of 1965 to over 400. Half of these were Americans, the rest were from all over the world. This growth foreshadowed the problems the government would have as the public awoke to the war and the toll it would take on the nation.

Officials in Saigon recognized that they would need to draw up a new system to handle the influx of correspondents. In fact, pressures had been mounting for a reexamination of information policies since the spring and summer of 1964. By that point the tensions between the U.S. mission and the press were high, the war was not going well, and both military and civilian officials began to realize that current press policies were in many instances doing them more harm than good. Investigation of the military's public affairs operations revealed several organizational problems as well as a poor understanding of how to deal with the press. Officials felt that the information program needed to be centralized under one person. Barry Zorthian, a USIA official, was made chief public affairs officer for the U.S. mission and was given the order to make the needed improvements in Saigon's relations with the press.[30]

Zorthian then set to work with the recently appointed commander of U.S. forces in Vietnam, General William C. Westmoreland, to restructure the public affairs effort in Saigon. Their changes were made in the hope of regaining journalists' trust as well as balancing critical press reports with more positive assessments of the situation in Vietnam. Considerations of operational security certainly existed and were sharpened by the thought of greater numbers of reporters coming to Vietnam. Operational security, however, had not been a problem thus far and was not the focus of Zorthian's and Westmoreland's planning. Among other things, the changes they made included greater efforts to get journalists to the scene of military engagements and to disseminate official speeches and stories about positive aspects of the conflict. Zorthian's and Westmoreland's plans were approved by the State Department and their polices came to be identified by the phrase "maximum candor."[31]

Unfortunately for officials, installing the policies of maximum candor did not convince journalists that openness and honesty were established fact. As the conflict grew more complicated and the United States more involved throughout 1964 and into 1965, journalists began to protest that the government was not actually interested in loosening its information policy.[32] The *Wall Street Journal* offered a typical assessment of the situation in early 1965: "Time after time high-ranking representatives of government—in Washington and in Saigon—have obscured, confused, or distorted news from Vietnam, or have made fatuously erroneous evaluations about the course of the war, for public consumption. . . . Yet the contradictions, the double-talk, the half-truths released in the name of the United States government about the Vietnamese War are not the fault of the USIA alone. The problem goes back to the Pentagon, to the State Department, and to the White House."[33]

Continued tensions between the government and the press, especially over U.S. actions in Laos in 1964, threatened the Johnson administration's diplomatic efforts as well as its ability to keep the conflict in Vietnam out of the public view. Officials said little about U.S. air strikes in Laos to keep details out of the news, but the press complained loudly.[34] The *Washington Post* editorialized: "Does the government really have the naiveté to believe that its hand in these operations can be concealed?"[35] Another obstacle created to staunch the flow of operational details was to put the air base at Da Nang off limits to journalists except when accompanied by a military information officer. U.S. officials tried to explain that this was a South Vietnamese initiative and that military security, not news management, had been the motivation. Correspondents again reacted negatively, and remained quite able to get very accurate information from other sources.[36]

Despite Zorthian's and Westmoreland's best efforts, there was no appreciable improvement in press coverage, especially from Washington's perspective. Knowing that problems could worsen once U.S. forces were fully committed to combat, Westmoreland and Zorthian called for a conference of military and civilian officials to be held in Honolulu, Hawaii in March 1965 to discuss the future of public affairs policy.

At the top of the list for discussion was whether or not censorship could solve the problems plaguing the government. Several issues seemed to favor the imposition of censorship. First, although there had been (and would be) very few instances in which journalists revealed tactical military information of use to the enemy, concern persisted over the press and operational security. In military eyes in Saigon and Washington, the difficulty of maintaining operational security was becoming more pronounced as the war expanded in size and scope and greater numbers of journalists came to Vietnam.[37] Second, and of greater importance at the time, political pressures created by press coverage of the war were encouraging officials to consider that censorship might be a preferable alternative to allowing journalists free rein in Vietnam. Johnson and other Washington officials were outraged by press coverage of the air campaign and troubled by its revelations of the Marines' activities. Press discussion of Vietnam, and particularly critical comments about how well things were going, made life difficult for Johnson as he tried to conduct a limited war without stirring the public consciousness. Too much news about Vietnam would give critics of Johnson and his policies more ammunition to use against him, and would make judgment of the success or failure of the intervention easier, thereby raising the political stakes for the president. Chairman of the Joint Chiefs of Staff General Wheeler wrote to Westmoreland in response to press discussion of Johnson's decision to send the Marines to Vietnam: "It is a fact, that the situation in the US is exacerbated and pressures upon highest authority [Johnson] increased by press coverage of items such as these cited above." He added in his next message, "It may well be that nothing short of press censorship will serve this end [easing pressure on Johnson]."[38]

However tantalizing the idea of censorship appeared at times, there was an overwhelming case for not instituting it. First, congress would have needed to declare war to provide the legal foundation for imposing censorship. As noted, however, declaring war was definitely not something Johnson wanted to encourage. In addition to concern that the public would not approve of a sudden escalation of the war, Johnson feared the risk to his Great Society legislation should the country move to an all-out war footing. Johnson told a biographer: ". . . History provided too many cases where the sound of the bugle put an immediate end to the hopes and dreams of the best reformers: the Spanish-American war drowned the populist spirit; World War I ended Woodrow Wilson's New Freedom; World War II brought the New Deal to a close. Once the war began, then all those conservatives in the congress would use it as a weapon against the Great Society. . . ."[39] The large expenditures of both dollars and political capital would, he worried, leave him incapable of fulfilling his domestic agenda.[40]

A second problem with imposing censorship was the expected uproar from the press should censorship be instituted after so many years without it. Officials at the Honolulu conference were very aware of the government's credibility problems with the press, and did not think that imposing greater restrictions would improve government/press relations. In addition, any censorship program would have had to allow South Vietnamese participation. But because of their poor track record with the press, U.S. officials felt that the South Vietnamese were likely to abuse their position as censors, and that the political fallout from those problems would also outweigh censorship's usefulness.[41]

The final major difficulty with censorship would have been the extreme logistical requirements. Not only would the military have had to ensure control over all communications and transportation within South Vietnam, but Military Assistance Command, Vietnam (MACV) would also have had to fly over the necessary equipment to view and edit television film, and a large staff of bilingual personnel would have to be trained and maintained to carry out the many duties required by a system of censorship.[42]

For these reasons the conference quickly rejected censorship and reaffirmed an open approach to public affairs. Though perhaps lacking the ultimate security of censorship, adopting an open approach to dealing with the press seemed to offer at least two advantages. First, by continuing the policies of "maximum candor," officials could claim that they wanted to ensure that the public was well informed on Vietnam. Second, by having journalists abide voluntarily by groundrules in exchange for access to military briefings and transportation, the government would be afforded some control over their actions. In the event that a journalist reported anything that compromised operational security, his or her accreditation could be revoked. In this way operational security, if not political security, could be reasonably maintained.[43]

After circulating through the State Department and White House, the recommendations of the conference were adopted. For the most part, the new policy only modified slightly the policies of maximum candor. Over the next several months, the policy was fine-tuned to account for those issues raised by the introduction of more U.S. forces and the greater coverage of combat that accompanied this buildup. The policies were then issued in written form by the Defense Department.

The guidelines were quite simple and did not represent a major restriction for journalists. In order to be accredited by MACV to cover the war, journalists would have to abide voluntarily by a number of groundrules whose purpose was to ensure the maintenance of operational security. Concerning combat information, journalists were expected not to identify specific units going into battle, the exact nature or size of those units, nor the precise number of casualties suffered by a unit in an engagement. Casualties would only be reported as light, moderate, or heavy.[44] Journalists also agreed not to reveal troop movements until the military had determined that the enemy was clearly aware of them. With regard to reporting on the air campaign, journalists could not release information about the kind of aircraft involved in an ongoing mission, their numbers, destinations, tactics, or possible future targets. The military would, however, announce general information concerning these figures—tons of bombs dropped by what types of planes and with what success—after the planes had safely returned. In exchange for following the guidelines, journalists would benefit from military transportation from Saigon to various remote areas in Vietnam, room and board from military units in the field, twenty-four-hour-a-day access to information at the MACV in Saigon, daily briefings and occasional backgrounders on the war's progress, and most importantly, would not find their news copy subject to censorship.[45]

The result of these press policies was that covering the war was made as easy as it could have been for journalists. The military, in fact, went to great lengths to help reporters do their jobs. Testifying before Congress in 1966, Arthur Sylvester, the Assistant Secretary of Defense for Public Affairs, described the support MACV had provided journalists in the last twelve months,

> . . . the MACV information office has:
>
> Arranged more than 4,700 in-country trips by newsmen, to include ground and air transportation; Arranged for or conducted almost 6,900 briefings and 108 background meetings; Answered more than 32,000 telephone queries from newsmen; Been consulted individually by newsmen on 3,300 occasions; Conducted daily press briefings in Saigon, 7 days a week; average attendance—130 correspondents; Conducted the U.S. portion of the accreditation of all correspondents arriving in Vietnam. . . . We have established daily scheduled plane flights for newsmen out of Saigon to eight major areas throughout the country. We have installed sole-user teletype circuits within Vietnam to assist MACV and the press in providing information, transmitting news copy, and answering questions.[46]

This impressive list of logistical and informational assistance did not include the more informal and hard to measure aid given to correspondents, especially by units in the field, which provided journalists with information as well as security, room, and board.

The press for the most part concurred with Sylvester about the help it was getting from the military. A *Chicago Tribune* reporter remarked on the transportation situation, for example: "Military transportation of all types is open to the reporter for the asking. He even gets preference on scheduled flights carrying troops and supplies. If no scheduled flight is available, the reporter need only wait on an air field and sooner or later a plane will come along. The pilot happily gives the reporter a lift."[47]

PROBLEMS REMAIN

Despite the relatively friendly and helpful nature of its public affairs policies the problems plaguing the government did not go away. Publicity, of course, was increasingly difficult to avoid as journalists streamed into Vietnam, matching the deployment of U.S. forces. Once American troops had been sent into battle, their actions and fate immediately became the most important story in the nation, one that would be covered intensively regardless of what the president might have wanted. Johnson, however, was determined to keep the public from realizing that the United States was irretrievably committed to fighting a war in Asia for as long as possible. To admit the stark truth about the situation would have been to turn 180 degrees from the statements he had made during his 1964 election campaign. At a stop in New Hampshire Johnson had declared that, "I have not thought that we were ready for American boys to do the fighting for Asian boys."[48] The United States would thus be taking over what Johnson had assured the public was a Vietnamese problem.

Despite such assurances, Johnson made the decision early in 1965 to send two battalions of Marines into South Vietnam to protect the US air base at Da Nang, from which the US was launching air strikes against targets in North Vietnam, Cambodia, and Laos.[49] Soon after he also gave Westmoreland the authority to send the Marines out to defend the base in depth, and to pursue the Viet Cong when encountered. These new orders reflected a substantial change in mission. Rather than announcing the change publicly, and in spite of the openness of the military's public affairs policies, however, Johnson endeavored to keep the nature of Marines' mission and the immanent escalation of the war to include ground combat out of the public spotlight.[50] Until that point, increasing bombing of North Vietnam had been the only publicly acknowledged expansion of the war effort. To talk about a land war in Asia still did not seem a wise thing to do. As Secretary of State Rusk noted privately at the time, "The president felt that he must not force the pace too fast, or congress and public opinion, which had been held in line up to now through the president's strenuous efforts, would no longer support our actions in Vietnam."[51]

Johnson's orders, embodied in National Security Action Memorandum 328 of April 1965, made successful implementation of a open public affairs program essentially impossible. It is worth quoting at length from that document here:

> 5. The President approved an 18-20,000 man increase in US military support forces to fill out existing units and supply needed logistic personnel.
> 6. The President approved the deployment of two additional Marine battalions and one Marine air squadron and associated headquarters and support elements.
> 7. The President approved a change of mission for all Marine battalions deployed to Vietnam to permit their more active use under conditions to be established and approved by the Secretary of Defense in consultation with the Secretary of State. . .
> 11. The President desires that with respect to the actions in paragraphs 5 through 7, premature publicity be avoided by all possible precautions. The actions themselves should be taken as rapidly as practicable, but in ways that should minimize any appearance of sudden changes in policy, and official statements on these troops movements will be made only with the direct approval of the Secretary of Defense, in consultation with the Secretary of State. The President's desire is that these movements and changes should be understood as being gradual and wholly consistent with existing policy.[52]

In a memo to Secretary of State Dean Rusk, Maxwell Taylor, ambassador to South Vietnam, revealed the motivation for such a public relations strategy and how it would be implemented by the U.S. mission in Saigon:

> Under the circumstances we believe that the most useful approach to press problems is to make no, repeat, no special public announcement to the effect that U.S. ground troops are now engaged in offensive combat operations, but to announce such actions routinely as they occur. As the marines move from their present posture of securing the Da Nang airbase "in depth" to actions which can be related only indirectly to Da Nang, military spokesmen will be queried about whether the marine mission has changed and will answer that, while we never discuss the future, current operations speak for themselves. Eventually, of course, the fact that the marines or other ground troops are engaged in offensive combat will be officially confirmed. This low-key treatment will not obviate [all] political and psychological problems . . . but will allow us to handle them undramatically, as a natural consequence of our determination to meet commitments here.[53]

Johnson also argued publicly that the infusion of Marines did not represent a change in course. When asked at a press conference, "Mr. President, does the fact that you are sending additional forces to Vietnam imply any change in policy. . . ?" Johnson simply replied, "It does not imply any change of policy whatever. It does not imply any change of objective."[54] With these efforts Johnson was able to mute most speculation for several months, but eventually predictions of escalation did make the front pages, to be proved correct when Johnson finally announced the planned buildup of U.S. forces publicly in July of 1965.[55]

By attempting to shun publicity and by misleading journalists as to his intentions, Johnson in 1965 took a large step down the path toward destroying his credibility with the press on Vietnam. In addition, by forcing the U.S. mission in Saigon to follow this public relations ploy, the Johnson administration also degraded the military's credibility. Instead of letting the more open press policies in Saigon improve official credibility, the administration's desire to avoid publicity and critical reporting led to the widening of the credibility gap.[56]

Worse, from the administration's view, 1965 marked the arrival of television on a daily basis in Vietnam. Television's power and the problems it could cause presidents was revealed almost immediately. Morley Safer, a reporter for CBS, accompanied marine units on a mission to eliminate all resistance and enemy infrastructure in Cam Ne, a supposed Viet Cong stronghold. Marines were told to destroy any hut from which they received enemy fire. Safer described what happened as the film showed a Marine casually lighting a thatched hut roof on fire with his Zippo lighter:

> It first appeared that the marines had been sniped at before and that a few houses were made to pay. Shortly after, one officer told me he had orders to go in and level the string of hamlets that surround Cam Ne village. And all around the common paddy fields [camera focuses on a roof being lit by a flamethrower] a ring of fire. One hundred and fifty homes were leveled in retaliation for a burst of gunfire. In Vietnam like everywhere else in Asia, property, a home, is everything. A man lives with his family on ancestral land. His parents are buried nearby. These spirits are part of his holdings. . . . Today's operation shows the frustration of Vietnam in miniature. There is little doubt that American fire power can win a military victory here. But to a Vietnamese peasant whose home means a lifetime of backbreaking labor, it will take more than presidential promises to convince him that we are on his side.[57]

Safer's report from Cam Ne became one of the defining images of the war and was a symbol to many of the devastation the United

States wreaked in Vietnam. The reaction from the Johnson administration was immediate. Arthur Sylvester, Assistant Secretary of Defense for Public Affairs, called CBS News president Fred Friendly to insist that Safer be recalled, arguing that Safer was biased against the military and that because he was a Canadian citizen he did not have the proper appreciation of the situation in Vietnam.[58]

Frustration and tension with the press thus persisted after 1965. As the war heated up there were inevitably more problems, and more casualties, to report. Civilian officials also worried how the public would react to the yet larger numbers of troops planned for Vietnam. In late 1965, therefore, Washington officials discussed plans to sustain the fragile public support for the war, primarily focusing still on ways to keep the facts of the U.S. build-up from confronting the public head on.[59]

Even as they did so, however, actions taken in Vietnam served cross purposes, facilitating journalists' access to information and to combat zones. MACV's logistical and communications infrastructure was inadequate to meet the needs of the rapidly growing press corps. In response, Sylvester carried out several improvements in early 1966, making travel to remote areas in Vietnam easier, improving the communications within Vietnam, and upscaling the information center at Da Nang, which had become a popular spot for journalists with the expansion of the air war in the north. The accreditation process was also liberalized, so that journalists only needed a letter from their editor in order to get access to the many benefits the military provided.[60] These improvements made it easier for journalists of all kinds to cover the war, making the administration's task of playing down the war that much more difficult.

The administration's various attempts to ensure positive coverage eventually raised suspicions in Congress. In August 1966 Senator J. William Fulbright, chairman of the Senate Committee on Foreign Relations, held a hearing to investigate news policies in Vietnam. According to Fulbright, "Almost continuously over the past two years the Defense Department has been charged by responsible journalists and newspapers with managing, or mismanaging, the flow of news from Vietnam."[61] Statements at the hearing by Fulbright and others made it clear that the Johnson administration was implicated thoroughly in those charges. In defense of the administration and Defense Department policies, Arthur Sylvester argued that the military was in fact doing all it could to provide the press with logistical support and information.[62]

Jack Raymond of the *New York Times* seconded the cooperativeness of the military with respect to access to the battlefield and complained that the real problem in covering Vietnam lay not with public affairs policy itself, but with the government's attempts to assert things that journalists found simply were not true. Raymond wrote, "Far more serious are the sporadic clashes between the press and officialdom over the very facts of the war. Dispatches from Vietnam from time to time have questioned the accuracy of official statements. In retaliation, government spokesmen—military and civilian officials alike—have questioned the competence, good judgment and even patriotism of correspondents. As a consequence, an undercurrent of doubt greets much of the news from Vietnam, official and unofficial."[63] The committee seemed somewhat less than convinced by Sylvester's testimony that government news policies were truly open and not geared toward manipulating news coverage. Nothing came of the hearings, but their very existence revealed that the administration's attitude and policies toward the press were causing concern and doubt in many circles.[64]

By 1967 domestic antiwar sentiment had begun to grow, along with concern that the United States was not making the sort of progress envisioned against the communists. Press reports began to reveal cracks in the administration's unity on Vietnam policy. Even television, which until this point had rarely questioned official reports of progress, began to reveal the doubts many people were having.[65] Realization of these trends struck fear into the administration. First, both Johnson and others believed strongly that public dissent would lengthen the war because it convinced Hanoi that the United States did not have the political resolve to continue. As Henry Cabot Lodge, Ambassador to Vietnam, noted, "[demonstrations] make Hanoi think all they have to do is hang on and we'll fall apart."[66] Second, officials had begun fearing that Johnson's reelection would be at risk if the public became convinced that the war was deadlocked. As a result, the administration took every opportunity to attack its critics and to portray the war in a favorable light, while encouraging the U.S. mission in Saigon to do the same. As Hammond notes, "In conjunction with the administration's efforts, the Military Assistance Command and the US mission in Saigon strove continually to temper news stories that tended either to reflect poorly on the South Vietnamese government or to embarrass President Johnson."[67] These efforts, however, did not produce the desired results.

In an effort to combat criticism of the war and growing perceptions of stalemate, Johnson twice drafted Westmoreland to travel to Washington to speak publicly about the war's progress in 1967. On his first trip in April, Westmoreland spoke in positive terms about the progress of the war before a gathering of newspaper editors, but caused an uproar both in Congress and the press by adding that he was dismayed by the "unpatriotic acts at home" of those opposed to the war.[68] Johnson was promptly accused of bringing Westmoreland home for the purely political purpose of quieting dissenters, although one commentator noted that it was more credible to hear from Westmoreland than Johnson.[69] By deleting reference to the question of home front unity, Westmoreland put a damper on this criticism in his second speech, given before a joint session of Congress. Westmoreland delivered what many considered an excellent speech, again offering a very optimistic assessment of the war.[70]

Westmoreland's performances gave Johnson a brief boost in the polls, but they hurt Westmoreland himself, as he had feared.[71] Prior to his trip to Washington, Westmoreland was a highly credible and trusted source for journalists. Much of what he told reporters on background would end up in newspapers almost verbatim. Westmoreland's trip to Washington, however, damaged his credibility. The military had now been fully absorbed into the political sphere. As Hammond notes, "Suspecting that Westmoreland had become a tool of the Johnson administration, newsmen replaced their favorable coverage with more skeptical appraisals."[72]

After a short honeymoon during which the public seemed to believe that the war was going fairly well, doubts began to creep back into press coverage. It became increasingly clear to many that South Vietnam was not carrying its own weight in the war, and the press offered many pessimistic accounts to this effect. Further, it seemed that the communists were ably matching increased U.S. efforts with increased efforts of their own. By the middle of 1967, most observers in the media were pronouncing the war a stalemate.[73]

Officials in Washington and Saigon, however, believed that the war they were losing was actually on the public relations front. Westmoreland's distress over the impact of public relations is evident in an entry from his diary at the time: "There is . . . an amazing lack of boldness in our approach to the future. We are so sensitive about world opinion that this stifles initiative and constantly keeps us on the defensive in our efforts to portray ourselves as a benevolent power that acts only in response to an initiative by the enemy. Therefore we become victims of our own propaganda and subject to political attrition."[74] President Johnson was also beginning to take an even more serious interest in the war's public image. Thus officials once again stepped up their efforts to convince the public that the war was going well.[75]

The administration's determination to improve public opinion of the war was felt in Saigon. Johnson urged the mission in Saigon to "search urgently for every occasion to present sound evidence of progress in Viet Nam."[76] Ward Just of the Washington Post noted the motivations for the White House pressure: "Quantify us some hearts and minds, the Administration has in effect told its agents in Saigon, or lacking that, give us a measure of how the war is being won. Because if the American people are not convinced that the war is being won, dissent will grow, the polls will plunge, and the public demand to disengage would become irresistible."[77] In response the U.S. mission undertook an organized effort to showcase various forms of progress from the past two years. Successes from various nonmilitary initiatives were highlighted, and the declassification of captured enemy documents was sped along in order to show doubters that even the communists believed that the U.S .efforts were having an impact. These efforts were not enough to comfort Johnson, however, and he once again asked Westmoreland to come to Washington to respond to war critics.[78]

In Washington Westmoreland had several opportunities to promote his views, including testimony before the House Armed Services Committee, an interview on the television program "Meet the Press," and most importantly, as it turned out, a speech before the National Press Club.[79] At that speech, Westmoreland made his most optimistic projections of the war. He argued that the United States and South Vietnam had made substantial progress, that the enemy was wearing down and had not won a major battle in the last year.[80] As after his first public relations trip to Washington, Westmoreland's appearance before the National Press Club raised many questions; many in the press derided Westmoreland's appearances as blatant attempts to "sell the war."[81]

Despite such criticism, however, Westmoreland's remarks received widespread play in the media, and the "progress campaign" succeeded in assuaging much public doubt that the war was going well. Johnson's popularity rose eleven points after Westmoreland's visit and administration public relations efforts continued to cement the shift in public opinion.[82] Administration officials made the rounds of television and radio programs to shore up the image of progress and to rebut critics' charges.[83] By January of 1968 the administration was feeling somewhat more secure in its public standing, only to be stunned along with the public by the Tet Offensive.

Launched in the early morning hours of January 30, 1968, the Tet Offensive involved near simultaneous attacks on five of South Vietnam's most important cities including Saigon, thirty-six provincial capitals, sixty-four district capitals, fifty hamlets, and even a nineteen man suicide attack on the U.S. embassy in Saigon.[84] The attacks took place during the Tet holiday (the Lunar New Year), a time of great celebration and of a yearly cease-fire, catching ARVN troops almost completely off-guard and U.S. forces only somewhat less so. Suffering nearly 59,000 dead, the communists fought to hold ground they had taken and continued harassing U.S. and South Vietnamese positions. Although in most areas communist forces were quickly thrown back, fighting in several areas went on much longer, and the outcome in many places was not clearly known for some time. Action was particularly heavy at Hue and Khe Sanh, the latter of which became a beacon for press coverage as Marines there were pinned down for seventy-seven days before U.S. air strikes finally liberated them. The United States and South Vietnam also suffered heavy casualties—the highest numbers seen in such a short period thus far in the war. The United States lost almost 4,000 men and South Vietnam almost 5,000.[85]

Although the attacks achieved tactical surprise against the U.S. and South Vietnamese forces, and despite the unprecedented allied losses, Westmoreland immediately began assuring the press that Tet in fact was a grave blow to the enemy.[86] Westmoreland argued that the offensive represented a recognition by the communists that U.S. military pressure was winning the war, and that drastic measures were needed to tilt the political balance in their favor as a military victory was impossible. Whereas historians now agree with Westmoreland's assessment of the situation, the media painted a much different picture of events.

As Peter Braestrup has forcefully argued, the media portrayed Tet as a defeat for the United States and a blow to the Johnson administration's strategy for pursuing the war. Braestrup has argued that the Tet crisis played against journalism's inherent weaknesses. In short, the press jumped to the conclusion that Tet was a defeat before it could have possibly known for sure.[87] And despite the mistakes made in the rush to report breaking events, Braestrup argues, few news organizations made efforts to correct them later. Thus, once Tet had been reported a failure, it remained a failure. In addition, in its rush to find drama and good television pictures, the press swarmed to cover the battles at Hue and Khe Sanh. Braestrup notes that stories from Saigon, Hue, and Khe Sanh represented 90% of all battlefield coverage, even though those battles accounted for only 15% of the total activity of allied forces.[88]

Braestrup also argues that television, for the first time capable of truly covering the war firsthand during these battles, transmitted to the public a distorted picture of what was happening at Tet. The images from those scenes, the bloodiest and most chaotic of the war so far, overwhelmed any comforting or positive predictions made by officials.[89] Another observer of the Tet period, Don Oberdorfer, argues that Tet was television's first "superbattle." By 1968, he notes, there were 100 million television sets in use in America, with a potential audience of 96% of the population. Viewing rates, especially during the winter months, were very high. Estimates show that nearly 20 million homes tuned into CBS and NBC news programs every night during the first weeks of Tet. For the first time, television brought the shock of battle into the living rooms of a massive number of homes. The impact of this fact on public opinion, leaders assumed, was tremendous.[90] Finally, Stanley Karnow also notes the special character of television, "But newspaper accounts paled beside the television coverage, which that evening [January 31] projected the episode [U.S. embassy fight], in all its vivid confusion, into the living rooms of fifty million Americans. There, on color screens, dead bodies lay amid the rubble and rattle of automatic gunfire as dazed American soldiers and civilians ran back and forth trying to flush out the assailants."[91]

Aside from any inadequacies of journalistic practice and judgment, however, responsibility for the press reaction to Tet lay heavily with Lyndon Johnson. The administration had, after all, spent the latter part of 1967 trying very hard to convince the public that the war was being won. Westmoreland himself had played a central role in lending the public relations blitz credibility. When television reports from Saigon showed the U.S. embassy under attack, both the press and public found the General's optimism, past and present, hard to swallow.[92] As George Herring notes, "Televised accounts of the bloody fighting in Saigon and Hue made a mockery of Johnson and Westmoreland's optimistic year-end reports, widening the credibility gap, and cynical journalists openly mocked Westmoreland's claims of victory."[93] Newsweek added, "Both in Vietnam and America [the enemy attacks] aroused searing doubts about U.S. strategy in the Vietnamese war and about the man entrusted with its execution—Gen. William Westmoreland. These doubts, however, did not appear to extend to the Administration, most of whose members continued to insist publicly that the enemy had suffered a major defeat. . . ."[94]

In Washington officials responded defensively to press coverage of Tet. Johnson responded by claiming that the enemy had been dealt a blow and denying that the communists had won a political or psychological victory over the United States, but for the most part let his subordinates do the talking.[95] Secretary of State Rusk showed a frustration many felt when he berated journalists at a press conference: "Whose side are you on? Now, I'm secretary of state of the United States, and I'm on our side! None of your papers or your broadcasting apparatuses are worth a damn unless the United States succeeds. They are trivial compared to that question. So I don't know why, to win a Pulitzer Prize, people have to be probing for the things that one can bitch about when there are two thousand stories on the same day about things that are more constructive."[96]

For Johnson, Tet represented the ultimate failure of his public relations strategy for the war. The public in 1967 had been unsure that he was guiding the country to a quick and certain end to the war. In trying to maintain support for the war, Johnson had glossed over the sacrifices the war would yet demand. His failure to warn the public about the possibility that the enemy still had a lot of fight left, and his inability to convince people after Tet that he had a plan that could end the war, left him without credibility and without support.

From Johnson's perspective, the most important symbol of this loss of support was CBS anchorman Walter Cronkite. Cronkite, the "most trusted man" in America, traveled to Vietnam during Tet to get a firsthand look at the situation. Reporting from Vietnam in a CBS special on the crisis, Cronkite dashed the administration's attempts to persuade the public that the war was going well:

> . . . It seems now more certain than ever that the bloody experience of Vietnam is to end in stalemate. . . . To say that we are closer to victory today is to believe, in the face of the evidence . . . optimists who have been wrong in the past. To suggest we are on the edge of defeat is to yield to unreasonable pessimism. To say that we are mired in stalemate seems the only realistic, yet unsatisfactory, conclusion. . . . But it is increasingly clear to this reporter that the only rational way out would be to negotiate—not as victims, but as an honorable people who lived up to their pledge to victory and democracy and did the best they could.[97]

Johnson felt that once he had lost Cronkite, he had lost middle America. After watching Cronkite's report Johnson is reported to have said, "It's all over."[98] In the wake of Tet Johnson's approval rating sank to an all-time low of 36%, and support for his handling of the war dropped to 26%.[99] On March 31, after a reassessment of his Vietnam strategy, Johnson appeared on television to discuss the situation in Vietnam, announcing a new peace proposal and shocking the nation with the news that he would not run for another term as president.[100]

Johnson's successor, Richard Nixon, thus inherited a poisoned government/press relationship, with government and military credibility at its lowest ebb. Although Saigon public affairs policies remained open and for the most part cooperative in terms of access and logistics, Nixon's approach to public relations, like Johnson's, would often contradict those policies.[101] What he might have gained in credibility through reliance on an open relationship with the press, Nixon disregarded in favor of secrecy and attempts to circumvent the press.[102] And, like Johnson, Nixon's Vietnam policies aroused great domestic protest, leading American society into a period of unparalleled divisiveness.

After Tet, press coverage became distinctly less favorable to the war effort and the government. Nixon could not count on the sort of patriotic coverage, especially from television, that Johnson had enjoyed early on in the conflict.[103] But Nixon did not wait for the press to report favorably on his actions. Nixon, like Johnson, went to great lengths to promote his war policies. In fact, Nixon sought time on television so frequently to discuss his Vietnam policy that the Federal Communications Commission felt obliged to give opponents of the war an opportunity to give their views under the Fairness Doctrine.[104] Of Nixon's television appearances, the most effective was probably the November 3, 1969 "silent majority" speech. In that speech, Nixon castigated domestic critics of the war, defended the United States' commitment to South Vietnam, spelled out his plans for Vietnamization, and asked the silent majority of Americans who supported the war effort to stand behind him. The speech raised public support for the war appreciably, giving Nixon political breathing room, and fueled Nixon's belief in using television as a tool to mobilize public opinion.[105]

Later, Nixon would try to use television to deflect the opposition he knew he would face over the Cambodian incursion, also undisclosed until the last moment. Nixon argued, "If when the chips are down, the world's most powerful nation acts like a pitiful helpless giant, the forces of totalitarianism and anarchy will threaten free nations and free institutions throughout the world."[106] By this point, however, Nixon had run up against the limits of television's usefulness. Instead of support, Nixon watched the antiwar movement stage the largest demonstrations of the war. Congress also showed its displeasure, by voting to terminate the 1964 Tonkin Gulf resolution that had allowed Johnson to escalate the war in the first place.[107]

Nixon's attempts to control Vietnam press coverage are best symbolized by his secret decision to approve and carry out a massive fourteen-month bombing campaign of communist positions in Cambodia in 1969-1970. The military had long wanted permission to extend the air war against Cambodia, a neutral country, in order to disrupt and destroy communist logistical efforts and headquarters located there. Thus far considerations for public and international reaction had restrained such action, but Nixon gave the military the go-ahead.

The administration and the Pentagon kept the operation hidden from public view by creating an elaborate system of accounting for the air strikes, with the official Pentagon histories showing that other targets had been struck instead of those actually hit in Cambodia. Although early on the *New York Times*, based on leaks from sources in the administration, reported that the United States had bombed Cambodia to obstruct communist supplies coming into South Vietnam no notion of the scale of the bombing was offered, nor did reports discuss the fact that such attacks were in essence widening a war Nixon was professing to be ending.

With the Nixon administration and the military refusing to comment in any way on such missions, the issue died. In fact, in 1969 the reports failed to stir any public reaction. The news accounts did, however, enrage Nixon and Kissinger, who worried about public and international reaction should the bombing become widely acknowledged publicly. Their concern led to the illegal wiretapping first of Nixon national security aide Morton Halperin, and later of several journalists and other government employees.[108] As William Shawcross notes, "The secrecy, the wiretaps, the burning and falsification of reports, were principally intended to conceal the administration's widening of the war from the American people."[109]

It was not until four years later that Congress discovered the deception and its scale, after an Air Force major wrote letters to the Senate Foreign Relations committee telling members of his role in the operation. In 1973, the revelations had a much greater impact, fueling congressional and public antagonism for Nixon, who was by that point reeling from the Watergate scandal.[110]

The military, in an awkward position fighting a war many Americans simply wanted to end, by 1970 had begun to withdraw into itself. Public information officers, though often bitter toward the press, stopped trying to "sell the war" as had been done previously so frequently.[111] General Creighton Abrams, who took over from Westmoreland in 1968, tended to let the war speak for itself, rather than attempt to put a good face on events. He also preferred to take a less public tack with journalists. As Major General Winant Sidle (USA, Ret.), head of the Military Assistance Command Office of Information from 1967-1969, noted, "Westy liked to have press conferences; he liked to have backgrounders; he liked to get on television. I'm not knocking Westy at all, but it turned out in the end to be somewhat counterproductive. Now General Abrams took an entirely different view of this. He had no press conference the whole time I was there . . . (but) he spent literally hundreds of hours in one-on-ones with every significant newsman in Vietnam who wanted to talk to him."[112] Abrams, unlike Westmoreland, also resisted attempts to draft him into a more political role in the public view.

Despite a lower-key public affairs effort in Saigon, military and other officials were still plagued by the press and its coverage of events in Vietnam. The My Lai massacre and Lt. Calley's conviction for "at least 22 murders" received extended attention in 1969 and the public's view of the military soured further.[113] Journalists after 1968 also began to travel in greater numbers to North Vietnam to report on the war from there. The first person to do so had been Harrison Salisbury of the *New York Times* in 1966. The animosity he had engendered among officials with his reporting had not been forgotten. Many, especially in the military, felt that any reporting from the other side in war was an act of treason.[114] As Peter Braestrup notes, journalists reporting from North Vietnam were seldom critical of their hosts, a fact which further frustrated U.S. officials.[115] In addition, officials believed that many of the journalists who went to Vietnam after Tet were firmly opposed to the war and were interested in promoting that view in their writing. Nixon's Cambodian incursion of 1970 and the bombing of Laos in 1971 reinvigorated antiwar forces at home, and coverage of the domestic dissent produced the least favorable press coverage of the war.[116]

CONCLUSIONS

Both on paper and in practice, the government's policies for dealing with the press during Vietnam were the least restrictive in U.S. history. For the first time in the century the government had not implemented censorship on battlefield reporting. Moreover, the military was in fact quite helpful to journalists covering the war, providing transportation, accommodations, and information to thousands over the years.

That public affairs policies were so open was largely the result of political considerations stemming from the Vietnam strategies of the Kennedy and Johnson administrations, which looked first to keep news of the conflict and U.S. involvement in Vietnam out of the public consciousness and later attempted to convince the public that all was well. Ironically, perhaps, the fact that press policy was so unrestrictive helped hasten the deterioration of the government/press relationship. Instead of enhancing journalists' trust in military and civilian officials, the lack of restrictions allowed the press to discover and report that the war was not going the way government spokesmen were claiming.

As the next chapter will illustrate in detail, Vietnam provided those in both the government and the press with dramatic evidence of the political power of the press. But whereas all agreed on its potential for influence, a violent disagreement arose in the wake of the war over whether that power had helped or harmed the nation. Johnson and Nixon undoubtedly both took away the lesson that the press had far too great a power to disrupt and obstruct their conduct of the war to the detriment of the national interest, as well as to hurt them politically. Moreover, many concluded that things had simply been made worse by the lax press policies which allowed uncensored reporting from the battlefield. On the other hand, journalists and others began to argue that without the freedoms it had enjoyed the press would have been unable to tell the public the truth about the war when government officials were offering overly rosy claims about its progress. This acrimonious debate over the impact of the press has only intensified since the war as the power of the press in all areas of American politics has risen dramatically over the last twenty-five years.

ENDNOTES

1. David Halberstam, *The Powers That Be* (New York: Dell, 1984), p. 716.
2. General William C. Westmoreland and Admiral Sharp, *Annual Report on Vietnam*, 1967, p. 274.
3. Peter Braestrup, *Big Story: How the American Press and Television Interpreted the Crisis of Tet in 1968 in Saigon and Washington* (New York: Westview Press, 1977), pp. 2-6; David Halberstam offers a personal account of reporting the war in *The Making of a Quagmire* (New York: Random House, 1965); William M. Hammond, *The Military and the Media, 1962-1968* (Washington, DC: US Army Center for Military History, 1988), pp. 11-65; Philip Knightley, *The First Casualty: From the Crimea to Vietnam* (New York: Harvest, 1975), pp. 374-381; and James Aronson, *The Press and the Cold War* (Indianapolis: Bobbs-Merrill, 1970), pp. 180-205.
4. Hammond, *The Military and the the Media*, pp. 135-143; Hammond's work is the Army's official historical study of the subject. Because it is the only work that relies primarily on primary historical sources to examine Vietnam public affairs, I make extensive use of it in this chapter. Those interested in greater detail than is offered in this chapter should consult Hammond's volume.
5. p. 11
6. Daniel C. Hallin, *The "Uncensored" War: The Media and Vietnam* (Berkeley: University of California Press, 1986), p. 28; for Hallin's discussion of the reporting of the early years, see pp. 26-58; Almost all writers on the subject agree on this point. Other examples are Philip Geyelin, "Vietnam and the Press: Limited War and an Open Society," in Anthony Lake, ed., *The Vietnam Legacy: The War, American Society and the Future of American Foreign Policy* (New York: New York University Press, 1976), pp. 166-193; Kevin Williams, "Vietnam: The First Living-Room War," in Derrik Mercer, ed., *The Fog of War: The Media on the Battlefield* (London: Heinemann, 1987), pp. 213-260; and John Mecklin, *Mission in Torment* (New York: Harper & Row, 1965).
7. Aronson, *The Press and the Cold War*, pp. 180-205. Aronson offers a more aggressively critical analysis of both government and press in the early 1960s.
8. Ibid., p. 181; for background history on the agreements and how administrations viewed them see Herring, *America's Longest War*, pp. 29-57, 82-84.

9. Herring, America's Longest War, pp. 82-84; This analysis is noted in "Fears on Vietnam Rising," *New York Times*, February 12, 1962.
10. Tom Wicker, *On Press* (New York: Viking, 1978), p. 92.
11. Troops in Vietnam were in fact upset at the time that the public did not appreciate the risks they were taking in Vietnam. The government's information policy kept news of their efforts out of the papers and discouraged officers from saying anything about their role. See Homer Bigart, "Denial of Purple Heart to G.I. Angers 'Copter Men in Vietnam," *New York Times*, April 24, 1962; and David Halberstam, "Curbs in Vietnam Irk U.S. Officers," *New York Times*, June 3, 1962; Also see "Salinger Tells How Kennedy Tried to Hide Vietnam Build-Up," *U.S. News and World Report*, September 12, 1966, p. 103.
12. Cited in Hammond, *Military and the Media*, p. 15.
13. Ibid., p. 15; Mecklin, Mission in Torment, pp. 111-119; Thomas Sorenson, *The Word War: The Story of American Propaganda* (New York: Harper & Row, 1968), p. 191.
14. Assistant Secretary of State for Public Affairs Roger Hilsman testified the cable was not an attempt to get newsmen to write any particular stories and thus did not represent news management; see "Vietnam New Coverage," in Hearings before the Foreign Operations and Government Information Subcommittee of the House Committee on Government Operations, 88th Congress, 1st session, May 24, 1963, pp. 387-420; and "US Information Problems in Vietnam," House Report 797, 88th Congress, 1st session, October 1, 1963.
15. Hallin, *The "Uncensored" War*, p. 9.
16. Hammond, *The Military and the Media*, p. 69.
17. 31 Americans died in Vietnam in 1962, 77 in 1963, cited in Hallin, *The "Uncensored" War*, p. 28.
18. Ibid., pp. 24-25.
19. From a memo from Rostow to Secretary of State Dean Rusk, cited in Hammond, *The Military and the Media*, p. 70.
20. This distinction has become widely accepted among those studying the period. See William M. Hammond, "The Press in Vietnam as Agent of Defeat: A Critical Examination," *Reviews in American History*, June 1989, pp. 312-323; Hallin, *The "Uncensored" War*, p. 28; Aronson, *The Press and the Cold War*, pp. 182-183; Knightley, pp. 374-381.
21. Cited in Aronson, *The Press and the Cold War*, p. 216.
22. For a brief summary of press pessimism about South Vietnamese forces and government, including excerpts from news stories, see Hallin, *The "Uncensored" War*, pp. 39-43.
23. Hammond, *The Military and the Media*, p. 70; also see Hammond's discussion of negative press coverage and officials reactions to it, pp. 70-80.
24. Cited in Hammond, *The Military and the Media*, p. 12.

25. Cited in Braestrup, *Big Story*, pp. 2-3.
26. Herring, *America's Longest War*, pp. 134-135, for example.
27. Hammond, *The Military and the Media*, p. 16.
28. See, for example, Peter Braestrup's background paper in *Battle Lines: Report of the Twentieth Century Fund Task Force Report on the Military and the Media* (New York: Priority Press Publications, 1985), pp. 63-64; the unreliability of the follies is discussed in almost every account of military/media relations.
29. Cited in K. Williams, "Vietnam: The First Living-Room War," p. 255.
30. Hammond, *The Military and the Media*, pp. 74-80.
31. Ibid., pp. 80-85.
32. Ibid., pp. 102-103
33. *Wall Street Journal*, April 23, 1965, cited in US Congress, Senate, Hearings Before the Committee on Foreign Relations, "News Policies in Vietnam," 89th Congress, 2nd session, p. 64; Senator Fulbright offered this and several other articles in the same vein for consideration during the hearings.
34. Hammond, *The Military and the Media*, pp. 87-91; for the press response see *Chicago Tribune*, "Still Managing the News," June 15, 1964; *Aviation Week Magazine*, "The Credibility Gap," June 15, 1964.
35. "The Price of Secrecy," *Washington Post*, June 17, 1964.
36. Hammond, *The Military and the Media*, pp. 133-142.
37. Ibid., pp. 139-140.
38. Ibid., p. 160.
39. Doris Kearns Goodwin, *Lyndon Johnson and the American Dream* (New York: Harper and Row, 1976), p. 252.
40. Herring, *America's Longest War*, pp. 108-143; and on Johnson's continuing efforts to balance Vietnam and domestic legislation see Kathleen Turner, *Lyndon Johnson's Dual War: Vietnam and the Press* (Chicago: University of Chicago Press, 1985).
41. Hammond, *The Military and the Media*, p. 145; Braestrup, *Battle Lines*, p. 66; and *Vietnam: 10 Years Later* (Defense Information School, Ft. Benjamin Harrison, 1984), pp. 52-53.
42. Ibid., pp. 144-145
43. Ibid., p. 145
44. Dale Minor notes that the rule on casualties reporting seesawed. There was so much skepticism of how the terms light, moderate, and heavy were being applied that MACV switched back to using specific numbers, only to return to the policy during the Tet Offensive, when it was determined that revealing actual numbers during a battle could aid the enemy. See Minor, *Information War* (New York: Hawthorn Books, 1970), p. 50.
45. "News Policies in Vietnam,"pp. 66-113; also, Hammond, *The Military and the Media*, pp. 133-148.
46. "News Policies in Vietnam," pp. 67-68.
47. Arthur Vessey, "Reporter Finds Viet War Easy: Providing," *Chicago Tribune*, June 20, 1966.

48. Braestrup, *Big Story*, p. 7.
49. On Johnson's decisions to extend the U.S. commitment and to deploy ground troops, see Herring, *America's Longest War*, pp. 108-143; Hallin, *The "Uncensored" War*, pp. 59-101; Karnow, *Vietnam: A History*, pp. 395-426; and Berman, *Planning a Tragedy*.
50. Herbert Y. Schandler notes that "efforts were made to make the change as imperceptible as possible to the American public . . ." in *The Unmaking of a President: Lyndon Johnson and Vietnam* (Princeton: Princeton University Press, 1977), pp. 20-22; Hallin, pp. 59-101.
51. Hammond, *The Military and the Media*, p. 151.
52. From National Security Action Memorandum 328, April 6, 1965, signed by McGeorge Bundy and addressed to the Secretary of State, Secretary of Defense, and the Director of Central Intelligence, cited in Philip Geyelin, "Vietnam and the Press," pp. 166-167.
53. Berman, *Planning a Tragedy*, pp. 57-58.
54. Hallin, *The "Uncensored" War*, p. 61
55. Ibid., pp. 80-101.
56. Journalists pounced on Johnson for his dissembling. See, for example, Arthur Krock, "In the Nation: By Any Other Name, It's Still War," *New York Times*, June 10, 1965; Charles Mohr, "War and Misinformation," *New York Times*, November 26, 1965; James Reston, "Washington: 'Candor Compels Me to Tell You . . .'" *New York Times*, November 17, 1965.
57. CBS News broadcast August 5, 1965, cited in Hammond, p. 188.
58. Hammond, *The Military and the Media*, pp. 185-193; Donovan and Scherer, pp. 79-83.
59. Hammond, *The Military and the Media*, pp. 207-208.
60. Ibid., p. 232.
61. "News Policies in Vietnam," p. 63.
62. Ibid., pp. 66-113
63. Jack Raymond, "It's a Dirty War for Correspondents, Too," *New York Times*, February 13, 1966.
64. Aronson, *The Press and the Cold War*, p. 226.
65. Hallin, *The "Uncensored" War*, pp. 163-167; Turner, *Dual War*, pp. 170-211; Karnow, *Vietnam: A History*, pp. 479-514.
66. John H. Fenton, "Lodge Finds War Hurt by Critics," *New York Times*, April 27, 1967.
67. Hammond, *The Military and the Media*, p. 265.
68. Ibid., pp. 287-290.
69. Max Frankel argued that Westmoreland was, in essence, doing something Johnson could not politically afford to do himself in "Johnson and the General," *New York Times*, April 28, 1967; see also John Herbers, "Morton Accuses Johnson of Stifling Debate on War," *New York Times*, April 28, 1967; and James Reston, "Washington: Blessed Are the War Makers?" *New York Times*, April 28, 1967.
70. Tom Wicker, "Westmoreland Tells Congress US Will Prevail," *New York Times*, April 29, 1967; "Transcript of the Westmoreland

Speech," *New York Times,* April 29, 1967; John Herbers, "Congress Expects War Escalation," *New York Times,* April 19, 1967; Westmoreland gives his own interpretation of the speech in *A Soldier Reports,* pp. 224-229.

71. Westmoreland notes in his memoirs that he had serious reservations about going to Washington and entering the political sphere; *A Soldier Reports,* pp. 224-225.
72. Hammond, *The Military and the Media,* pp. 289-290.
73. Ibid., pp. 296-299; Hammond notes several several articles echoing this theme: Tran Van Dinh, "A Look at the Vietnamese Armies," *Christian Science Monitor,* June 15, 1967; "The War: Taking Stock," *Time,* July 14, 1967; "The War in the Delta," *Newsweek,* August 14, 1967; Merton Perry, "Their Lions, Our Rabbits," *Newsweek,* October 9, 1967; and Everett G. Martin, "Vietnam: Last Chance," *Newsweek,* September 25, 1967.
74. Cited in Hammond, *The Military and the Media,* p. 282.
75. Herring, *America's Longest War,* pp. 181-185.
76. Cited in Herring, *America's Longest War,* p. 183; also see Hammond, *The Military and the Media,* p. 328.
77. Cited in Dale Minor, *The Information War,* p. 69. Minor notes that other opinions about the war's progress were evident in the press. For example, Hanson Baldwin, military analyst for the *New York Times* was writing at the same time that North Vietnam could no longer be seeking a military victory. See Minor, pp. 69-74
78. Hammond, *The Military and the Media,* pp. 328-333.
79. On Westmoreland's trip see Braestrup, *Big Story,* pp. 48-61; Oberdorfer, *Tet!* (Garden City, NY: Doubleday, 1971), pp. 102-108; Westmoreland, *A Soldier Reports,* p. 234.
80. Westmoreland's speech is reprinted as Appendix I in Braestrup, *Big Story.*
81. James Reston, "Washington: Communique from the Home Front," *New York Times,* November 17, 1967; Joseph Kraft, "Westmoreland's Trip, Swing by LBJ Have Common Themes," *Washington Post,* November 14, 1967; Hedrick Smith, "Optimists vs. Skeptics," *New York Times,* November 24, 1967; Ward Just, "The Heart Mind Gap in Vietnam War," *Washington Post,* November 19, 1967.
82. Louis Harris, "Johnson Regains Popularity," *Philadelphia Inquirer,* December 4, 1967.
83. Hammond, *The Military and the Media,* pp. 338-339.
84. The best single work documenting Tet is Don Oberdorfer, *Tet!* (Garden City, NY: Doubleday, 1971).
85. Don Oberdorfer, *Tet!,* citing official U.S. figures in the dedication page.
86. Braestrup, *Big Story,* pp. 120-123; for Westmoreland's views of Tet in hindsight, see *A Soldier Reports,* pp. 310-334.
87. Ibid., pp. 508-529.

88. Ibid., Braestrup, *Big Story,* p. 218.
89. Ibid., pp. 509-520.
90. Oberdorfer, *Tet!* pp. 159-160, 238-277.
91. Karnow, *Vietnam: A History,* p. 526.
92. Braestrup readily admits this point; *Big Story,* pp. 48-74, 468-471.
93. Herring, *America's Longest War,* p. 191.
94. Braestrup, *Big Story,* p. 141.
95. Johnson urged Westmoreland, for instance, to say something positive every day during the crisis to ease the shock in the United States. Braestrup, *Big Story,* p. 468
96. Aronson, *The Press and the Cold War,* p. 245.
97. Oberdorfer, *Tet!,* p. 251.
98. Halberstam, *The Powers That Be,* pp. 716-717.
99. Braestrup, *Big Story,* p. 501.
100. Johnson told the country, "I have concluded that I should not permit the presidency to become involved in the partisan divisions that are developing in this political year. . . . Accordingly, I shall not seek, and I will not accept, the nomination of my party for another term as your president." Karnow, *Vietnam: A History,* p. 565.
101. Interview with William M. Hammond, April 18, 1994. Hammond notes that public information officers tended to be less knowledgeable about the war after Tet, less likely to tolerate opposing viewpoints about the war from the press, and generally less helpful to journalists on an individual basis. Official policies did not change much, however.
102. Works that examine Nixon's relationship with the press more generally include Joseph C. Spear, *Presidents and the Press* (Cambridge, MA: MIT Press, 1984); Marilyn A. Lashner, *The Chilling Effect in TV News* (New York: Praeger Publishers, 1984); William E. Porter, *Assault on the Media: The Nixon Years* (Ann Arbor: University of Michigan Press, 1976); and Joe McGinniss, *The Selling of the President* (New York: Pocket Books, 1970).
103. Hallin, *The "Uncensored" War,* pp. 167-210.
104. Broadcasting is a federally regulated industry. The Federal Communications Commission created the Fairness Doctrine in order to ensure that although the number of available television channels was limited, the number of political viewpoints broadcast would not be. With Nixon on television so frequently to promote his views on Vietnam, it was felt that under the regulations opposing viewpoints should be given airtime.
105. Herring, *America's Longest War,* p. 230; This speech also led to Agnew's series of attacks on the press. Nixon was extremely upset at the instant post-speech analysis of his remarks by the networks. He felt that they were ruining his ability to speak directly to the public in his own words. He thus gave Agnew the task of publicly attacking the "nattering nabobs of negativity," and the liberal

establishment press. Agnew's attacks fared quite well with the general public, but did little to improve the administration's relationship with the press. See, for example, Hallin, *The "Uncensored" War*, pp. 181-191; Spear, *Presidents and the Press*, pp. 114-121.

106. Herring, *America's Longest War*, p. 236.
107. Herring, *America's Longest War*, pp. 237-239; William Shawcross, *Sideshow: Kissinger, Nixon and the Destruction of Cambodia* (New York: Touchstone, 1987, Revised Edition), pp. 128-160 on the "incursion" and and the reaction in the United States.
108. Shawcross, *Sideshow*, pp. 19-35.
109. Ibid., p. 94.
110. Ibid., pp. 34-35.
111. Braestrup, "Covering the Vietnam War," *Nieman Reports, 1970*, pp. 8-13; Interview with William M. Hammond, April 18, 1994. The second volume of the Army's official history of Vietnam military public affairs, also written by Hammond, *Public Affairs: The Military and the Media, 1968-1973* (Washington, DC: Center of Military History United States Army, 1996).
112. Cited in Braestrup, *Battle Lines*, p. 71.
113. For discussions of My Lai see Knightley, *The First Casualty*, pp. 390-397; Seymour Hersh, "The Story Everyone Ignored," *Columbia Journalism Review*, Winter 1969-1970, pp. 55-58.
114. William V. Kennedy, *The Military and the Media*, pp. 87-90; Salisbury even being in North Vietnam was a problem for many. But worse, he reported that the United States had been hitting civilian targets and killing North Vietnamese civilians in Hanoi, something U.S. officials had denied. His statistics came from North Vietnamese government documents but without noting that they were the source of his story. Even journalists who supported Salisbury's trip to Hanoi felt that this was a big mistake. See Hammond's discussion of Salisbury's trip, *The Military and the Media*, pp. 274-279; *Columbia Journalism Review*, "A Salisbury Chronicle," Winter 1966-67, pp. 10-13.
115. Braestrup, *Battle Lines*, p. 72.
116. Hallin, *The "Uncensored" War*, pp. 181-210.

3

The Legacy of Vietnam and the Growth of Media Power

Those who argue that Vietnam had a major impact on current wartime press policies are correct, but not for the reasons they cite. The most mindful student of the Vietnam experience with respect to the press was not the military but the White House. Though the military did expend a great deal of energy learning from Vietnam, that energy was directed at becoming a more effective fighting force, not at becoming better public relations agents. And more importantly, the most critical relationship to break down during Vietnam was not that between the military and the media as is almost universally assumed. The critical breakdown was in fact between the White House and the press, and even more broadly between the institutions of government and the press. The predominantly calm and trusting relationship between the institutions of government and the Fourth Estate was the primary casualty of Vietnam, replaced by an atmosphere of mistrust and skepticism that now pervades their interaction.

Driving and shaping the emergence of the new White House media strategy (and, I believe, of political-military strategy more generally, though to a lesser extent as well) is growing presidential wariness of what might be called Mueller's Dictum. Mueller's Dictum states simply that as casualties rise, public support for war, and thus for presidents, inevitably will fall. John Mueller, a political scientist, showed twenty-five years ago that public support for the Korean and Vietnam wars dropped fifteen percentage points for every order of magnitude increase in casualties. Thus, for example, as casualties (dead and wounded) in Vietnam grew from 1,000 to 10,000, and again as they went from 10,000 to 100,000, support for the war dropped fifteen percentage points. Presidents have not, of course, read Mueller's work. Rather, they and others saw for themselves the disaster of Vietnam and appear to have concluded that the public has little stomach for long and bloody wars. Such an experience goes a long way to explaining the origins of America's new approach to waging war from a politico-military perspective, but by itself fails to explain why an aggressive policy of press restrictions and public relations has become a fundamental element of that new approach.

Mueller argued that public disillusionment with war grew simply as a result of mounting casualties, but modern presidents disagree. Presidents believe that the link between casualties and opinion is heavily influenced by how the media presents the war and its costs to the public. Despite Mueller's insistence that in fact the media, and television in particular, have nothing to do with the level of public support for war, presidents fear that negative coverage of war, especially television coverage, could destroy public support, make successful resolution of a conflict impossible, and ruin their presidencies.

To presidents the press represents an increasingly certain threat even to the "quick and painless" warfighting strategy they have adopted to minimize political and military vulnerabilities. Presidents fear that even a successful, low-casualty conflict could be ruinous to their political fortunes if television managed to transmit footage of even a few soldiers losing their lives in the wrong way or at the wrong time. Where Mueller sees a tidy, logrithmic relationship between reality and opinion, presidents see an irrational and emotional connection. Intense media coverage of even a few casualties, they believe, can shake public confidence in the president and the mission. Presidents thus fear sustaining even low levels of casualties when the media will be there to witness and report them.

And although presidents have always feared the power of press coverage of war to damage the national interest as well as their own political fortunes, their fears have intensified since Vietnam for two main reasons. First, the volatile role played by the press during Vietnam gave rise to an acrimonious debate over the impact of wartime coverage and for the first time split the government and press into competing camps. Since Vietnam the government/press relationship has become ever more adversarial, making presidents more certain than ever that reports from the battlefield will do damage to their own efforts as well as the national interest. This fear has motivated the White House to seek greater controls over what the media reports.

Second, the government/press split and the mistrust and fear it engendered in the White House have been dramatically intensified by the rising power of the press in politics and its consequences. Since Vietnam the press has become a more powerful player in all aspects of the political process and presidents have come to rely more more heavily than ever on media strategies to build and maintain public support for their efforts and governance. As their belief in the importance of shaping and controlling even day-to-day press coverage of their actions on a daily basis has grown more entrenched, so have their fears of what might happen were an unfettered and uncensored press to be allowed to report from the battlefield. The rising importance of the press could by itself account, I believe, for the increased efforts by the White House's to control the press in times of war. Coupled with the breakdown in the government/press relationship, however, the new power of the press has provided almost irresistible motivations for presidents to seek to impose harsh restrictions on press access to the battlefield and to use the resulting information dominance to maximum public relations advantage.

In sum this chapter argues that presidents operate and wage war today in a political environment very different from that which they encountered either during Vietnam or before. The new environment, in which the mass media play a more powerful, pervasive, and adversarial role, has forever changed the way presidents will seek to deal with journalists in time of war. In the wake of Vietnam and with a generation's worth of accumulating evidence of the political power of the news, especially of negative news, presidents and their advisors believe that it would be foolish to prepare for war without preparing for the press.

This chapter fleshes out this argument first by outlining the debate that broke out over the role and impact of the press in Vietnam and by documenting the adversarial relationship between the government and the press that it helped spawn. It then discusses in detail how the rising power of the press has exacerbated these tensions and heightened presidential fears of wartime coverage, thereby pushing the White House inexorably toward the new, more aggressive and restrictive press policies seen from Grenada through the Gulf war. Later chapters then provide the historical support for this argument by documenting the White House's central and primary role in the development of those policies.

THE DEBATE OVER PRESS POWER AND THE EROSION OF THE GOVERNMENT/PRESS RELATIONSHIP

The media's performance and perceived impact during the Vietnam War set off an acrimonious debate whose echoes are still loud and clear today and that, later chapters will show, has had a longstanding influence over the way the White House has dealt with the press both in general and, more particularly, during crises and conflicts. On one side presidents, government officials, military officers, and many conservatives felt that the press had "lost the war" or at least had made its effective prosecution impossible while at the same time wrecking havoc on several presidents politically. On the other side, journalists, led by those who had reported the war firsthand, as well as many liberals, believed that the free press, unchecked by restrictions or censorship, had proved itself to be a powerful protector of the national interest through its ruthless pursuit of the truth in the face of persistent government efforts to hide the war from the public, to sugarcoat its consequences, and to overstate U.S. successes. The press, they argued, had helped educate the public about the true nature and costs of the war and in so doing had helped bring the misguided and ill-fated war to a quicker end than otherwise would have been the case.

The Vietnam War did not mark the first time that people had worried about the potential dangers of unrestrained press coverage of war. The tight censorship imposed in both of the World Wars, of course, was guided by just such concerns. And in each of the previous wars during this century most journalists saw themselves as part of the "American team" and went along willingly with censorship, agreeing for the most part that the national interest was best served by government-controlled press coverage so as not to disrupt American morale on the homefront or to give aid and comfort to the enemy in any way. As late as the Korean War, in fact, the journalists in the war zone asked the military to impose censorship after the press corps found a more relaxed policy too much responsibility.[1]

This changed drastically, however, with Vietnam. The press no longer believed that the national interest was served by censorship. As Daniel Hallin notes, ". . . it was a war in which journalists clearly did not think of themselves simply as 'soldiers of the typewriter' whose mission was to serve the war effort."[2] The press began to argue in essence that journalists, not the government, should make the decisions about what should be news, and that the truth, rather than the impact of that truth, should guide a journalist's actions. Malcolm Browne, a journalist who covered Vietnam in the early years reflected on this new perspective in a 1965 article, "Our concern is not what effect a given piece of news will have on the public. Our concern is to get the news before the public, in the belief that a free public must be an informed public. The only cause for which a correspondent must fight is the right to tell the truth and the whole truth."[3]

Vietnam thus represented the first time a war had been openly reported in the twentieth century and the first time that the press had argued that the benefits to the nation of a free press during time of war outweighed its potential dangers. Among those who believed that the press had had an extremely negative impact on the national interest during the Vietnam War, this new attitude generated both outrage and a great deal of concern for what might happen in the future if the media were allowed to report without censorship again. At the White House, in particular, thoughts of such an institutionalized, dedicated, and powerful threat to the national interest and to the president's political well-being have made the imposition of press restrictions an obvious strategic choice. On the other side many journalists and liberals more generally became so convinced that the White House had failed to act in the public interest throughout the war that for them the role the press had played in Vietnam took on almost mythical importance. These tensions have lent far greater urgency and acrimony to the modern debate than it has ever had before.

This section of the chapter examines the arguments made by each side in this debate since Vietnam. In part it is an effort to analyze systematically what I will call the national interest/free press debate. More importantly, though, it serves to illustrate how the Vietnam war helped to erode the government/press relationship and thus to sow the seeds of the more aggressive and restrictive White House media strategies of recent conflicts.

The National Interest Camp

Presidents, military officers, and conservatives have argued that the negative, bloody, sensational reporting of Vietnam biased the public against the war, gave aid and comfort to North Vietnam and the Viet Cong, and bolstered opponents of the war at home, all of which weakened the president's ability to wage war effectively and helped lead to U.S. failure in a war to which it had committed tens of thousands of lives, billions of dollars, the credibility of its political leadership and its international reputation.

The national interest camp argues that much of the damage done by the press during Vietnam stemmed from the fact that the press came to view its mission as that of an adversary or critic of government whose only interest was to report the news without any reference to its impacts. Gone were the days when journalists identified with the American cause; now journalists identified with journalism, and saw the pursuit of "the story" as a higher calling than duty to their nation. This lack of patriotism aggravated military officers and civilian officials committed to fighting a war against the specter of communism. S.L.A. Marshall, a retired general then covering military affairs for the Detroit News, noted the breakdown of the old system,

> In the days of yore the American correspondent . . . was an American first, a correspondent second. This old-fashioned standard seems to have been forgotten in South-East Asia. Some old-timers still play the game according to the rules. There is a new breed that acts as if it believes a press ticket is a license to run the world.[4]

Worse in the eyes of the national interest camp, however, was its widely held belief that journalists not only lacked a sense of patriotism, but in fact that a majority of them were personally opposed to the war effort and had abandoned the journalistic tenet of objectivity to criticize the war in their reports. Major General Winant B. Sidle argues years after that

> The quality of reporting from Vietnam suffered from advocacy journalism. Too many reporters, especially the younger ones, arrived firmly convinced that the war was unjust, immoral, or whatever, and that the US should not be there. This trend became more noticeable after Tet. These advocacy journalists seemed to think that Americans are incapable of reaching sound, reasoned opinions based on plain old factual, complete and objective reporting. So the reporter tried to convince his audiences via his *news* coverage that his opinions should be their opinions.[5] (Sidle's italics)

And, in a widely noted episode from a background briefing in Washington during the Tet Offensive, Secretary of State Rusk angrily revealed the depth of official frustration with an unpatriotic press:

> There gets to be a point when the question is, whose side are you on? I'm the Secretary of State, and I'm on our side. . . . None of your papers or your broadcasting apparatuses are worth a damn unless the United States succeeds. They are trivial compared to that question. So I don't know why, to win a Pulitzer Prize, people have to go probing for things one can bitch about when there are 2,000 stories on the same day about things that are more constructive in character.[6]

The national interest camp argues that the press coverage generated by this adversarial style of reporting was overly critical of the military, presidents, and the U.S. cause generally, was extremely violent and bloody, especially on television, and most often failed to put events in context for the public. As General Westmoreland argued in his memoirs,

> . . . television's unique requirements contributed to a distorted view of the war. The news had to be compressed and visually dramatic. Thus the war that Americans saw was almost exclusively violent, miserable, or controversial: guns firing, men falling, helicopters crashing, buildings toppling, huts burning, refugees fleeing, women wailing.[7]

Hawkish journalist Richard Fryklund of the Washington Star put it this way:

> Television's day-to-day coverage of the war in Viet Nam—uncensored, biased and deeply emotional, is becoming a national problem. . . . The presence of the camera can "create" news where none otherwise would have existed. . . . The interviewed soldier who understates has no impact. He sells no soap. His little segment is dropped, and something with maximum drama is substituted. . . . The Viet Cong have a policy of deliberate torture and assassination. . . . But they don't permit uncensored television coverage, and their people don't have sets. Our side permits reporters and cameramen to go everywhere and record everything.[8]

Over time, argues the national interest camp, this violent, emotional, and negative coverage of war turned the public against the war despite the fact that a large majority had supported it for years. In short, the American public is squeamish, and if television cameras in particular reveal the underside of war, public support for war will decline *even for worthy causes.* As he made clear the day after his nationally televised speech to the nation in which he announced that he would not seek another term, Lyndon Johnson was a committed member of this camp:

> As I sat in my office last evening, waiting to speak, I thought of the many times each week when television brings the war into the American home. No one can say exactly what effect those vivid scenes have on American opinion. Historians must only guess at the effect that television would have had during earlier conflicts on the future of this Nation: during the Korean war, for example, at that time when our forces were pushed back to Pusan; or World War II, the Battle of the Bulge, or when our men were slugging it out in

> Europe or when most of our Air Force was shot down that day in June 1942 off Australia.[9]

Others observers since Johnson, such as E. L. Patullo, have been more blunt:

> The root problem is that in a war zone one sees only the part of the truth that makes rational men and women abhor war—the awful fact of humans preparing to kill, killing, and being killed. Excluded from the picture is the chain of events that has persuaded the nation to resort to force.[10]

Thus, if the United States is to stand its ground, television pictures must not show our troops fighting, the harsh conditions under which they fight, and most important of all, they must not show American troops dying.

The second way in which the national interest camp believes that this type of press coverage may damage U.S. national interests is by giving domestic opponents of the president ammunition with which to attack him. In Washington a president's power rests to a great extent on perceptions of his public approval and support. War coverage that is unfairly and preponderantly negative in tone and focused on the horrors of war may embolden the president's political enemies to attack him more vigorously. If they can point to sagging public approval of the president's policies, even if they are temporary and media-induced rather than "rational" calculations of the national interest, critics of the president will have a greater chance of success in derailing his policies. At the same time, allies of the president may also take their cues from critical media reports and their support for him, at least in public, may wane. Both of these dynamics make it harder for a president to do what must be done to lead the nation in time of war.

This fear was realized, argues Peter Braestrup, in the wake of the Tet Offensive, as the press, particularly television, framed the crisis as a stunning defeat for the United States and thereby ignited far more vocal congressional and public opposition to the war than had existed previously. The reaction to Tet coverage not only cost Lyndon Johnson politically but made it impossible for him to take advantage of the military opportunity the crisis in fact represented according to General Westmoreland. It also would narrow the range of options Richard Nixon could later choose from in attempting to fight the war.[11]

Subsequent heavy coverage of such media-fueled "domestic dissent," often symbolized during Vietnam by television coverage of protests in the streets, may in turn cause another serious problem. By focusing so intensely on policy debates and challenges to presidential authority, argues the national interest camp, the media may signal to an enemy that the United States lacks or has lost the resolve to carry through. This danger is particularly relevant in situations like Vietnam and the limited conflicts that have characterized the post-Vietnam era. The American strategy in Vietnam was not to win an outright military victory but to fight long enough and impose great enough costs on North Vietnam that its leadership would decide to give up their battle for control of the South. As a consequence presidents deemed the North Vietnamese perceptions of American resolve critical and worried continually that press coverage might give the impression that they lacked the will to continue fighting in Vietnam.[12]

The national interest camp took up this line of argument again during the Gulf war. Throughout the tense standoff of Desert Shield before the war, President Bush hoped to convince Saddam Hussein that the United States and the international community would cut off all of Iraq's ties to the outside world, thereby causing great harm to the Iraqi people, economy, and military, until he left Kuwait. Later, Bush hoped that by threatening military action to eject Iraq's forces if they were not withdrawn by the January 15th deadline he could win Hussein's compliance without actually having to risk U.S. casualties. Again, the success of such coercive efforts was believed to rest at least in large part on the credibility of Bush's threat. But as debate in the United States over whether to continue with an embargo or to use military force escalated and was reported on extensively in the press, national interest camp observers worried that Iraq would get the wrong message. Political scientist Barry Posen summed up their fears:

> Had it taken place in October, when the proposal was first broached in the press, the country could have had a serious discussion of the merits and demerits of a prolonged embargo—a "long siege." But now, this debate will do more harm than good. It will wrongly help to convince Saddam Hussein that the coalition will not attack.[13]

Another way in which sensational, negative, and horrible coverage of war may damage the national interest is through its dampening effects on both civilian and military morale. Stories about defeats, antiwar demonstrations, or lingering debate over the rationale for fighting in the first place may wrongly convince people that the nation's sacrifices are wasted or misguided. It may also convince troops that the public has little confidence in their abilities or, worse, cares little about their well being. Because the combination of a disillusioned public and a demoralized military can only make winning a war more difficult, argues the national interest camp, such coverage should be minimized or altogether avoided.

Censorship during World War II did just that. It was not until 1942, for instance, that an American newspaper first showed a dead American soldier, and any news which criticized U.S. forces or their fighting prowess was apt to be struck by the censor's blue pencil. During Vietnam, however, critical coverage of the war led many to argue that the press had caused a rift between the public and the government, especially the military, and that America's fighting effectiveness was thereby diminished.[14]

Finally, the national interest camp has long argued that an unfettered press corps roaming around the battlefield poses a great risk to operational security. Ironically, with such a long list of complaints about press performance in Vietnam, violations of the reporting guidelines designed to ensure operational security were rare. Despite the press' strong track record in Vietnam, however, military officers and officials in the White House now argue more vehemently than ever that concerns for operational security demand tighter controls on the press. A great deal of this concern has emerged in reaction to the advances in media technology that now make it possible for journalists to report in real-time from anywhere on the globe. Military officers worry that journalists, many if not most of whom know very little about military affairs or fighting wars, are simply unprepared to make informed decisions about what material is safe to report and what is not, even if they are given a set of general guidelines to help them. This fear is then compounded by the fact that new technologies allow and encourage journalists to report news live or with far less time given to analyzing what they have just witnessed, thereby increasing the likelihood that something of use to the enemy will slip through. In addition, since Vietnam the cost and time involved in traveling around the world have decreased dramatically, ensuring that ever more journalists will be looking to report the news from the battlefield rather than from home.[15]

The Free Press Camp

Journalists and many liberals interpreted the impact of the press in diametrically opposite fashion. The free press camp argued that it was in large part the very fact that the press was free and uncensored that allowed it to carry out its prescribed mission of government watchdog effectively and allowed the public, in turn, to pass reasoned judgment on U.S. policies. Many believed that the press had proved itself to be a crucial brake on government officials out of touch with public opinion and the true "national interest." The free press camp argued that it was not biased or sensational press coverage but simply the reality that the United States was disastrously failing to win the war and never would that convinced the public that it was time to get out.

In an article written during the fall of Saigon in 1975 James Reston of the *New York Times* articulated the media's growing awareness of their powerful influence and at the same time made the case that the free press was essential to ensuring the national interest rather than a threat to it:

> The reporters began by defending the policy of American intervention, but reported facts that suggested it wouldn't work. Presidents Johnson and Nixon vilified them for challenging the official line that all was going well, and refusing to "get on the team," but in the end, the reporters came nearer to the truth in Vietnam than the officials.
>
> There may be an important lesson here: It is no longer possible for a free country to fight even a limited war in a world of modern communications, with reporters and television cameras on the battlefield, against the feelings and wishes of the people.
>
> Maybe the historians will agree that the reporters and the cameras were decisive in the end. They brought the issue of the war to the people, before the Congress or the courts, and forced the withdrawal of American power from Vietnam.
>
> One result is that the reporters of the press and radio and television are now being blamed for the defeat of American policy and power in Indochina, which is another way of challenging the whole idea of democracy.[16]

The free press camp has in turn challenged each point made by the national interest camp, beginning with the claim that the press corps was biased against the war. What the national interest camp read as bias the free camp argues was in fact simply the blunt truth about American failures to get the job done in Vietnam. Only after years of government obfuscations and attempts to paint a rosy picture of the war did journalists begin to challenge official statements and predictions. David Halberstam, for example, felt by the Kennedy administration to be one of the sharper thorns in its side in the early years of the war and widely regarded as representative of the antiwar slant of correspondents in Saigon, noted in his 1965 book that "I believe that Vietnam is a legitimate part of that global commitment. A strategic country in a key area, it is perhaps one of only five or six nations in the world that is truly vital to U.S. interests."[17]

The free press camp also disagrees that press coverage of the war was overly sensational, inaccurate, or particularly violent and argues that if the public is firmly committed to a cause then television reports, even violent ones, will not shake their faith. On the first count many journalists have argued vehemently that the press in fact did an excellent job of getting the facts straight and telling the public what was happening in Vietnam. Charles Mohr, correspondent for the *New York Times* argued, "Not only ultimately but also at each major milestone of the war, the weight of serious reporting corresponds quite closely to the historical record."[18] In addition to comparing its product to the historical record, a fairly stiff challenge for journalism, the free press camp has used a more pointed index of press performance during Vietnam—comparing the accuracy of press reports with the accuracy of government pronouncements of the time. It became an article of faith for many journalists and others that the press was usually closer to the truth than the government, even before the Johnson administration made the credibility gap a household phrase.[19] As David Halberstam viewed it, ". . . we had to be critical of the representatives of our government who created a policy of optimism about the war that simply was not justified. There was no choice for us. We had our duty to our newspapers, the public that reads them, and that was to tell the truth."[20] Not all government officials have disagreed with this assessment. Barry Zorthian later admitted of the 1964-1968 period, "More often than not, the press was more accurate in covering the situation in Vietnam than the official government public reports—at least until Tet."[21] And William Hammond, author of the Army's official history of public affairs in Vietnam, notes that David Halberstam's memoirs of the early Vietnam years "reads like the author saw the State Department's classified file on the period."[22]

Many journalists have also defended their record during Tet, the period of coverage most criticized by the national interest camp. Charles Mohr has taken issue with Peter Braestrup's conclusions about the performance of the press at Tet, arguing that the public and Congress interpreted Tet to be a defeat not as a result of the coverage of it but as a result of the Johnson administration's earlier public relations efforts to convince the public that the enemy was incapable of launching such an attack. Even television had its defenders. Leonard Zeidenberg, writing for *Broadcasting*, argued that "All three networks did remarkable work in covering the Communists' massive Tet Offensive of 1968 . . ."[23] And John Laurence, a CBS correspondent who covered Tet, disputes Braestrup's charge that journalists' work suffered during the crisis: "I recall that the men and women of the American press corps went about the job of trying to get the story in a professional, hardworking, and dedicated way. And—with one or two minor exceptions—they maintained the old tradition of 'grace under pressure.'"[24]

On the question of whether negative and violent footage turned public opinion against the war, the free press camp argues first that Vietnam coverage was neither so ugly as often asserted nor responsible for an "irrational" turn of public opinion against the war. First, in an analysis of the images accompanying television reports of the war, Lawrence Lichty has argued that only a minute portion contained "bloody" footage of war, casting doubt on the national interest camp's argument that television carried death and destruction into living rooms on a regular basis and thereby turned opinion against the war.[25] Further, Daniel Hallin, in the most complete study to date of media coverage of the war, argued that the press was not nearly so critical of the government as the national interest camp presumes and that press coverage only became more questioning of the war after political elites and the public had already turned against it.[26] Clarence Wyatt's study of newspaper coverage of the war supported Hallin's account, arguing that the majority of press accounts from Vietnam relied heavily on government sources and reflected far more of the government's viewpoint than many critics of press coverage would like to believe.[27]

And finally, on the question of press impact on public opinion in particular, John Mueller has shown that public support for Vietnam followed the same pattern as during Korea, falling in proportion to rising casualties, despite the vast differences in television coverage of the two wars and the fact that most Americans did not yet have television sets during the Korean War. This evidence, argues Mueller, strongly suggests that television did not have the negative impact on public opinion that the national interest camp has argued.[28]

On top of this, the free press camp argues that television coverage of the horrors of war does not have the power often claimed. Colonel Harry G. Summers, author of an influential analysis of political-military strategy during Vietnam, argues that the effect of television images cannot be considered without accounting for the public's previously held beliefs about the value of the war's objectives. Just as Germany's strategic bombing failed to break the British spirit and just as Allied bombing failed similarly to turn Axis publics against their governments, Summers argues, so do critics wrongly assume that televised horrors will provoke a public turnabout. If the public believes the goal is worthwhile and the costs justified, it will pay the necessary price despite the pictures.[29]

The free press camp also challenges the argument that coverage that spurs domestic dissent and debate is unhealthy for the nation in time of war. In contrast, argue many, times of crisis and conflict may demand more discussion. As with Vietnam, without open debate over the best course of action, American policy makers may lose sight of the limits that public opinion will eventually set on their actions. And if it is the government rather than the press that decides what it to be published about the progress of the war, much important information about the war will go unknown. The free press camp argues that Vietnam and most other conflicts reveal a clear tendency for presidents and militaries to blur the truth and deceive the public for political reasons and that a free and uncensored press is the best safeguard against the dangers of ignorance. And because Congress also depends so heavily on the press for information during foreign policy crises and war, to allow a president to control over press coverage is to allow him too much leverage in his relationship with the other branch of government involved in foreign policy making. Daniel Hallin offers the standard free press camp warning about the need for open debate: "Those who imagine that political elites would govern better without the press and public looking over their shoulders should look back to the decision-making process of the early 1960s that led to American intervention in Vietnam."[30]

Journalists also continue to argue that the press does not represent a risk to operational security despite advances in technology. A recent survey of journalists who cover defense issues found that 75% of them felt that the news media can be trusted with information that might jeopardize operational security if reported.[31] Journalists often point back to Vietnam for proof of their case. As noted, even official observers have admitted that Vietnam raised very few of the dangers the national interest camp worries about. Barry Zorthian noted that "In the four years [1964-1968] that I was in Vietnam with 2,000 correspondents accredited . . . we had only four or five cases of security violations . . . of tactical military information."[32] William Hammond has gone even further: "We could not confirm even one breach, never one where the enemy was able to take advantage, where they didn't have other ways of knowing."[33]

Finally, the free press camp also disputes the charge that uncensored press coverage will harm morale. During war the public takes a proprietary interest in its military. The public wants to know that its sons and daughters are being wisely employed in battle, and that they are doing well. In contrast to the national interest camp, however, the free press camp believes that the best way to ensure the public's confidence in its political and military leaders and morale is by providing accurate and plentiful information about the military's condition and its progress. As the Twentieth Century Fund Task Force on the Military and the Media argued:

> Imperfect though it is, our independent press serves as the vital link between the battlefield and the home front, reporting on the military's successes, failures, and sacrifices. By doing so, the media have helped to foster civilian involvement and support, which presidents, admirals, and generals have recognized as essential to military success.[34]

The Deterioration of Government/Press Relations Since Vietnam

Vietnam not only made it clear to national interest observers that an uncensored press could damage American interests and hurt the president politically, it also drove a wedge between the government and press and gave rise to an era of adversarial relations and mutual mistrust that has only gotten worse since then. The national interest/free press debate was a precursor, in fact, to a larger argument about the role of the press in politics, in which presidents again took the side of those who argued that the press had grown too powerful and had a tendency to disrupt policy making for the worse rather than the better, and journalists overwhelmingly tended toward the opposite view.

Officials and journalists are now far more likely to view their relationship as adversarial rather than cooperative all the time, not just during war. This has pushed the government toward greater wartime restrictions on the press for a simple reason: Officials have become more likely to see the press as a hostile force that must be subdued or evaded in order to achieve policy successes.[35] They do not believe that the media will portray their policies in a favorable light in the absence of concerted government public relations efforts. This fear has a sound basis. In fact, journalists no longer place the same level of trust in government statements and actions that they once did. The press once equated presidential intentions with the national interest. Journalists now force presidents to prove that their actions will benefit the nation. They are more likely to criticize policies with negative stories and to offer their own analyses of White House actions rather than simply accept the president's statements at face value.

The mistrust and adversarial relations engendered during Vietnam under Lyndon Johnson only intensified under Nixon, who feared and hated the press more than any president before or since. As noted in the previous chapter, Nixon's dealings with the press on Vietnam were hardly any more successful than Johnson's, although he initially enjoyed the benefit of a media honeymoon as a result of his campaign pledge to seek peace rather than victory in Vietnam. Nixon created his own problems as he talked about "Vietnamization" and "peace with honor" while seeking in secrecy to expand the war to Laos and Cambodia to force the North Vietnamese to give concessions at the peace negotiations. When journalists discovered that both they and the public had been duped, trust deteriorated further.[36]

Nixon's biggest contribution to the continuing decline of comity and trust between the government and press, however, were his many difficulties in dealing with the Washington press corps on a daily basis, which hit their peak, of course, with Watergate. Nixon, who had never had an easy time with the press, dating back to his days as Eisenhower's vice president, came into office and was soon frustrated with how the press covered his administration. As former Nixon speechwriter William Safire recounted, "I must have heard Richard Nixon say 'the press is the enemy' a dozen times."[37]

All presidents, of course, have had troubles with the press. Nixon, however, went to greater lengths to deal with the problem than any before or since. As Marilyn A. Lasher wrote in a study of Nixon's relations with the press:

> Lawsuits, tax audits, FBI investigations, threats, subpoenas, license challenges, retaliation, and power plays became the hallmarks of [Nixon's] dealings with the press. By orchestrating a barrage of anti-media efforts, the Nixon White House was able to chill dissent in political commentary delivered on network television evening news programs. . . .[38]

In 1969, upset over press coverage of antiwar demonstrations, Nixon had Vice President Spiro Agnew launch a public attack against television, chiding the networks for their "instant analysis" of presidential speeches and for their overly negative coverage of government. These attacks, often covered by the networks live and heavily covered by newspapers, in fact engendered a great deal of support from the public, but served to set journalists and the Nixon administration further at odds.[39] As Paul Weaver wrote, "These tactics not only didn't work, they seemed only to confirm the press in its new determination to be independent, which in context meant critical."[40]

Thus, when the Watergate scandal broke in 1973, journalists had little sympathy for Nixon. Throughout the year in which Watergate dominated the headlines and nightly newscasts, the administration's relations with the press deteriorated into a state of near war.[41] White House briefings grew tense and hostile, and the administration in vain explored every avenue to generate positive publicity for the president before he finally resigned to avoid impeachment on April 1974.[42]

Although Nixon's resignation perhaps marked the end of the darkest days of the government/press relations, it by no means signaled a clean slate. Presidents since have been no friends of the press, nor have journalists come to trust politicians and government institutions any more. As Thomas Patterson writes, "Although Watergate and Vietnam are viewed as the high point in critical coverage of our leaders, they merely marked the beginning of a steady rise in negative news."[43] Grossman and Kumar note that no president since Lyndon Johnson has enjoyed over 50% positive coverage in the *New York Times*, *Time*, or on CBS even in their first year, when coverage is at its most favorable.[44] This increase in critical coverage has done little to improve relations. As Paul Weaver pointed out, "Increasingly newsmen began to say that their job was to be an autonomous, investigative adversary of government and to constitute a countervailing force against the great authority of all established institutions."[45] As subsequent chapters will discuss in detail, both the Reagan and Bush administrations held extremely negative views of the press and felt that the press was very much an adversary which had to be reckoned with if they were to achieve their political goals.

THE RISE OF MEDIA POWER

Along with the deterioration of the government/press relationship emerged a more fundamental trend—the rise of media power in politics more generally—whose dynamics have in many ways radically altered American politics and that have greatly intensified presidential fears of media coverage during crisis and conflict. The rise of media power has, through various means, helped create a political environment in which presidents and their senior advisers sense that the media now represent a far more complex and dangerous threat not just to the national interest during war but to presidential political success. Occupants of the White House and their staffs now believe more than ever that they must, at least to some degree, shape news coverage of their actions if they are to be successful in their efforts in any arena of politics, not just in times of war.

The Growing Importance of the Press in Politics

The transformation of the press into a larger, more influential, more critical, and more independent actor in American politics has given presidents an increased interest and incentive in shaping the news coverage of their administrations. The stakes for influencing news coverage have risen as the media play a greater role in the policy process. Presidents know that a victory on the battlefield means nothing if they do not win the battle for public opinion through the media. And because the press has become politically more sophisticated and because other actors have learned how to gain access to the media to stake their claims, setting the public agenda and managing news has become more difficult. Presidents used to set the agenda simply by being the president. Now they must work harder to do so. Presidents have found that setting the agenda and getting their message to the public during war is much easier when the press is restricted than when it is free.

The press since Vietnam has become a larger and more influential force than ever in the policy process. Dom Bonafede noted this change in 1982,

> The press emerged from Vietnam and Watergate more confident–arrogant, in the view of its critics—and freer than ever from some of its self-imposed restraints. The news media today are bigger, more diverse, more influential and more controversial.[46]

Although not confusing size with importance, the growing role of the media in politics has been matched by its growing numbers. After World War II the Washington press corps numbered about 3,000. By the mid 1980s the number of newspeople in the capital was over 10,000.[47] Between 1968 and 1984 the number of radio and television reporters in Washington grew fourfold. This increase followed from the growing audiences for television news, and the need to cover the ever-growing number of programs and activities of the federal government.[48]

This pervasiveness, in turn, has helped spawn a more intrusive press, one which inspects and judges our government more thoroughly now than ever before. The journalists of today are also better educated than their counterparts twenty years ago, and the number of specialists in the press corps, able to follow arcane twists in policy, has risen substantially, making it much more difficult for the government to escape scrutiny by releasing incomplete or misleading information.[49] There is thus more pressure on policy makers to reveal the inner workings of government and details of policy than in the past. It has become much more difficult for the government to keep things secret or to delay the press in reporting any newsworthy item.[50] Even the private lives of public officials have largely become public domain.[51]

The press has also grown increasingly resistant to attempts by outsiders to manage the news. Journalists have always bridled at government (or other outside) control over the news, but over the last thirty years the major news organizations have become more independent. Jay Blumler summarized the journalistic desire for autonomy:

> Media power is not supposed to be shared: that's an infringement of editorial autonomy. It is not supposed to be controlled: that's censorship. It's not even supposed to be influenced: that's news management![52]

Observers have offered several reasons for the media's increased independence. Grossman and Kumar credit the growing financial and political power of these organizations with providing this independence.[53] Others see it as a result of the Vietnam/Watergate era, when journalists became disillusioned with their traditional role as "neutral transmitters" of government statements. When journalists stopped trusting that government press releases were honest, they perceived the need for greater distance from government and for a greater level of analysis of government actions and words.[54] Daniel Hallin notes that this independence may also have roots in the more general erosion of public confidence in institutions which began in the 1960s.[55]

Further, the president and White House in particular must cope with a much greater level of coverage than in the past. Michael Grossman and Martha J. Kumar found that the *New York Times* increased its White House coverage 50% in the 1968-1978 period compared to the 1953-1968 period, and *Time* nearly doubled its coverage over the same period.[56] Television, in particular, has been responsible for raising the visibility of the president and the White House.[57] The president makes perfect television; he offers high drama in a form all Americans can identify, and the logistics of covering the president are far less challenging for the networks than covering large numbers of scattered beats.[58] Grossman and Kumar found that over the period from 1968 to 1978, CBS ran an average of four stories about the president each night. Even more importantly, the president's stories tend to come early in the newscast, thereby making a bigger impression on the audience about their importance.[59]

Even more importantly, perhaps, with the demise of political parties as unifying and educational instruments, television and the print press have taken over the role of informing the public about the government's activities and providing judgments of the president's performance.[60] The press' power to set the agenda—to determine what politicians and the public will think and talk about—has grown as the press has inserted itself further into the policy process.[61] In the past, presidents had an easier time setting the agenda, with the press corps more often taking its cue from him. Now, however, as larger numbers of journalists prowl the sprawling federal government for news, presidents and other government agencies find it dramatically more difficult to focus the public's or Congress' attention on their preferred agenda. This trend is exacerbated by the fact that some journalists have become celebrities in their own right; reports and commentary from network stars can shine uncomfortable spotlights on public figures and organizations.[62]

As a consequence of its rising influence the press has become a more critical element of the political system. Television, especially, has become the linchpin of presidential strategies of governing.[63] Presidents know that their policy initiatives will be won or lost in the press. Negative press coverage could halt a program, thwart a cabinet nomination, or force a retreat in negotiations with congress. Martin Linsky interviewed senior government officials and found that they were in consensus on the growing importance of the press to public policy. Linsky found that not only do officials spend more time dealing and thinking about the press now than before Vietnam, he also found that those who had served in government primarily after Vietnam were more likely than others to report that the press had a "dominant impact" on the policy process.[64]

It is thus more important than ever that a president and his administration look good in the press and on television. As the media's importance in politics has risen, presidential efforts to manage news have intensified. The results are clear at the White House. Gary Orren notes that 25% of Reagan's senior staff was engaged in public relations or dealt with the media in some way.[65] But the White House's focus on the press is more fundamental than simple numbers can illustrate. As Lee Atwater, a senior political strategist in the Reagan White House later observed, "I can't think of a single meeting I was at for more than an hour when someone didn't say, 'How will this play in the media?'"[66] As we will see in subsequent chapters, this preoccupation with solving the press problem has carried over to wartime. As General Colin Powell warns, "Once you've got all your forces moving and everything's being taken care of by the commanders . . . turn your attention to television because you can win the battle or lose the war if you don't handle the story right."[67]

Advancing Media Technology

Accelerating presidential concerns and fears of the media has been the breakneck pace of technological change which has given journalists increasingly powerful tools to gather and disseminate news from around the globe, including the battlefield. Though the media's technological advances have raised concerns for officials throughout history, the pace of change and the growth of new media capabilities since Vietnam is unparalleled. Writing just before World War I in response to press coverage of the Spanish-American war, war correspondent Richard Harding Davis summarized the impact of technological change on the future of war, reporting:

> The fall of the war correspondent came about through the ease and quickness with which today's news leaps from one end of the earth to the other. In the days of the Crimea, of the Civil War, of the Franco-German and Russo-Turkish wars, the telegraph and cable were inadequate and expensive, and the war correspondent depend-

> ed largely upon the mails. In consequence, before what he wrote appeared in print the events he described had passed into history, and what information he gave could in no way benefit the enemy. But the day his cable from Cuba to New York was relayed to Madrid the war correspondent received his death sentence. . . .[68]

Davis' argument carries even greater weight today. The lightning-fast march of technology has transformed the media's newsgathering capabilities in the last twenty years and has magnified the government's incentives to keep the press away from the battlefield.[69] Advances in computers, satellites, fiber optics, minicams, and other areas have combined to allow the media to bring us news live and in color from anywhere on the globe, including the front line, sharpening fears of negative and horrible war coverage and altering the relative usefulness of censorship and restricting access.[70]

In earlier wars, the press agreed to give the government the ability to censor its materials (or agreed to self-censor, as in Vietnam) in return for access to the war zone and aid in transmitting their dispatches back home. In this way, the military, and thus the White House, could be assured nothing was published that would threaten operational security. Today, however, technology makes it possible for a journalist to transmit his story, his photos, and even his television footage back to the United States from almost anywhere in the world. A journalist no longer needs military assistance to send his material to his organization (which previously gave the military confidence that all material had been reviewed), nor does he need to even leave the battlefield. The bargain struck between access and censorship is thus no longer valid. Now, even if the government imposes censorship, unless the military keeps close track of all journalists, the military cannot be sure that it has reviewed everything.[71] As a result, officials have found it easier simply to keep the press away from the battlefield entirely, rather than risk the press using its technical capabilities to report from the front.

Officials worry that such uncensored reporting will be more likely to damage operational security and aid the enemy.[72] A reporter going live from a battle area could, in his rush to get on the air, disclose information that could damage operational security, simply because he did not stop to think about the consequences.[73]

Military and civilian leaders have long harbored particular concerns about television coverage of war. And with recent advances in media technology, their concerns have been amplified. During Vietnam television crews consisted of a reporter and two cameramen. The camera, to which the reporter was connected by a short wire when taping, weighted almost ninety pounds. Today television cameras weigh as little as fourteen pounds, are carried on a shoulder, and are easy to take almost anywhere.[74] With their greater mobility, television reporters are more able to cover the very action presidents fear most—combat. One Marine colonel noted at a conference on military/media issues: "My nightmare is that if the press can report instantaneously, parents will see Johnny's brains getting blown out on CNN."[75]

Some also complain that live television news from the battle zone is likely to lack even the rudimentary explanation and context necessary to understand a conflict. Without such context, it is argued, the public may be unduly swayed by images and forget or dismiss the logic behind the rational for U.S. action. Research shows that this concern has some merit. Live coverage of the Gulf War by CNN focused heavily on breaking events, but offered very little background about why they were happening.[76]

Further, the immediacy of the news today makes foreign policy more difficult to manage, especially during crisis situations. Lloyd Cutler, former White House counsel for Carter, argues that television coverage often robs the government of time to deliberate thoroughly when making decisions. Although newspapers have had similar impact in the past, television has an unsurpassed ability to alert the public and to spur presidents to quick action.[77] It seems fitting therefore that today almost all senior officials have a television nearby tuned to CNN, especially in a crisis, and often find that they, too, learn some things more quickly through that than other official intelligence channels. Chris Kent notes this reality in his article on CNN:

> As one US assistant secretary put it, "That's the first thing we here [in the administration] when something important happens—turn on CNN." Not long ago the Washington Post reported that Chief of Staff John Sununu had quipped at a recent staff meeting that "he had learned more about the attempted coup in Panama from watching Cable News Network than from Webster's Central Intelligence Agency."[78]

In Vietnam, television news lacked the immediacy that makes it such a powerful political force today. Vietnam footage shown during the nightly news was at least twenty-four hours old, often older. Without easy and inexpensive access to satellites in Vietnam, film had to be flown to Tokyo, from where it could then be sent to New York. The first same-day coverage seen from Vietnam was not until 1969. And the cost of using the satellite link for speedy news transmission was prohibitive except in exceptional circumstances.[79] The delays between events in Vietnam and their appearance on television news gave officials more time to make decisions than they are often allowed today.

Americans and their news organizations, furthermore, have become accustomed to the benefit of speed allowed by this technology.

Everyone will long remember the vivid images from the Berlin Wall *as it came down* in 1989, from Moscow during the attempted coup in 1991, and from Tienanman Square in China, as human rights protesters battled tanks in the streets.[80] In each case television cameras were there, bringing the entire world up to date on what was going on each day. Thus, although seeing television footage days later may have been the norm during Vietnam, today very little film of breaking events over a day old now makes it to the evening news.[81] Television correspondents in particular, whose primary professional concern is getting their stories on the air and getting them there before the competition, thus have a great incentive to resist government efforts to slow the pace of news.

Press Coverage of the Deteriorating Foreign Policy Consensus

The incentives for presidents to manage news during war have also grown stronger as a result of press coverage of the deteriorating consensus on American foreign policy. When political and military leaders agree on the need for military action, presidents will have a relatively easy time leading the nation into war. When elites disagree, however, the president faces a much more difficult task. Not only must he convince important political leaders that military action is necessary, he must do so under fire from critical press coverage. As Daniel Hallin and many others have noted, press coverage tends to reflect the debates and beliefs of political leaders. When they agree, the press is unlikely to challenge the justifications for U.S. policy. When they disagree, however, the press will report the misgivings of the critics.[82] Negative press coverage can then compound the difficulty a president has keeping his political allies on board and his enemies at bay.

During the darkest days of the Cold War, the broad outlines of U.S. strategy were clear, and few questioned a president's foreign policy decisions made within that framework.[83] American involvement in World War II, Korea, and even the war in Vietnam (at first) enjoyed bipartisan support in the United States. Presidents enjoyed generally favorable press coverage in these periods.

During Vietnam, however, the elite consensus over the war broke down. Press coverage became more negative, and the government/press relationship suffered.[84] After the war, Congress began to take a more active role in foreign policy, its members fearing that the president had gained too much power over its conduct.[85] The press has responded by holding post-Vietnam presidents to very high standards when considering involving the United States in another engagement. Every conflict since has fueled debate over whether the United States should pursue a military option.[86] Not only has this meant greater political opposition to presidents, but this opposition has been duly recorded by the media, often infuriating policy makers. Most recently, with the dissolution of the Soviet Union and the collapse of the Warsaw Pact, the Cold War compass directing U.S. foreign policy has disappeared entirely. The room for debate over strategy, as well as tactics, has increased dramatically. The task facing presidents who would lead the nation to war has become much more daunting.[87]

Increasing White House Efforts to Manage the News in Peace and War

At the same time White House fears about the destructive power of the press have risen, however, it has also recognized the correspondingly greater benefits for those who manage to dominate or influence press coverage on an issue. In an age of media-dominated politics public relations strategy sits on par with political strategy in the Oval Office. Presidents have come to view the media, especially television, as integral elements of their strategies for governing, for building public support, and for claiming credit for their successes. And just as they turn to the media in peacetime, so do they turn to public relations strategies in time of war. Public relations in fact represent a necessary complement to press restrictions. Keeping journalists away from bad news is but a first step, one which can only reduce the amount of negative press coverage of war. The second step presidents must take is to generate positive news coverage of conflict in order to justify their actions, convince the public that the cause is just and the costs bearable, and to ensure that a military victory redounds to their political benefit.[88]

Since Vietnam presidential appreciation of the growing importance of the media has led successive White House staffs to develop sophisticated strategies for public relations to combat the media's power. By many accounts, they have done so with great success. As Grossman and Kumar noted in 1981, "the recent history of the office of the president is in large part a history of the expansion of the resources that presidents have to get their message to the public."[89] Joseph Spear went so far as to say that "During this period [the 1970s] the chief executives virtually mastered the media."[90] This success has led in turn to a reliance on using public relations to build public support, to sway recalcitrant Congresses, and to maintain high levels of presidential approval. Their peacetime efforts to deal with the press have then been imported directly to wartime public relations campaigns.

Presidents believe that the aggressive use of the press has become increasingly essential simply to stay even, to avoid being drowned in criticism, to buoy presidential approval, and to keep the administration focused on its political agenda.[91] To play the public relations game successfully, a president must be media savvy. As Richard Cheney, former Ford chief of staff and Bush Secretary of Defense, told an interviewer, "The most powerful tool you have is the ability to use the symbolic aspects of the presidency to promote your goals and objectives. . . . You don't let the press set the agenda. The press is going to object to that. They like to set the agenda. They like to decide what's important and what isn't important. But if you let them do that, they're going to trash your presidency."[92] Further than that, however, presidents have found that skilled dealings with the press are also a powerful tool for building public support for their policies and for dealing with recalcitrant Congresses.[93] The result has been a steady rise in the sophistication of presidential efforts to manage the news coverage of their actions, and an increasing reliance on public relations to solve problems facing their administrations. It would be unthinkable today for a president to consider policy actions without simultaneously considering media strategy.

The evolution of a structured and sophisticated White House media operation began in earnest under Nixon. In an attempt to use the press to their advantage, Nixon and his staff initiated many of the routines carried on by every president since. For instance, Nixon's staff started compiling a daily news summary from television and newspaper stories to keep a close eye on press coverage. The administration made a routine of calling journalists to complain about mistakes and perceived bias or distortions in their reporting to influence future coverage by making them think twice about taking such a tack in the next story. In the administration's efforts to avoid the mediation of Washington journalists, many of whom Nixon considered unfriendly to his cause, senior officials often took their messages directly to local media outlets, who tended to be far less critical and more likely to report the administration's preferred themes. The most powerful version of this tactic was Nixon's repeated appearance on television during prime time for presidential addresses. By avoiding day-time press conferences in which journalists could ask hostile questions or selectively report Nixon's words to the public later that night, Nixon felt he could send his message directly to the public. With some minor exceptions and fine tuning, all presidents since Nixon have embraced his White House communications apparatus and public relations tactics.

Most observers agree that during the Reagan administration news management hit its stride. As I will discuss more thoroughly in Chapter Four, Reagan's presidency was consciously and skillfully packaged for television. David Gergen, communications director for Reagan, put it this way: "We wanted to control what people saw, to the extent that we could. We wanted to shape it and not let television shape it. . . . I mean, large aspects of government have become staged, television-staged, and there is a real question who is going to control the stage. Is it going to be the networks or the people who work for the candidate or for the president?"[94]

George Bush, although in no sense a great communicator like Reagan, nonetheless showed that he and his team had learned and borrowed from Reagan during his 1988 election campaign. Bush's advisers included experienced hands in the government/press struggle, and they first displayed their skills by using television far more effectively than Bush's opponent, Michael Dukakis.[95] Later, Bush showed his considerable sophistication on media issues during both the Panama and Persian Gulf crises. His use of the press in both cases helped him build overwhelming public support for actions which initially did not appear popular.[96]

CONCLUSION

Analyzing the debate that erupted in the wake of Vietnam over the role of the press during war and outlining the rise of media power since the war offers three central insights. First, the most critical piece of history with respect to modern White House strategies for dealing with the press is not in fact the Vietnam War, but the dramatic rise of the media's power in almost every realm of politics since then. Second, the most important and lasting legacy of the Vietnam War in terms of the media was not the breakdown in military/media relations as the conventional wisdom maintains, but the fundamental split between the government and press over the proper role of the press during war and the eventual souring of government/press relations more generally. Finally, when taken together, the rise of media power and the erosion of the government/press relationship have created a political environment in which presidents and their senior advisers clearly believe that they must seek control over the news, at least to some degree, in order to achieve their goals. The next three chapters illustrate the White House's attempts to control the press and shape the news to avoid threats both to the national interest and to presidential political interests.

ENDNOTES

1. Knightley, *The First Casualty* (New York: Harcourt Brace Jovanovich, 1975); Loren Thompson, "The Media versus the Military: A Brief History of War Coverage in the United States," in Thompson, ed., *Defense Beat* (New York: Lexington Books, 1991); Peter Braestrup, *Background Paper in Battle Lines* (New York: 20th Century Fund, 1985).

2. Daniel C. Hallin, *The "Uncensored" War* (Berkeley: University of California Press, 1986), p. 6.
3. Malcolm Browne, "Covering the War in Vietnam," *Columbia Journalism Review*, March/April 1965.
4. Quoted in R. Dudman, "What Ethics for Combat Reporting?" *Columbia Journalism Review*, Winter 1970-71, p. 35.
5. Sidle, "The Role of Journalists in Vietnam: An Army General's Perspective," in Salisbury, ed., *Vietnam Reconsidered*, p. 111.
6. Quoted in Aronson, *The Press and the Cold War*, pp. 244-245.
7. Westmoreland, *A Soldier Reports*, p. 420.
8. Quoted in William Kennedy, "Third View," pp. 39-40 from a December 7, 1965 article in the *Washington Star* by Fryklund.
9. "Remarks in Chicago before the National Association of Broadcasters," April 1, 1968, Lyndon B. Johnson, *The Public Papers of the President of the United States, 1968* (Washington, DC: Government Printing Office, 1969).
10. Patullo, "War and the American Press," *Parameters*, Vol. XXII, No. 4, Winter 1992-93.
11. Braestrup, *Big Story*, pp. 465-507.
12. Herring, *America's Longest War*, pp. 144-185, 225-230.
13. Posen, "Saddam Must Get Word: He Will Lose," *Boston Globe*, Nov. 25, 1990.
14. Knightley, *The First Casualty*; Thompson, "The Media Versus the Military."
15. Frank Aukofer and W. P. Lawrence's report on the relationship between the media and the military, *America's Team, The Odd Couple* (Nashville, TN: Freedom Forum First Amendment Center at Vanderbilt University, 1995), pp. 5-15
16. *New York Times*, April 1975.
17. David Halberstam, *The Making of a Quagmire* (New York: Random House, 1965).
18. Mohr, "Once Again—Did the Press Lose Vietnam?" *Columbia Journalism Review*, November/December 1983, p. 56.
19. Sydney Schanberg, "The Saigon Follies, or, Trying to Head Them Off at Credibility Gap," *New York Times Magazine*, November 12, 1972.
20. Quoted in Aronson, *The Press and the Cold War*, p. 195.
21. Zorthian, "The Press and Government: I," in Salisbury, ed., *Vietnam Reconsidered*, pp. 136-137.
22. Hammond, *The Military and the Media*, p. 393.
23. Leonard Zeidenberg, "Vietnam and Electronic Journalism: Lessons of the Living Room War," *Broadcasting*, May 19, 1975, p. 29.
24. John Laurence, "The Tet Offensive: Another Press Controversy: III," in Salisbury, ed., *Vietnam Reconsidered*, pp. 172-176.
25. Lichty, "The War We Watched on Television: A Study in Progress," *American Film Institute Report*, Vol. 4, No. 4, Winter 1973; also Lichty, "Video Versus Print," the *Wilson Quarterly*, Vol. 6, No. 6; and Michael Mandlebaum, "Vietnam: The Television War," *Daedulus*, Vol. 111, Fall 1982.

26. Hallin, *The "Uncensored" War*; Similar arguments are made by George Bailey, "The Vietnam War According to Chet, David, Walter, Harry, Peter, Bob, Howard, and Frank: A Content Analysis of Journalistic Performance by the Network Television Evening News Anchormen 1965-1970" (Unpublished Ph.D. thesis, University of Wisconsin, Madison, 1973); Oscar Patterson III, "An Analysis of Television Coverage of the Vietnam War," *Journal of Broadcasting*, Fall 1984; Todd Gitlin, *The Whole World is Watching: Mass Media in the Making and Unmaking of the New Left* (Berkeley: University of California Press, 1980).
27. Wyatt, *Truth from the Snares of Crisis: The American Press in Vietnam* (Unpublished Master's Thesis, University of Kentucky, 1984).
28. Mueller, *War, Presidents and Public Opinion* (New York: Wiley, 1973). Mueller's analysis is buttressed by a study done by Burns Roper for Peter Braestrup's book *Big Story*. Roper analyzed the polls before, during, and after Tet and found that coverage of the crisis did not have much impact, if any, on public support for the war.
29. Summers, "Western Media and Recent Wars," *Military Review*, May 1986, p. 10.
30. Hallin, *The "Uncensored" War*, p. 215.
31. Lawrence, *America's Odd Couple*, p. 183.
32. Zorthian, "The Press and Government: I" in Salisbury, ed., *Vietnam Reconsidered*, pp. 136-137.
33. Hammond, *The Military and the Media*, p. 393.
34. *Battle Lines: Report of the Twentieth Century Fund Task Force on the Military and the Media*, p. 4.
35. Linsky, *Impact*, p. 46.
36. For an excellent account of Nixon's Cambodia policies and their fallout, see William Shawcross, *Sideshow: Kissinger, Nixon, and the Destruction of Cambodia* (New York: Simon and Schuster, 1987 ed.); Stanley Karnow's excellent book is also useful, *Vietnam: A History* (New York: Penguin, 1984).
37. William Safire, *Before the Fall* (Garden City, NY: Doubleday, 1975) p. 352.
38. Marilyn A. Lasher, *The Chilling Effect in TV News* (New York: Praeger Publishers, 1984), p. 5.
39. Nixon's troubled relationship with the media spawned numerous books. On this period see, for example, Joseph C. Spear, *Presidents and the Press* (Cambridge, MA: MIT Press, 1984); William Porter, *Assault on the Media: The Nixon Years* (Ann Arbor: University of Michigan Press, 1976); and Maltese, *Spin Control . . .*
40. Paul H. Weaver, "The New Journalism and the Old—Thoughts after Watergate," *Public Interest*, Vol. 35, Spring 1974, p. 79.
41. Maltese, *Spin Control*, pp. 120-125.
42. Spear, Chapter 7.
43. Thomas E. Patterson, "Trust Politicians, Not the Press," *New York Times*, December 15, 1993, p. A27.

44. Grossman and Kumar, *Portraying the President*, p. 261.
45. Weaver, "The New Journalism . . .", p. 80.
46. Dom Bonafede, "The Washington Press—Competing for Power with the Federal Government," *National Journal*, April 17, 1982, p. 664.
47. Ibid., p. 664.
48. Gary Orren's introduction in Martin Linsky, *Impact: How the Press Affects Federal Policymaking* (New York: W. W. Norton, 1986), pp. 3-4. Numbers for the press corps in Washington are available in *Hudson's Media Contacts Directory* (Washington, DC: Howard Penn Hudson and Mary Elizabeth Hudson, 1994).
49. Stephen Hess, *The Washington Reporters* (Washington, DC: Brookings Institution, 1981), pp. 64-65.
50. On how much more cozy the relationship between officials and reporters was in the 1960s, see Linsky, *Impact*, p. 42; and especially James Reston, *Artillery of the Press* (New York: Harper & Row, 1967).
51. This fact has become clear from all recent presidential election campaigns, as well as in confirmation hearings and other daily government business. See Larry J. Sabato, *Feeding Frenzy: How Attack Journalism Has Transformed American Politics* (New York: Free Press, 1991).
52. Jay Blumler, "Purposes of Mass Communication Research: A Transatlantic Perspective," *Journalism Quarterly*, Vol. 55, Summer 1978. It should also be noted that Blumler is not entirely in favor of such freedom for the press. He wonders who will ensure that the press does not abuse its powers.
53. Grossman and Kumar, *Portraying the President*, pp. 305-306.
54. Weaver, "The New and the Old," pp. 74-80; also see J. Boylan, "Declarations of Independence," *Columbia Journalism Review*, November/December, 1986, pp. 32-41. An excellent discussion of this can also be found in Michael Schudson, *Discovering the News: A Social History of American Newspapers* (New York: Basic Books, 1978), pp. 160-194.
55. Daniel C. Hallin, "Sound Bite News: Television Coverage of Elections, 1968-1988," *Journal of Communication*, Vol, 42, No. 2, Spring 1992, pp. 5-24; for a similar argument see Thomas Patterson, *Out of Order* (New York: Knopf, 1993).
56. Grossman and Kumar, *Portraying the President*, pp. 256-259.
57. Ranney, *Channels of Power*; Stephen Hess, *The Washington Reporters*, p. 98; and Alan P. Balutis, "The Presidency and the Press: The Expanding Presidential Image," *Presidential Studies Quarterly*, Vol. 7, Fall 1977.
58. Michael Schudson, "The Politics of Narrative Form: The Emergence of News Conventions in Print and Television," *Daedalus*, Vol. 111, Fall 1982, pp. 97-111.

59. Grossman and Kumar found that 23% of all White House stories came before the first commercial break, television news' version of the front page. *Portraying the President*, p. 259.
60. Ranney, *Channels of Power*, pp. 109-113; Graber, *Mass Media and American Politics*, 4th edition (Washington, DC: Congressional Quarterly Press, 1993), pp. 4-12, 250.
61. The literature on agenda setting is now voluminous. The initial classic work on the media's power to influence what people are thinking about is Maxwell McCombs and Donald L. Shaw, "The Agenda-Setting Function of the Mass Media," *Public Opinion Quarterly*, 1972 (data); for a good discussion of the media's power to set the policy agenda, see Cook et al.,"Media and Agenda Setting: Effect on the Public, Interest Group Leaders, Policy Makers, and Policy," *Public Opinion Quarterly*, Vol. 47, 1983, pp. 16-35; and Shanto Iyengar and Donald R. Kinder, *News That Matters: Television and American Opinion* (Chicago: University of Chicago Press, 1988).
62. On the rise and power of modern journalistic celebrities see James Fallows, *Breaking the News: How the Media Undermine American Democracy* (New York: Vintage Press, 1996); Barbara Matusow, *The Evening Stars: The Making of the Network News Anchor* (Boston: Houghton-Mifflin, 1983). Also see Benjamin I. Page, Robert Y. Shapiro, and Glenn R. Dempsey, "What Moves Public Opinion?" *American Political Science Review*, Vol. 81, No. 1, March 1987, pp. 23-43. Page et al., find that commentary by leading news anchors can have a larger effect on opinion than presidents at times.
63. There is an expanding literature on the increasing use of the media by the White House. See, for example, John A. Maltese, *Spin Control: The White House Office of Communications and the Management of Presidential News* (Chapel Hill: University of North Carolina Press, 1992); Hedrick Smith, *The Power Game: How Washington Works* (New York: Random House, 1988); George C. Edwards, *The Public Presidency: The Pursuit of Popular Support* (New York: St. Martin's, 1983); Samuel Kernell, *Going Public. . .* , Michael B. Grossman and Martha J. Kumar, *Portraying the President: The White House and the News Media* (Baltimore, MD: Johns Hopkins University Press, 1981).
64. Linsky, *Impact*, p. 46. Linsky also found that current policy makers were twice as likely as pre-1973 officials to spend more than ten hours a week dealing with media issues.
65. Orren, in Linsky, *Impact*, p. 4.
66. Smith, *The Power Game*, p. 402.
67. Cited in Bob Woodward, *The Commanders* (New York: Pocket Star Books, 1991), p. 130.
68. Quoted in Charles Brown, *The Correspondents' War* (New York: Scribner, 1967), pp. vii-vii.
69. Abrams, Arterton, and Orren, *The Electronic Commonwealth* (New York: Basic Books, 1986).

70. A good review of the technology available as of the Gulf War and how it can be used is Linda Jo Calloway, "High Tech Comes to War Coverage: Uses of Information and Communications Technology for Television Coverage in the Gulf War," in *Contributions to Military Studies*, Vol. 148, 1994, pp. 154-172.
71. On this point see *The Military and the Media: The Continuing Dialogue* (Robert R. McCormick Tribune Foundation, 1993), pp. 49-50.
72. The Sidle Panel report, a review of Grenada public affairs, discusses these concerns. The report is reprinted as the appendix in Battle Lines, pp. 161-178; also see Jonathan Friendly, "Debate Rises About Curbs On Grenada," *New York Times*, November 20, 1983, p. A35.
73. Anna Banks, "Frontstage/Backstage: Loss of Control in Real-Time Coverage of the War in the Gulf," *Communication*, Vol. 13, 1992, pp. 111-117.
74. The amateur videotape recording of police officers beating Rodney King in Los Angeles, seen repeatedly on national network news, exemplifies this growing power of new media technologies to be everywhere and see everything.
75. *The Military and the Media: The Continuing Dialogue*, p. 49.
76. Robert H. Wicks and Douglas C. Walker, "Differences Between CNN and the Broadcast Networks in Live War Coverage," in Greenberg, ed. *Desert Storm and the Mass Media* (Cresskill, NJ: Hampton Press, 1993). For more detail on CNN during the Gulf War see Perry M. Smith, *How CNN Fought the War: A View from the Inside* (New York: Birch Lane Press, 1991).
77. Lloyd Cutler, "Foreign Policy on Deadline," *Foreign Policy*, #56, Fall 1984, pp. 113-128; Austin Ranney, *Channels of Power*, pp. 113-128; Martin Linsky finds the same process at work, especially in his study of the Love Canal case. *Impact*, pp. 71-81, 87-118.
78. Chris Kent, "CNN Makes Its Omnipresence Felt," *Washington Journalism Review*, p. 14.
79. Peter Braestrup, *Big Story* (New Haven: Yale University Press, 1977), pp. 33-39; Edward Fouhy, "The Effect of the Vietnam War on Broadcast Journalism: A Producer's Perspective," in Harrison E. Salisbury, ed., *Vietnam Reconsidered* (New York: Harper & Row, 1984), pp. 89-93.
80. Donovan and Scherer, *The Unsilent Revolution* (New York: Simon Schuster, 1991).
81. John Fialka notes that television studios had to discard (archive) thousands of feet of Gulf film because it didn't make it back to the U.S. in time to be news.
82. Hallin, *The "Uncensored" War*. W. Lance Bennett provides a very useful discussion of this tendency which he terms "indexing" in "Toward a Theory of Press/State Relations in the United States," *Journal of Communication*, Spring 1990.
83. On the president's ability to get his way without difficulty on foreign policy during the Cold War, see Aaron Wildavsky, "The Two

Presidencies," in Wildavsky, ed., *Perspectives on the Presidency* (Boston: Little, Brown, 1975), pp. 448-461.

84. Hallin, *The "Uncensored" War*, pp. 174-210. Hallin found that early press coverage of Vietnam, when consensus on the need to act in Vietnam was high, was very accepting of U.S. policy. Criticism of particular efforts in South Vietnam was more common. This finding is reinforced by the testimony of several journalists who covered the war. See, for example, David Halberstam, *The Powers That Be* (New York: Knopf, 1979). After the 1968 Tet Offensive, when elites began speaking out more against the war, press coverage followed. This is discussed at greater in Chapter 2. Also see the companion piece to Wildavsky's noting the breakdown of consensus on foreign policy, Donald A. Peppers, "The Two Presidencies: Eight Years Later," in Wildavsky, ed., *Perspectives on the Presidency* (Boston: Little, Brown, 1975), pp. 462-471.
85. See, for example, Wallace Earl Walker, "Domesticating Foreign Policy: Congress and the Vietnam War," "Did Vietnam Policymaking Make a Difference?" in G. K. Osborn et al., eds., *Democracy, Strategy, and Vietnam: Implications for American Policymaking*, pp. 105-120; James M. Lindsay, "Congress and Foreign Policy: Why the Hill Matters," *Political Science Quarterly*, Vol. 107, No. 4, 1992-93, pp. 607-628; and James L. Sundquist, *The Decline and Resurgence of Congress* (Washington, DC: The Brookings Institution, 1981), esp. pp. 91-126, 238-273.
86. The debate over each conflict will be reviewed in later chapters.
87. Current U.S. debate over what should be done in Somalia and Bosnia reflect the standards to which politicians, especially the president, are being held. See Chapter Six.
88. Walter Lippmann makes this point is his discussion of the First World War. See Lippmann, *Public Opinion* (New York: Harcourt, Brace and Co., 1922), pp. 23-36.
89. Grossman and Kumar, *Portraying the President*, p. 7.
90. Spear, *Presidents and the Press*, p. 1.
91. Kernell, *Going Public*, pp. 83-110. Kernell argues that the development of going public is one of the most important changes in the presidency over the last fifty years.
92. Maltese, *Spin Control*, p. 2.
93. Kernell, *Going Public*, pp. 51-81 on the president/press relationship is particularly useful here.
94. Smith, *Power Game*, pp. 403-404.
95. Maltese, p. 216.
96. Chapters 4 and 5 on Panama and the Gulf War will detail this thoroughly.

4

Grenada: The "Off the Record" War

The 1983 U.S. invasion of Grenada marked the turning point in modern wartime press policy. Breaking with the policies of Vietnam, the Reagan administration and the military kept the press off the small island of Grenada and away from the action for the first forty-eight hours of the operation. It marked the first time in U.S. history that the press had not covered a war firsthand, prompting *Newsweek* to label Urgent Fury an "off-the-record" war.[1] The administration and the military became the sole sources of information about the conflict; independent analysis was impossible. The high level of public support for the invasion in turn was attributed by some to the barring of the press from the island. Reagan public relations maestro Michael Deaver later claimed that the public approved of the action because "they didn't have to watch American guys getting shot and killed. They can't stand that every night."[2]

Journalists and most other observers at the time pinned the blame for the harsh treatment of the press on the military, reasoning that its bitter memories of Vietnam were still so strong that it had shut the press out in Grenada as revenge. After Vietnam, many argued, military officers determined how they would restrain the press next time to avoid a repeat of that troubled experience. Drew Middleton, *New York Times* military correspondent, summed up the conventional wisdom: "The majors and commanders of the Vietnam War who believed the media had worked against the American command there had become influential generals and admirals determined not to expose the Grenada operation to what they continue to view as a hostile adversary."[3]

On the surface, this argument seems strong. The military's list of complaints about the press in Vietnam was long and it seems logical that the military would have wanted to do something to improve its lot the next time out. Moreover, observers noted that Grenada came on the heels of the British experience in the Falklands, in which the government censored press dispatches, did not allow television to cover the conflict, and purposely misled the press in order to deceive the Argentineans. The U.S. military, some argued, had learned from the British experience how to solve their problems from Vietnam. And indeed, British officials remarked after the Falklands conflict that the American troubles in Vietnam spurred their restrictive press policies.[4]

As straightforward and obvious as this argument is, however, it is false. Although Vietnam certainly taught the military that the press could cause problems during war, by no means did the military "learn" how to solve those problems. As determined as Middleton and others may believe officers were to keep the press from ruining the Grenada operation, they nevertheless had *no plans* in place before the conflict to deal with the press in such a contingency. Instead, efforts to cope with the media were made only in the period directly before H-Hour and after the invasion had begun. Thus, although Vietnam certainly had a great impact on the military's relationship with the media, it did not lead directly to new and improved plans for dealing with the press in any fashion, much less in a fashion so restrictive as in Grenada.

I will argue in this chapter that the Grenada episode provides several pieces of evidence that illustrate the inaccuracy of the conventional wisdom and that reveal the first signs that the White House, not the military, would be the central force behind post Vietnam press restrictions. First, as noted, the military did not have any plans in place before Grenada to deal with the press. This clashes with the assumption of many critics that Grenada represented the culmination of organized military efforts to find an answer for Vietnam. This is an important point on which to be clear. It is one thing to assert that the military's disposition toward the press has been affected by Vietnam, or that individual officers' decisions were influenced by their experiences there. It is an entirely different and far more serious matter to claim that the military as a whole laid plans to undermine and restrain the constitutionally protected institution of the free press. That said, other military professional concerns did operate to make restricting the press an attractive option to the military on the ground in Grenada even without the precedent of Vietnam.

Second, recent admissions from military and civilian officials involved add to the rather scant evidence available at the time and together they strongly suggest that the White House, not the military, made the critical decisions for dealing with the press during the invasion. This evidence is further buttressed by an examination of the Reagan White House's more general approach to dealing with the press which, in accordance with the trends outlined in the previous chapter, stressed both an adversarial relationship with reporters and an intense and continual struggle to control news coverage of Reagan and his administration's activities. As important as controlling press coverage was for the administration during peacetime, it is impossible not to believe that it must have become even more so during the conflict when American lives and the president's political fortunes were on the line.

Finally, the changes in public affairs made after the invasion provide further evidence that neither Grenada nor future press policies were a simple reaction to Vietnam. To avoid the bitter military/media dispute that arose during Grenada, the military turned back to the guidelines used in Vietnam as part of an attempt to ensure a smoother relationship in future conflicts. The military's willingness to do so defies the overly simple argument that the military somehow learned not to do what had been done in Vietnam.

After a brief summary of the historical and political background of the Grenada conflict, this chapter assesses the military's planning for public affairs and its implementation of its plans during the conflict, arguing that the conventional wisdom fails to accurately describe and explain the historical record. It then builds the case for White House dominance over wartime press policy development through an analysis of the Reagan White House's influence over Urgent Fury public affairs and its approach to dealing with the press during Grenada. Of particular importance here is how closely the Reagan administration's strategy for dealing with the media on an everyday basis matched its behavior during the crisis. Next the chapter discusses the impact of the press ban and other restrictions on how the press covered the invasion and, finally, it traces the development of military public affairs policy after Grenada to reveal that the military itself did not reject Vietnam era press policies as so many have asserted.

BACKGROUND

Trouble had been brewing on the small island of Grenada since 1979, when Maurice Bishop and the leftist New Jewel Movement[5] took control of the government in a bloodless coup d'état while Prime Minister Sir

Eric Gairy was out of the country. Bishop was a very popular figure in Grenada, but began to chart a course for his country that would make him very unpopular with the United States.[6]

Although Bishop and the new People's Revolutionary Government promised to hold elections soon after taking power, they never did. Instead, within weeks Bishop had suspended the constitution, moved to shut down the press, put political opponents in jail, disbanded the police and army, and had created the People's Revolutionary Army (PRA). More disturbing, however, was Grenada's move to establish close relations with Cuba and the Soviet Union, along with reports soon thereafter that Cuba was shipping arms to Grenada. Seeking to avoid outright confrontation, the Carter administration settled for giving economic aid to every Caribbean nation but Grenada with the hope that this might influence the PRG to become more democratic. But because the PRG showed few signs of being cooptable the administration ended up simply downplaying the issue.

A year later when Reagan took office, however, increased attention was given to Grenadian activities. Conservatives worried about Grenada's movement into the Cuban and Soviet orbit, as well as its continued militarization. The PRA now claimed over 2,000 members, making it by far the largest armed force in the Caribbean and the cause of concern to Grenada's neighbors. Bishop's rhetoric had a distinctly anti-American tone and Grenada was not shy about its allegiance to the Soviet Union—voting against the U.N.'s declaration on the Soviet invasion of Afghanistan. To Reagan officials, Grenada represented the same type of threat posed by Nicaragua and El Salvador. Committed to combating the spread of communism in the Western Hemisphere, the administration adopted a more aggressive policy of isolating Grenada economically and politically in order to induce its leaders to turn away from the Soviet Union and Cuba.

By 1981 the United States had cut off all diplomatic ties with Grenada and was working to obstruct Grenada's flow of aid from the international community. The administration even tried flexing some military muscle in the area, staging a large NATO maneuver in the Caribbean, code-named "Amber and the Amberdines" in unsubtle reference to Grenada and the Grenadines. The PRG simply used the occasion to denounce the American effort to destabilize their economy, claiming that the exercise was a tune-up for an immanent U.S. invasion.

These efforts led some observers to claim that Reagan's policies had helped drive Grenada further into the arms of the Cubans and Soviets. Hugh O'Shaughnessy writes, for example, "It is ironic that the Cuban-Grenadian relationship should have been fostered by Washington, whose constant harping on the supposed strategic threat from a tiny Eastern Caribbean island caused the New Jewel Movement to militarize their society more than they might otherwise have done."[7] U.S .efforts may indeed have frightened the PRG, though it is hard to believe the Grenadians actually imagined defending themselves against the United States. And on the political side, Robert Pastor makes a convincing case that Bishop and company had been dedicated to following a Marxist-Leninist path since taking power.[8] Either way, subsequent events would drive the two nations yet further apart.

In March 1983 during his famous Star Wars television speech, Reagan showed the nation satellite photos of a runway being built on Grenada with Cuban aid and workers. He claimed that "The Soviet-Cuban militarization of Grenada can only be seen as power projection into the region."[9] Grenadian officials protested that they were building the airport to promote increased tourism, and replied to Reagan with their own angry rhetoric.

Then, in late May of that year, Bishop made a trip to the United States, ostensibly to revive their bitter relations. The primary rationale behind this effort was probably Grenada's sagging economy.[10] Accounting for 40% of its GNP, tourism in Grenada had dropped off markedly since Bishop took power, due in large part to poor relations with the United States. Although he asked to be received by President Reagan, his request was denied, and he met instead with Assistant Secretary of State Kenneth Dam and National Security Adviser William Clark. By all accounts the meeting was routine, with Bishop expressing his interest in improving U.S.-Grenada relations and the U.S. officials warning Bishop on the unacceptability of Soviet influence in the Caribbean. Neither side seems to have been moved by the meeting to change its views; U.S.-Grenada relations remained strained.

By October 1983, relations *within* Grenada were not well, either. A split had evolved between Bishop and his deputy, Bernard Coard. Coard had the support of a majority of the PRG Central Committee and of General Hudson Austin, commander of the PRA. On October 13th, Bishop was put under house arrest by the Coard faction. Six days later a crowd of Bishop supporters, reportedly as many as 10,000, went to Bishop's home and freed him. They then marched with Bishop to Fort Rupert in St. George's, ending up in a face-off with soldiers of the PRA. The soldiers fired on the crowd, killing about fifty civilians. Bishop was taken into custody again, this time to be shot hours later along with five other ministers, including his wife. General Austin and a group called the Revolutionary Military Council claimed control of the island and declared a shoot-on-sight curfew. The execution of Bishop on the 19th and subsequent actions by the RMC initiated the chain of events that would culminate with the October 25 American invasion.

Grenada's neighbors, never happy with Bishop's ascent to power, were very unhappy with the situation in Grenada after the 13th of October. Never before in the region had there been a military-backed coup, and Grenada's military was the only serious armed force in the region. Caribbean leaders convened in Barbados on the 15th under the auspices of CARICOM, the regional economic organization, to discuss the situation. Of the options discussed, economic and political sanctions were unanimously supported, though no consensus was reached about any military options.

The smaller OECS (Organization of Eastern Carribbean States) nations threatened most by recent events, however, along with the more hawkish governments of Barbados and Jamaica, met separately from CARICOM and agreed to request U.S. military intervention. After Bishop's arrest, Prime Minister Tom Adams of Barbados had discussed with U.S. officials the possibility of a mission to rescue him. The day after Bishop's murder, Adams had privately asked the United States to intervene. Then, on the 21st of October, the group of OECS states along with Barbados and Jamaica transmitted a request for military intervention to the United States. This action, by most accounts, paved the way for the final decision by Reagan to go ahead with a full-scale invasion.

Whereas Caribbean nations worried about possible threats from Grenada, the United States was far more concerned over the presence on Grenada of the St. George's Medical School, attended by nearly 600 American students. As the State Department received reports of chaos in the streets and the shoot-on-sight curfew enforced by the anti-U.S. Revolutionary Military Council now in control of the country, the specter of a hostage situation arose. With the Carter administration's Iran hostage debacle fresh in mind, administration officials feared a replay in Grenada. At the State Department an interagency group chaired by Assistant Secretary of State Langhorne Motley began monitoring events on October 13th.

As the turmoil continued in St. George's, U.S. officials began to argue that the administration should plan for an evacuation of the medical school students. On October 17th at a meeting of the Restricted Interagency Group monitoring Grenada, Undersecretary of State Lawrence Eagleburger recommended that the Joint Chiefs of Staff begin to draw up contingency plans for evacuation of U.S. students.[11] On October 19th, following the demonstrations and Bishop's death, U.S. Ambassador Milan Bish warned the State Department that US citizens in Grenada might be facing "immanent danger." In addition, the CIA had no agents in Grenada to provide timely intelligence, forcing the administration to deal with added uncertainty about the safety of U.S. nationals. In response to this news, Secretary of State George Shultz recommended to Reagan a military takeover of Grenada.[12]

On October 20th, in response to the rush of events and Ambassador Bish's warnings, the Special Situation Group of the National Security Council was convened, chaired by Vice President Bush.[13] One participant at that meeting, Constantine Menges, special assistant for Latin American affairs, writes that the group gave serious attention to the Iran hostage analogy, and that those present considered a military solution necessary.[14] *Time* magazine quoted a participant as saying everyone was "gung-ho" about an invasion.[15] After the meeting National Security Adviser Robert McFarlane briefed Reagan, who ordered plans for a military takeover of Grenada to move ahead. Reagan also gave Bush approval to divert the aircraft carrier USS Independence and the USS Guam, carrying Marines for duty in Beirut, to the Caribbean. The operation by now had been code-named "Urgent Fury."

Late on Friday, October 21st, the OECS formally requested U.S. intervention, having been urged to do so by Ambassador Bish, whose task, undoubtedly, was to help provide full justification of any U.S. actions. Word of the OECS request was passed to President Reagan at around 3 a.m. on October 22nd. Later that morning Reagan signed a draft of a National Security Decision Directive authorizing an invasion.[16] Reagan, along with Shultz and McFarlane, was on a long-planned golf outing in Augusta, Georgia. They had determined that to change plans could alert Grenada and Cuba to possible U.S. actions. Reagan would keep in touch with Washington by secure telephone link.

At 9 a.m. on October 22nd the Special Situation Group met to review the situation with Reagan participating for about five minutes by phone. An updated NSDD was passed around at the meeting, offering three bases for the decision to intervene in full force:

1. Ensuring the safety of American citizens on Grenada.
2. In conjunction with OECS friendly government participants, the restoration of democratic government on Grenada.
3. Elimination of current, and prevention of further, Cuban intervention on Grenada.[17]

Efforts to keep Urgent Fury quiet were tragically enhanced by the early morning news on Sunday the 23rd of the bombing of the Marine barracks in Beirut, which left 241 Marines dead. Reagan returned to Washington immediately. During the day, Sunday, Reagan met with the National Security Planning Group to discuss both Beirut and Grenada. In the wake of the bombing the political risks of the Grenada operation loomed larger. How would the public react to more casualties? Would people see Grenada as merely an attempt to assuage the frustration of Lebanon? Reagan resolved to go ahead. It seems clear that he saw a window for taking decisive action not only to protect American lives, but to strike a blow against communism in the Western Hemisphere. Reagan reportedly told Bush, "If this was right yesterday, it's right today, and we shouldn't let a couple of terrorists dissuade us from going ahead."[18]

The invasion began in full force near dawn on October 25th, as Marines and Army Rangers hit the beaches and parachuted onto Grenada's two airports. The invading force would secure the airfields to ensure Cuba could not reinforce Grenada by air, then move to rescue both Governor General Paul Scoon and the American medical students, after which they would take control of the capital. Resistance was expected to be fairly light, although intelligence on both the terrain and the disposition of Grenadian forces was quite poor. In addition, there were questions about whether the Cuban construction workers were perhaps in fact military personnel. To avoid taking any chances, Urgent Fury planned for substantial reinforcements to the landing force soon after H-Hour. U.S .casualties turned out to be relatively light (29 dead, 152 wounded), and most of the fighting was over within two days, at which point all that remained was to flush out General Austin and Bernard Coard, both of whom had gone into hiding.

Meanwhile, the U.S. media watched in frustration from afar, stranded in Barbados by the decisions of the Reagan administration and military leaders. The press was not allowed onto Grenada until forty-eight hours after the initial assault, when almost all of the fighting was over. At that point the military began letting small groups of journalists take military-led tours of the island, frustrating the hundreds more waiting to see the situation for themselves. It was not until five days after the invasion began that all journalists were allowed to travel to and stay on Grenada as long as they wanted. What the public saw and read about the first days of the invasion, therefore, was determined in great part by what U.S. civilian and military officials decided to make known.

THE MILITARY COMES TO GRENADA WITHOUT A PLAN

Journalists and other observers argued that Grenada press restrictions were the result of the military's efforts to avoid "another Vietnam." This argument, however, usually involved no more than a recitation of the obvious, though superficially compelling, fact that the military resented the media for their role in Vietnam and blind acceptance of the White House's not-very-credible avowal during the invasion that the press ban had been the military's idea. To critics, the military restrictions on the press were simply the inescapable and logical result of its lessons from

Vietnam. Jacqueline Sharkey, for example, made the typical argument that "the decision to ban the press reflected the abiding dislike that many military commanders had for the media in the wake of Vietnam, and their belief that if media access had been more tightly controlled, the coverage would have been more positive."[19]

The historical record, however, contradicts this view. A closer look at the history of military public affairs before and during Urgent Fury reveals four reasons to discard the common belief about the military's role in restricting the press. First, the military never took the steps to make its public affairs policies more restrictive after Vietnam that its critics assume it must have. Second, nor did the military come to the invasion of Grenada with a preconceived plan for keeping the press away from the battlefield, as one would expect from an institution harboring two decades of hatred and seeking revenge. Third, a complete ban on the press, even according to the conservative scholar Peter Braestrup, was unnecessary to maintain either operational security or journalists's safety, the two rationales for the press ban offered by the administration and the military at the time. Such restrictions were, however, entirely consistent with the Reagan administration's general approach to dealing with the press and certainly would have mitigated the potential dangers of press coverage from the invasion. And finally, in the wake of Urgent Fury the military did at last revise its public affairs planning policies, but turned to Vietnam as the proper template for future policies, not Grenada, as the conventional wisdom has assumed.

Military Public Affairs Planning Before Urgent Fury

Contrary to the assumptions of many journalistic and academic critics, the military did not take concrete steps after Vietnam to solve the problems it had with the press. There was no decision to keep the press away from the battlefield in future conflicts, nor was a plan developed to restrain the press in any way. As General Winant Sidle, a veteran of the Saigon public affairs operation during Vietnam, noted shortly before the Grenada invasion of the military's response to Vietnam, "I'm not sure we learned too many lessons. They were there for the learning, but I haven't noticed any great change in how we are operating public affairs at the top level of government. We're still making the same old mistakes that we made in Vietnam."[20]

A study done by an officer studying at the Army War College corroborated this view. Lieutenant Colonel Clyde Hennies wrote in June 1983 that "it was discovered that the Army presently has no official *formalized* media training program (except for Public Affairs Officer

Specialty Code 46) for officers, lieutenant colonel and colonel, preparing to occupy positions of greater responsibility which have potential for frequent contact with and exposure to the media."[21] Hennies surveyed officers at the War College and found that the majority of them had never spent any time dealing with journalists and felt unprepared to deal with the media. Several other such studies by War College students made in subsequent years reiterate this theme.[22]

The lack of attention to public affairs at the level of the individual officer was matched by inaction at the organizational level. Far from preparing to restrict the press more heavily in the future than it had in Vietnam, the Army disbanded its reserve field censorship units in the 1970s, having decided that censorship was unlikely to be considered again. This left the Army without any organized way to implement censorship even if political leaders had decided to sanction it—hardly the act of a military bent on pursuing restrictive press policies.[23]

Second, the military went to Grenada with *no plans for dealing with the press whatsoever*. The military's lack of a plan to deal with a contingency such as Urgent Fury reveals among other things that very little thought had been given to the problems the military might face in such a situation and how it would want to deal with the press. Had restricting press access to the battlefield been a priority, however, one would at least have expected the military to be able to pull a contingency plan from the files detailing how this was to be accomplished. No such plan existed.

Making it even more unlikely that the military was solely responsible for banning the press from the island part is the fact that public affairs officers at Atlantic Command, who normally would have drafted the annex for the operation, were informed of the invasion only after it had begun. The Chief of Public Affairs at Atlantic Command, Captain Owen Resweber, was told of the possibility of an invasion on the 23rd, but did not receive orders to develop press plans until Wednesday the 26th, twenty-four hours into the operation, when Michael Burch, Assistant Secretary of Defense for Public Affairs finally received permission from Weinberger to initiate preparations to deal with the hoards of journalists who had already descended on Barbados, the closest nation to Grenada.[24]

With so little forewarning of the invasion and so little knowledge of what was going on in Grenada, it is simply hard to believe that the military would have made the unprecedented decision to bar the press entirely from a conflict for the first time in American history on its own. Taken together, the lack of a contingency plan and the last-minute nature of public affairs planning for the crisis indicate that the decision to bar the press from Grenada was not the product of an organized and premeditated attempt by the military to solve the press problems of Vietnam. They also reveal that the press ban decision came from a high enough level to circumvent the standard procedures for public affairs planning.

It would have been quite difficult, however, for anyone watching from outside the government at the time to understand this, because the White House took great pains to claim that the press ban was the military's responsibility. The administration gave the public and press two rationales for its decision to keep the press off Grenada and said that the decision had been made by the military. As Weinberger said in the first Pentagon press conference of Urgent Fury:

> The reason [for the exclusion] is of course the Commander's decision, and I certainly don't ever, wouldn't ever dream of overriding Commanders' decisions in charge of an operation like this, their conclusion was that they were not able to guarantee any kind of safety of anyone including of course anybody participating and that you have to maintain some kind of awareness of the problems going into areas where we don't know what kind of conditions totally will be encountered. Where the airport was obviously heavily overloaded with all kinds of activity and we just didn't have the conditions under which we thought we would be able to detach enough people to protect all of the newsmen, cameramen, gripmen, all of that.[25]

At the same conference, General Vessey, Chairman of the Joint Chiefs of Staff, offered another rationale for barring the press, which soon became the standard government explanation:

> I think that one of the most important reasons we didn't [let in the press] is the need for surprise in this operation. We were going in there very quickly and we needed to have surprise in order to have it successful.[26]

Later, Admiral Metcalf, the commander of Urgent Fury forces, backed up his superiors' statements, claiming responsibility for the decision and told the press he would keep journalists off the island until it was safe for them to go there, "I want to get you there, but by golly I'm going to insist that you can be supported when you get there."[27]

Few journalists believed the administration's public rationales for its actions. Conservative *New York Times* columnist William Safire, who supported the invasion, blasted the administration's press strategy:

> The excuses given for this communications power grab were false. Caspar Weinberger, with an inarticulate martinet at his side, pretended that reporting was denied because of concern for journalists' safety, which is absurd: The Reagan Administration would hail the obliteration of the press corps. Another reason advanced—that the military was too busy to provide the press with tender loving care—is an insult calculated to enrage journalists.[28]

In particular, the argument that the administration had barred the press from Grenada for its own safety struck journalists and others as ludicrous. Over fifty correspondents died covering the Vietnam War, and at the same time Grenada was taking place, CBS alone had over two dozen personnel covering war-torn Lebanon.[29] As CBS president Edward Joyce noted in congressional testimony during the invasion, journalists routinely signed waivers with foreign governments to absolve them of any responsibility for death or injury.[30] Given the strong historical precedent in both American and foreign conflicts, the idea that the Reagan administration suddenly felt such a strong responsibility for journalists' welfare seemed extremely unlikely.

Second, some journalists challenged the argument that the press would have posed a threat to operational security or given away the element of surprise. Safire again:

> The nastiest reason (for the press ban), bruited about within the Reagan bunker, is that even a small press pool would have blabbed and cost American lives. Not only is this below the belt, but beside the point: We know that the Cubans knew of the invasion plans at least a day in advance.[31]

The *New York Times* on the 23rd reported that, "Throughout the day, Grenada's Government radio broadcast statements that the island was calm but also warned that a 'military invasion of our country is imminent.'"[32] However, it is not clear that most of the media took Grenada's warnings seriously, as they were located well inside both the *Times* and the *Washington Post,* suggesting that one should not necessarily believe all one heard. Of course, events did transpire as Grenada radio predicted, and several days after the invasion Prime Minister Tom Adams of Barbados admitted that word of the invasion had leaked from the OECS meeting in Port of Spain at which the invasion had been discussed.[33] Finally, two weeks after the invasion Prime Minister Edward Seaga of Jamaica told reporters that the leader of the Revolutionary Military Council, Hudson Austin, had actually been told of the invasion plans thirty-six hours before Urgent Fury began, although he was not informed of the precise timetable.[34] Although the press could not have known the extent of the breach in operational security that had already occurred, many like Safire believed that keeping the press away from Grenada did little if anything to enhance security. And once the invasion was underway, this argument should have faded away.

Urgent Fury Public Affairs[35]

To argue that the military was not out for revenge against the press is not to argue that the military did not make life difficult for journalists once the invasion was underway. In fact, as we shall see in every case, the military, like the White House, has many reasons to prefer keeping the press away from the battlefield. These derive, however, not just from the memories of Vietnam as most have argued, but from various professional interests that make having control over battlefield information almost as attractive to the military as to the White House in an age dominated by television. Despite its lack of planning for dealing with the press, the military's public affairs performance during the operation proved that it appreciated a good press restriction as much as the next government agency and a review of Urgent Fury public affairs reveals that the White House receives a good deal of help from a military uninterested for various reasons in helping journalists do their job.

Contrary to what he himself said in a press conference during the invasion, Metcalf wrote a decade later that the "no press" rule was handed down to him from CINCLANT (though he has not said any more about how CINCLANT made the decision). Metcalf himself had only been informed he was to head the Joint Task Force thirty-eight hours before the invasion was to begin. He had not, by his own account, considered press coverage at all before that time. After being given this dictate and once the invasion had begun, Metcalf wrote that he had control over when the press would be allowed on the island. He based his decision on five criteria, none of which, he claimed, concerned problems of maintaining operational security:

1. Safety of personnel—soldiers, marines, students, and journalists—was the primary consideration. The media must not interfere with it.
2. Troops in a combat area should not be burdened with the responsibility for the safety of the media.
3. The media should not be exposed to hostile fire.
4. Media, if in the area of troops in combat, would be escorted by a PAO.
5. Accommodation for the media must be available whether ashore or aboard one of the ships.[36]

Although Metcalf was apparently given veto capability over press coverage of Grenada early on, once the students had been rescued and pressures from Congress and the press began rising to allow journalists on the island, it seems unlikely that Metcalf alone made the decision to lift the press ban. The timing of Metcalf's lifting of the press restrictions on Sunday is suspicious. Cries from Congress to let the press go to Grenada were growing, and on Saturday, October 29th, the House passed a nonbinding resolution recommending that the restrictions be lifted. In addition, there are suggestions that James Baker may have sped along the decision.[37] This fits what we know about the Reagan administration's approach to both public relations and to management. The administration had complete control over dealings with the press, but in general Reagan used a "hands-off" management style. Either way, Grenada seems to exemplify both of these characteristics. Civilians made or at least confirmed the big decisions—to launch an invasion and to restrict the press, but let the military work out the implementation of both with quite a bit of leeway.

As noted, military public affairs officers did not begin efforts to accommodate the press until twenty-four hours into the operation. Assistant Secretary of Defense for Public Affairs Michael Burch asked Atlantic Command staffers to put together plans to set up a Joint Information Bureau (JIB) in Bridgetown, Barbados. Admiral McDonald approved the plans and made the decision to send a public affairs team to Barbados later that day. A six-man team, led by Navy Commander Ron Wildermuth, set up the Joint Information Bureau on the 27th to cope with the roughly 370 journalists in Bridgetown trying to get to Grenada.[38]

The JIB soon received permission from Admiral Metcalf to send a small print-television pool, about fifteen people, to Grenada after the medical students had been evacuated. The pool arrived in Grenada at Point Salinas airstrip and was met by Captain Barry Willey, U.S. Army, a public affairs officer from the 82nd Airborne Division. The pool had arrived more than forty-eight hours after the invasion began. Only sporadic fire fights continued. Captain Willey then took the press on a bus tour to selected spots, none of which included units involved in fighting. Willey had not received any specific orders as to what to do with the pool; he himself had just arrived in Grenada that day. Further, there was no transportation or other support available to him for doing much more with the pool.[39]

The pool's trip seems to have been a hastily and ill-planned affair, reflecting both the lack of forethought given to press matters and the fact that the task force on Grenada was still busy wrapping up military matters and had little time to consider the press.[40] On the other hand, however, it also seems clear that the public affairs officers had a decent sense of what should happen with the pool. As Captain Willey told Braestrup in response to being asked if the press pool's itinerary had been planned in advance:

> Yes, I guess it was. We determined that they would be interested in seeing the immediate area around Point Salinas airstrip and some of the important aspects of the operations including the captured weapons warehouses and the prisoner compound, some enemy vehicles that had been knocked out at the end of the airstrip. It was not feasible at that time to take them very far away from the airstrip area.[41]

In another interview Commander Wildermuth told Braestrup:

> That first day when we were finished with the media tour . . . we allowed the media to interview students and even some U.S. AID people who were there, more or less interviews of opportunity. They couldn't talk to the Cuban prisoners. But we were held up two hours (in returning) the first day because of military action around the airport.[42]

These comments reveal that the military was still concerned about what the press saw and heard. In addition, Wildermuth's use of the phrase "allowed the media" displays a remarkable sense of confidence. While there is certainly a lively debate about the media's rights of access to the *battlefield,* there is no debate about whether the military has the legal authority to "allow" the press to conduct interviews. It does not.[43] The pools continued to be quite restrictive, with journalists unable to move around on their own without escorts, until Sunday the 30th by which time, as noted, the uproar over the restrictions had finally reached Congress. Only at that point could the press stay on Grenada as long as they chose without returning to Barbados.[44]

In the two days before the pools began, the military had implemented the press ban quite effectively. Soon after the invasion began, Admiral Metcalf ordered a ban on all civilian shipping and aircraft. The rationale offered for the action was that the military did not want to shoot at friendly aircraft and ships by mistake. Metcalf, however, made clear years later that the move was in fact a response to hearing that journalists were trying to reach Grenada by speedboat.[45] The other, and perhaps more useful purpose it served was to allow the military to shoo away any journalists trying to make their way onto the island. One group of journalists in a fishing boat did indeed make it, but others were turned away, intimidated by low passes and near misses with buoys dropped from

Navy planes. Back in Bridgetown, the press complained of harassment by military personnel at the airfield and that the JIB was of little use.[46]

But perhaps the most frustrating aspect of the military's approach to public affairs for the press was simply the lack of information. The military held very few press conferences, and revealed very little about what was going on at them. The JIB in Bridgetown was unable to get Metcalf to send over a briefer to give a daily update on the conflict to journalists there. Moreover, the JIB did not even have a direct communications link to Metcalf's headquarters or to the Army units based at Point Salinas on Grenada. This obviously did not encourage the timely flow of news and information to the press.[47]

What Metcalf did do, however, was to set up a system to send back reports gathered from the field to CINCLANT every half hour. It was this data that Washington relied on to analyze the invasion's progress and which it then relayed to the press, mainly in the form of press releases. As Braestrup notes, however, much of the information in these reports was of dubious quality, especially since almost all of the U.S. troops were facing combat situations for the first time.[48] At any rate, however, it put another layer between news of the events and the public. CINCLANT and civilian officials in Washington had a chance to determine what information they would give to the press and what they would keep to themselves.

The first press conference held by Secretary of Defense Weinberger and Chairman Vessey was held forty-eight hours after the invasion began, and represented the high point of the government's openness with the press during the conflict.[49] Weinberger gave few details and repeated the administration line on the justification for the action. It was at this time that Weinberger hung the mantle of responsibility for the press ban on the military's collective shoulder and argued that the safety of journalists and concerns for operational security demanded press restrictions.

The Weinberger-Vessey press conference, as uninformative as it was, was unfortunately the only game in town for a press corps unable to get to the story. Instead of daily briefings by Weinberger or Vessey on the progress of Urgent Fury, from this point on most information was given to the press in communiqué form, short press releases with bland wording such as the first of the invasion, "United States armed forces, in conjunction with forces of other countries of the Organization of Eastern Caribbean Countries, have just concluded their first 12 hours of operations in Grenada. Resistance has been encountered, but most objectives have been taken . . ."[50] It was these from which the newspapers had to write the daily wrap-ups and that television news programs would use as the central story about the invasion each day.[51]

In the days and weeks following the invasion, it became evident that the military's dealings with the press had been somewhat less than forthright. Several issues received less than open and honest discussion, including the performance of U.S. troops and the adequacy of U.S. planning, enemy and civilian casualties, and the extent of Cuban involvement in the fighting. This lack of candor was reported in the press, and several articles came out later attempting to uncover what the military had left unsaid or obscured. Few of these revelations, however, made the television news, and did not visibly diminish public support for the operation.

"US AGAINST THEM": THE REAGAN WHITE HOUSE AND THE PRESS DURING URGENT FURY

Having established that the military did not come to Grenada with plans or policies to restrict the press, an examination of the relationship between the Reagan White House and the press offers support for the case that the administration made the decision to bar the press from Grenada during the invasion's early stages. As we shall see, both the planning and execution of Grenada press policy looked a great deal like everyday Reagan White House media strategy and flowed from the same principles and motivations. As David Gergen, Reagan's Communications Director, noted in discussing the strategy for pushing the administration line on television during the invasion, "We had a whole phalanx of people out there. It's part of the process, and there's nothing unusual about it, though it was intense."[52] The Reagan administration harbored an adversarial attitude toward the press and considered control over press coverage integral to its governing strategy. The administration was heavily focused on controlling media coverage of the president and his administration on domestic issues and never made a move without considering how to deal with the press. Given the political stakes surrounding the first large-scale use of U.S. military force since Vietnam and operating within the context of the post-Vietnam media/politics environment, the White House had even more reason than usual both to pay a great deal of attention to the press and to impose harsh restrictions on press access to Grenada.

Reagan Administration Press Strategy: Us Against Them

The attitude of the Reagan White House towards the press is best summed up by a quote from White House spokesman Larry Speakes' memoir: "For my six years as White House spokesman, it was Us Against Them." It was no secret at the time that the Reagan administration went to great lengths to influence the daily news coverage of its activities in order to receive favorable treatment in the news and especially on television.[53] On Speakes' desk was a sign that read, "You don't tell us how to stage the news and we don't tell you how to cover it." The press, of course, was not always as accommodating as officials would have liked, and a president as controversial as Reagan always had critics ready to take their case to the media; the White House never took good press for granted.

White House communications strategy was directed by James Baker (Reagan's Chief of Staff), Richard Darman (Presidential Assistant), Michael Deaver (Deputy Chief of Staff), and David Gergen (Communications Director). Baker and Darman were involved most heavily with setting strategy, and Deaver and Gergen were responsible for implementation on a daily basis. Each of these men believed that the key to an effective presidency was the ability to sell one's policies to the public, and thus organized their communications efforts around fulfilling Reagan's political agenda.[54]

Planning the administration's attempts to shape press coverage started every morning with a "line of the day" meeting at 8:15, with Baker chairing and Darman, Gergen, Deaver, and Speakes participating. The object was to focus media attention on a particular policy, presidential initiative, or event favorable to the president. The line of the day was sent out via electronic mail and phone calls to all senior administration officials and press spokesmen of various departments. This was an attempt to make sure that everyone in the administration was talking about the same thing, making it more likely that the press would pick it up as news, and minimizing the chance that some other news item, possibly negative, would get front page coverage. In addition to the daily guidance, the White House gave each of the departments a press strategy for special issues. The White House meetings determined which agency would have the primary voice on an issue, when information would be withheld entirely, and when the President would take the lead. Typically, the White House gave cabinet members the point position on controversial issues, reeling stories back in for Reagan to publicize once good news had developed.[55]

Having set the line of the day, shaping television coverage of Reagan's presidency became the central element of the administration's public relations strategy. As Larry Speakes noted, "Underlying our whole theory of disseminating information was our knowledge that the American people get their news and form their judgments based largely on what they see on television."[56]

As a result of television's primacy, the administration worked hard to ensure that it had "good visuals" to accompany the stories they wanted told on the news. Without good film footage, events have a much harder time making it onto the nightly news. The Reagan communications team knew this well, and used their knowledge of the operating routines of the networks to plan how to get the most flattering images of Reagan onto the news[57] further advantage of television, from the administration's perspective, is that it focuses the viewer's attention on the image rather than the words being spoken. As Sam Donaldson of ABC told an interviewer, "a simple truism about television: the eye always predominates over the ear when there is a fundamental clash between the two."

An example often recited to illustrate the Reagan White House media strategy is a Michael Deaver inspired "road show" on education. In the wake of a government report criticizing the state of American schools and polls showing disapproving of Reagan's handling of education, the White House instigated a month-long media campaign to show that Reagan was active on education issues despite the fact that his latest budget called for cuts in spending for education. Deaver took Reagan around the nation setting up visually appealing and favorable situations in which to speak about education reform. Within three months, the polls reflected a shift to majority approval of Reagan's handling of education despite the fact that he had not taken (nor planned to take) any concrete actions nor changed his policies at all. As Deaver explained, ". . . the viewer sees Ronald Reagan out there in a classroom talking to teachers and kids, and what he takes from that is the impression that Ronald Reagan is concerned about education."[58]

In addition to its sophisticated approach to influencing news coverage, the administration also took a hard-line view towards the principles of a free press with respect to national security and matters of secrecy. Secretary of Defense Caspar Weinberger spoke for the administration when he noted that the First Amendment should not impinge on "the equally legitimate tradition of the government's need for secrecy, especially in national defense."[59] The administration's unprecedented efforts to limit the availability of information becoming public regarding security issues included an expansion of the classification guidelines to ensure that more information would be classified, a fight to weaken the Freedom of Information Act, lifetime censorship for government employees who had access to classified materials, and a proposal to use lie detector tests to identify bureaucrats who may have leaked news to the press.[60] As Floyd Abrams, a First Amendment lawyer, noted of the Reagan administration's attitude toward information and national security: "It is a view that not only focuses on security but equates security with secrecy, and treats information as if it were a potentially disabling contagious disease that must be controlled, quarantined, and ultimately cured."[61] These efforts to enhance the ability of government to keep information from the press, while not all successful, reveal the perspective from which the Reagan administration approached dealing with the media during Grenada. When trade-offs had to be made between issues of national security or defense, which the administration defined quite broadly, and the media's access to information, the administration gave far greater weight to the former.[62]

Reagan officials have expressed satisfaction with the press coverage the administration received during Reagan's first term. Michael Deaver went as far as to say that "Ronald Reagan enjoyed the most generous treatment by the press of any President in the postwar era."[63] Journalists for the most part agree with that assessment, often to their chagrin.[64] And one scholarly observer notes, "The art of message management was never carried to a higher form than during the Reagan years in the White House."[65] During the Grenada invasion, the press ban and subsequent restrictions on journalists' movements allowed the administration to set the media agenda by controlling information and access while offering its own packaged explanation for events. Thus, where it counted most, on the front pages and on television, the administration's views and positive images of the conflict went uncontested.

Controlling the Stage: White House Press Policy and Public Relations

In light of the Reagan's relationship with the press and the fact that the military did no planning for public affairs before Grenada we must ask how likely it is that the media-savvy White House, which considered news coverage one of its primary tools, would have left military public affairs officers to do the job of the White House communications team. Indeed, though we still lack much hard evidence on this question, it seems rather unlikely that those who believed the president would succeed or fail based on television news would let the military make such obviously critical decisions about the media that would directly affect Reagan.

Thus the most likely explanation is that Grenada simply reflected an extreme example of what David Gergen called "controlling the stage," the strategy by which the Reagan White House attempted to shape the way in which journalists reported on the administration's activities through dictating when, where, and under what conditions the press could cover the president. At the very least, the few direct admissions from officials available (aside from public statements made during the invasion) strongly suggest that the decision to bar the press from Grenada was not, as portrayed by Weinberger and others, simply a military decision. More than ten years after the fact Laurence Eagleburger, at the time Under Secretary for Political Affairs and part of the interdepartmental planning team that had monitored the situation in Grenada before the invasion, told an interviewer with respect to the press ban, "Don't blame Grenada on the Pentagon. It was a political decision. As far as I can recall, it came out of the White House, although maybe the Joint Chiefs were saying, 'Okay, it's not something we object to.'"[66]

Consistent with Eagleburger's remarks, a *New York Times* story run two weeks after the invasion reported Assistant Secretary of Defense for Public Affairs Michael Burch's admission that Weinberger had in fact affirmed the press ban after discussions with military leaders. Burch did not expand on the reasons for Weinberger's approval, but his statements confirmed that civilian leaders exercised ultimate control over the decision.[67] In addition Drew Middleton noted months later in an article that James Baker had also approved of the ban on Reagan's behalf.[68] These revelations were buried in the middle pages of the newspapers and went largely unnoticed. Nonetheless, they contradicted the arguments made by critics that the military had exercised autonomous control over press policy.[69]

These insights take on greater weight when viewed in the context of the White House's public relations activities during the invasion and together they reinforce the argument that political rather than national interest motives were the dominant force behind the press restrictions. With the press unable to get to the island and witness the action, the administration was able to frame the invasion and claim victory in ways that would have been impossible otherwise.

Setting the tone for the entire conflict, the administration's planning for Grenada public relations did not include its frontmen, spokesman Larry Speakes and the communications director David Gergen. They were informed about the invasion only after it had begun. Leaving Speakes and Gergen out of the loop, however, should not be interpreted as a sign that the administration was ignoring the problem of public relations. It was, in fact, a calculated move to keep the press from learning anything about the invasion. Eagleburger noted long afterwards that ". . . from the beginning of the discussions it was clear from the White House that we were not going to let the press know about the operation."[70] James Baker offered the same view, "That White House was leaking like a sieve, and there were American lives at stake. . . . It was my view that because the military operation depended on surprise, and lives therefore depended on surprise, we should make certain there was no risk of premature disclosure."[71] This statement reflects the distrust some of the top Reagan aides felt for Gergen in particular, who was seen as too close to the press and likely to give away information. Baker also argued that keeping Speakes out of the planning was a way of protecting him from having to lie to the press about the invasion.[72]

As Speakes notes in his memoir, however, the result was that he was indeed forced to mislead the press, albeit unwittingly. When reporter Bill Plante of CBS, acting on information from a "trusted source," asked Speakes if the United States were planning to invade Grenada, Speakes called Captain Robert Sims, spokesman for the NSC, to get information. Sims in turn went to John Poindexter, the deputy National Security Adviser. Poindexter, acting on Baker's orders, told Speakes to "knock it down hard," and that the idea was preposterous. Speakes repeated these very words to Plante and was upset to then have to announce the invasion at a noon press briefing on the 25th of October. In his view, and in that of many journalists, the credibility of the administration suffered greatly.[73] The credibility of the president's spokesman, many have pointed out, is based on the understanding that he has access to the president and the policy process. When he is lied to or left out of administration planning, reporters may stop trusting what they hear through him. This tactic agitated the press and strained its relationship both with Speakes and with other administration officials, but not as much as the press ban would.[74]

In a 9 a.m. statement to the press on October 25, four hours after U.S. troops had stormed the island, Reagan announced that the invasion of Grenada was underway, offering three reasons for the U.S. intervention:

> We have taken this decisive action for three reasons: First, of overriding importance, to protect innocent lives, including up to 1,000 Americans whose personal safety is, of course, my paramount concern. Second, to forestall further chaos. And third, to assist in the restoration of conditions of law and order and of governmental institutions to the island of Grenada.[75]

To forestall criticism that he might have acted rashly, Reagan also made clear that the U.S. action was in response to an "urgent, formal request from the five member nations of the Organization of Eastern Caribbean States to assist in a joint effort. . . ." Interestingly, Reagan did not make the announcement on television, prompting speculation that he was trying to keep his distance from the invasion should it go poorly.[76]

Reagan's emphasis on "Americans in danger" is not surprising. As H. W. Brands found in his analysis of U.S. foreign intervention, possible danger to U.S. civilians abroad has been a common theme of presidential rationales. However one might feel about the use of force in theory, it is difficult to argue with a president who acts to protect the lives of Americans abroad. A president using this rationale provides himself more political cover than if he relies solely on abstract political justifications.[77] Beginning with Reagan's announcement, this justification became the administration's first "line of the day." Accordingly, administration officials took every opportunity to push the "Americans in danger" theme.

Later on the first day of the invasion, Secretary of State George Shultz held a news conference to explain the administration's decision-making process and to reinforce the justification of the invasion. Shultz underscored the need to protect American lives and the fact that the OECS has requested U.S. help. He stressed that given the "atmosphere of violent uncertainty" on Grenada, the administration had to act before the situation worsened.[78] Shultz also tried to reject the notion that U.S. actions violated the charter of the Organization of American States, of which both the United States and Grenada are members, which provides in the Rio Treaty that "no state or group of states has the right to intervene directly or indirectly for any reason whatever in the internal or external affairs of any other state."[79] Shultz argued that the OECS member states who had requested the invasion were not party to the Rio Treaty and had instead their own regional treaty, and that therefore U.S. actions did not violate the OAS charter. Shultz failed to mention, though news articles did, that the OECS charter called for unanimous decisions on collective security issues, and that three members: St. Kitts-Nevis, Montserrat, and, of course, Grenada, did not vote on the decision to request a U.S. intervention.[80]

On the day after the invasion began, October 26, White House spokesman Larry Speakes reiterated the "Americans in danger" theme. He admitted that the United States had received diplomatic cables from the Revolutionary Military Council on Sunday and early Monday before the invasion, assuring the United States that all American lives and property would be safe and that the airport would be open to allow people to leave Grenada. Speakes claimed, however, that the airport was in fact closed on Monday the 23rd. "What they told us, we simply did not trust. There was no way we could be at all assured that their promises would have been kept. We had very real fears of a hostage situation." Without pointing to any specific examples of danger to American lives, Speakes' explanations echoed Shultz's earlier description of the situation on Grenada as being too dangerous to take chances.[81]

Unfortunately for the administration, however, the "Americans in danger" explanation failed to convince everyone. Democrats in

Congress were doubtful of the need to resort to military force; many doubted that enough had been done diplomatically to rescue the students. The chancellor of St. George's Medical School, Charles Modica, felt that the invasion was unnecessary. Modica stated at a news conference that the Revolutionary Military Council had assured school officials that the students would be safe. Before the invasion, a group of parents of medical students had asked the president to act cautiously, for fear that overt U.S. actions could endanger their children by provoking Grenada's military factions.[82]

Criticism of the U.S. intervention from abroad was wide-ranging and vocal. Few nations seemed to accept that the United States had justifiable cause for intervention in Grenada. Most of Latin American and America's NATO allies were immediately opposed to the action. Even Margaret Thatcher objected, less than a year after the Falkland Islands campaign.[83] A *New York Times* editorial summed up the doubts many had at the time: "If there were really a threat to United States citizens, a rescue would obviously be justified. But no threat has been demonstrated. And the invaders are not behaving like a land-and-leave rescue team."[84]

With its star justification in some early trouble, the administration tried another approach. The day after the invasion, a "senior Reagan Administration official" told the press that the intervention had blocked an impending military buildup on Grenada by Cuba. "I honestly believe we got there just in time," he said, providing a phrase Reagan would pick up the next evening in his televised speech on Beirut and Grenada.[85] Some administration officials also began suggesting that in addition to construction workers, there were perhaps as many as two battalions of Cuban troops on Grenada. The administration would soon claim, erroneously as it turned out, that there were over 1,000 Cubans on Grenada, about 400 more than the Cuban government had claimed. At a press conference the same day, General Vessey, Chairman of the Joint Chiefs of Staff, told reporters that the American forces had run into far greater resistance from the Cubans than anticipated. Secretary of Defense Weinberger added that U.S. troops had overrun what appeared to be a "major Cuban installation."[86] Over the next two days it was revealed that U.S. troops had discovered large caches of Soviet made weapons, as well as documents detailing plans to expand Cuban presence on Grenada, although these were not immediately made public.

Questions about this new justification were immediately raised. If the administration knew all along about Cuba's plans, why hadn't Reagan mentioned them in his initial announcement of the invasion? Despite doubts, however, the administration's new justification took some steam out of the initial questioning about the safety of the students and the administration's diplomatic efforts, most likely as it was intended to do.[87] With the government enjoying an information monopoly on Grenada, the press was forced to print the administration's arguments without independent verification or challenge. Standing pat with this explanation for the short duration of the fighting, the administration was relatively quiet. Reagan then elevated the Cuban justification to center stage in his televised speech on Thursday the 27th. His speech would put the final stamp of legitimacy on the already successful operation.

As the Reagan administration knew so well, television was the main battlefield on which it had to prove itself to the public. Happily for the administration, without any network television cameras on Grenada, the only footage of the invasion was provided by the Defense Department. And that film, full of positive images, was not released until two days after the fighting began, when the administration was already claiming success. This meant that the administration did not have to spend much time on spin control; it could instead focus on putting across its message in a proactive and positive manner.

Better yet, what network television cameras eventually did find was extremely favorable to the administration. On the day after the invasion the media covered the return of the first students from Grenada. As if directed by Michael Deaver, some of the first students to get off the plane dropped to their knees and kissed the ground, and proclaimed how glad they were to be back in the United States. This made for perfect television; it was run by all the national news programs, and provided the administration with powerful visual reinforcement for their actions. Left out of the television news, however, were those students who felt the invasion had not been necessary. Critics could never overcome those images with mere words.[88] As Larry Speakes wrote in his memoirs, when he saw that scene he shouted, "That's it, we've won!"[89]

Following the administration's routine practice of farming out the responsibility for public relations to the departments to draw fire and generate good news, Reagan had let Weinberger and the military do most of the little talking that took place during the initial fighting. Then, once good news was assured—the students rescued and happy to be back, the casualties light—Reagan appeared on TV to take the credit and to confirm his justifications. At this point he could also take full advantage of the discovery that, unknown to U.S. intelligence before the invasion, Grenada had formed secret military aid agreements with Cuba and the Soviet Union, and that Grenada had been stockpiling more weapons than such a small country should have needed for defense.[90] This allowed Reagan to forge a greater consensus by framing the invasion in terms of the fight against global communism and the Soviet Union, an issue which he had used to great advantage throughout his career, and one which could add legitimacy to the invasion despite niggling doubts about the pretext for the invasion. Reagan argued that "we got there just in time. . . ."[91] He wasn't referring, as it turned out, to the students whose safety had been his original rationale, but to the communists, who he feared had long viewed Grenada as a stepping stone for exporting terrorism to the Western hemisphere.

Some challenged even this justification, such as *New York Times* columnist Anthony Lewis. Lewis, in a column entitled "What Was He Hiding?" argued that Reagan appeared to be purposely keeping the public in the dark by not revealing proof of his claims that Grenada was in league with the Soviets.[92] Those in Congress who might have been inclined to challenge Reagan, however, were silenced by polls released the day after his address which showed that a majority of the public approved of the invasion and believed the students had been in danger. This majority grew over the next several days to an overwhelming 71% approval, at which point very few in Congress wished to challenge the administration's version of events.[93] Of course, because of the absence of the press from Grenada, there was little room for anyone to disprove administration claims anyway.

THE IMPACT OF GOVERNMENT MEDIA STRATEGY ON THE PRESS

In explaining the impact of administration press restrictions and public relations as well as the military's handling of public affairs during the conflicts studied here, I must first make clear that I *do not* purport to describe or explain the bulk of American news media coverage, its focus, its tone toward the conflicts or towards the presidents who led them, or towards the military. Nor have I undertaken a large-scale content analysis of press coverage of America's recent conflicts. Those topics and the content analysis methodology required to evaluate them are important and complex enough to demand a more thorough treatment than I can give them here.

Others have analyzed various aspects of the press coverage of the Grenada, Panama, and Gulf conflicts and tried to ascertain how positive or negative the coverage was toward the administration and why, or tried to show how reliant journalists were on government sources for information in their news stories. These studies conclude with the by now predictable mix of results—some find that the press is too critical of government, some find the press too easy on government officials.[94] All such studies, however, only nibble around the edges of the point I seek to make here. Because we cannot know how the press would have covered these conflicts in the absence of restrictions and public relations campaigns, it does little good to attempt to quantify the impact of the government's efforts to control the news. It would be ridiculous to argue, for example, that the news was 10% more favorable to Bush during the Gulf War as a result of his administration's efforts at news management. Nor is the newsmaking process something so well understood and predictable that we can even imagine all the ways in which government and media actions and reactions collide to produce the news. We cannot know, for example, the relative importance of press restrictions to the myriad other influences on the tone of news coverage operating at the same time, such as public opinion, the level of elite consensus in the United States, the success and relatively light human toll of the military efforts, and so on.

Despite these complicating factors, the cases make clear a more basic and very powerful point about the impact of government restrictions which I attempt to illustrate throughout this work: Government press restrictions and efforts to generate positive coverage made it impossible for the press to cover critical aspects of American involvement in military conflicts and thus made it more likely that the information reaching the public about the conflicts would be shaped by the administration officials and military leaders. As we will see in each case, the government managed to eliminate all but a trickle of firsthand combat coverage, in particular television coverage of combat, or even of American casualties in noncombat situations. In short, the restrictions ensured that the press would not cover what presidents fear most: the horrors of war. As a result, the press was forced to focus more heavily on those things they did have access to, which by no coincidence were quite often government press conferences, press releases, or military sponsored trips into the field where little or no action was taking place. This lack of access to the battlefield and to information also meant that the press could not report the full story of America's performance in the conflicts. It would not be until long after each that those things the government did not want to talk about: casualties, the damage caused by military actions, military miscues, and the like, were revealed to the public. Presidents seem to understand that the media's power lies not in vague statistics such as the balance of positive to negative stories, but in the impact that one vivid and wrenching television report can have, such as Morley Safer's story of the Marines burning down the village of Cam Ne with their Zippo lighters. Those who fear that television images of war will turn public opinion need not count how many times the president is criticized on the network news. Though no doubt frustrating, enduring such criticism would be a small price to pay to keep bloody combat footage out of the news. By keeping the press off the battlefield and by using their resulting information monopoly wisely, the Reagan and Bush administrations succeeded in ensuring at the very least that the media would not stir an emotional or "irrational" reaction from the public.

Given this, my efforts to analyze the impact of the press restrictions will be limited to two basic themes: First, to repeat in each case that they meant that the press never got to the battlefield to cover combat or to corroborate what the military and White House told them about the operations. And second, to note the many cases in which the restrictions coupled with public relations offerings served to obscure the true nature of the operation or the military's actual performance from the press and public. Taking these two strands together, we find that even if we cannot know in what other ways the administration's news management efforts proved successful, we have evidence at the most basic level that the restrictions keep the press from doing what most consider the job of a free press to be—to provide an independent check on our government.

Newsgathering and Press Coverage of Urgent Fury

During the Grenada invasion the press ban, coupled with the administration's close control over information concerning the conflict, wreaked havoc with the media's newsgathering operations with two primary results. First, the tight control over access to the island of Grenada allowed the Reagan administration to ensure that all of the images and words flowing from the invasion were either favorable or at least not threatening. Most obviously, the press ban meant that no journalist could provide the public with firsthand reporting of combat, no pictorial evidence of the fighting and its results. But just as importantly, it also meant that journalists had to rely even more heavily than ever on official sources to write their stories, thus enhancing the administration's control over the newsmaking process. With so little competition from journalists the Reagan administration had the field to itself in the first critical days of the operation and thus its preferred terms and images (invasion as "rescue mission," students kissing the ground, etc.) dominated discussion and shaped the news reaching the public. The administration's success in presenting the operation in a favorable light before the press could get the whole story was such that public support for the invasion never faltered despite revelations in later months questioning both the invasion's necessity and its conduct. Second, the media's lack of access to the battlefield and reliance on government information led to a distorted picture. Administration and military half-truths and omissions, reported without independent verification by journalists who were unable to get to Grenada, led to a rough draft of history unsuitable as a guide to further editions. The news coverage of the invasion, written primarily from government press conferences and press releases, did little to portray events as they actually occurred. As a result, many of the accidents, foul-ups, and even the rationale for invading the nation in the first place did not receive the coverage they deserved until long after the conflict had fallen from the front pages and the public had stopped paying attention.

The key element of the government's success was the fact that the press ban (and the military's subsequent handling of public affairs) made independent reporting impossible and thereby increased the media's reliance on official sources. When the press began arriving in Barbados, the closest they could get to Grenada, problems between the military and journalists arose immediately. The military gave the press very little help in covering the invasion, and interfered on several occasions with its attempts to cover events in Barbados at the airstrip from which U.S. forces were taking off for Grenada.[95] As one reporter for the *Wall Street Journal* noted, "The journalists are frustrated. The military men here won't talk. The embassy here, such as it is, refers all questions to the State Department. There are no briefings, no press releases, no nothing."[96]

Several intrepid journalists made attempts to go around the press ban by chartering boats to Grenada. Most failed as a result of Metcalf's cordon, but one group of six reporters did make it to Grenada on Tuesday the 25th. Unfortunately, Grenada had no facilities for filing reports to the United States as the telephone and telex lines had been disrupted. Worse, four of the journalists were invited to the USS Guam, Metcalf's command post, and instead of being able to file they were kept incommunicado for a day. Their stories from the invasion's early hours were filed only late Thursday night when they finally returned to Barbados.[97]

When the press pools finally began, taking them to Grenada, journalists had to deal with each other. Competition for spots on the initial pools was stiff because not many were available. Soon after the invasion began the JIB had counted over 400 journalists present in Barbados. This number, made higher yet by hundreds who claimed to be members of the press but were not, exceeded the number of journalists at any war in history except during the Tet Offensive in Vietnam.[98] Knowing that such a group could never have agreed on who to send with a pool, the JIB selected those who would go in the first days of the pool. This caused predictable grumbling among the press, but no one complained that the situation would be better without the pools.

Though better than nothing, the pools did not solve the media's problems, and in fact, being led around by the military simply made most journalists angrier. The first group to go over included fifteen journalists from various television, wire, and print organizations. As noted above, the public affairs officer in charge of dealing with the first pool followed Metcalf's guidelines. The pool members were severely limited in what they saw, where they went, and to whom they could talk.

Greater numbers of journalists were taken by the pool to Grenada in the following days, until finally on Sunday all restrictions were lifted, due in part to the political ruckus the restrictions had caused back in Washington, where congressional hearings provided a forum for angry media executives and senior journalists to vent their frustrations at the Grenada restrictions. Of course, by Sunday, the story everyone had come to find—the invasion—was long over. All that remained was to write about U.S. efforts to help stabilize Grenada's political system. This proved relatively uneventful and soon the press began to lose interest. Most of the press corps that had shown up were gone after the final JIB briefing in St. George's on November 23rd.[99]

Of all those covering Urgent Fury, the television networks faced the least appetizing situation. At least print reporters could search out nontraditional and foreign sources for stories—even if just for the inside pages. Television needed pictures, good ones, to go with the story, preferably dramatic action footage involving U.S. troops. Without access to Grenada, however, television had no such pictures.[100] World leaders objecting to the invasion through a press release don't make for good visuals. They do not often make the television news, especially during a conflict when everyone knows other more exciting things are happening. During the invasion, television news was stuck with showing maps, graphic illustrations, and their own correspondents reporting from various locations far from the battlefield.

With no access and little information of their own the press turned to the government for information and interpretation. And although the press always leans heavily on official government and military sources for information during wars and periods of armed conflict, in Grenada the media were almost completely dependent on them. As one journalist noted of press coverage of the fighting, "The major stories were written by reporters in Washington based on information given to them by State Department and other Government sources."[101] A study of Grenada press coverage by Brigitte Nacos adds weight to that analysis. She found that the *Chicago Tribune*, the *Washington Post*, and the *New York Times* relied almost exclusively on Reagan administration sources for their front page coverage of the acute phase of the crisis.[102] Journalist Hugh O'Shaughnessy, who was one of the few to temporarily evade the press ban, noted that *Time* and *Newsweek* also relied almost entirely on administration accounts of the invasion's planning and execution.[103]

This overreliance on official information meant that the public received through the press a sterilized and truncated version of events. What did not get any coverage, in either print or television outlets, as noted, was combat. The few stories describing combat that appeared in major news outlets were based solely on interviews done several days after the fact, rather than on any firsthand experience. Without access to the battlefield there simply could not be any real combat coverage.

Not only did the press restrictions ensure that there would be no television pictures of casualties, fighting, or the "dirty side of war," but the dearth of access ensured that the media would make a big deal out of whatever images they could get. During the invasion this factor played to the administration's advantage. Television's thirst for images created an opening for the administration and the military to provide the images that the public would see of Urgent Fury. It had long been military policy to send Audio/Visual crews in to document military operations for archival and other purposes. On October 27th, two days into the invasion, the Defense Department finally released to the networks CINCLANT footage of the operation—but only after President Reagan's television speech to the nation. Much to the networks chagrin, however, the footage was not at all what they would have preferred to run. Instead of combat footage, the film released by DoD featured not a shot, not a drop of blood, and no frightening images of war. As Tom Shales of the *Washington Post* put it, "Most of the film consisted of American students smiling, blowing kisses and flashing the "V" sign as they were escorted off the island under military protection. It looked like a bunch of kids coming home from camp."[104] Nonetheless, with nothing else to offer, all of the networks ran the DoD footage. Perhaps embarrassed by their inability to get to the story, none of the networks mentioned right away that a press ban had been instituted or that they had no firsthand reports to offer. Seemingly annoyed by the whole thing, Dan Rather on CBS made several references to the film having been "cleared by DoD censors."[105]

Not only did the government make firsthand coverage of combat and thus of American casualties impossible, it also evaded the issue of enemy and civilian casualties until long after the invasion. Whereas the administration officials of course made very clear that American lives were their highest priority, they made no mention of enemy casualties, to the point of refusing to speculate on their numbers.

A perfect example of the military's desire to avoid discussion of Grenadian civilian casualties was the military's silence on the U.S. bombing of a Grenadian mental hospital. The hospital, which evidently had no markings revealing its true nature, had been bombed by U.S. aircraft after they had been fired upon by PRA troops using the building as cover, killing forty-seven patients according to the news story. Admiral Metcalf, however, did not mention the incident until confronted with it after the story broke several days after the bombing through the efforts of a Canadian journalist. Metcalf argued at first that he had not been informed yet that it had been a hospital, but reporters were unconvinced. Many believed this was a attempt to avoid negative publicity by covering up mistakes. The Pentagon initially reported that the bombing had only killed twelve, not the forty-seven claimed in news reports, but revised its estimate upward over time.[106] Later, Metcalf admitted to knowing that it had been a hospital that U.S. forces bombed, but claimed he did not mention it because he was too busy with operational matters.[107]

In fact, the Pentagon and the Administration maintained until Sunday October 30th that there had been *no* civilian casualties. Because the press had no other source of information to turn to for an alternative number, no news story had a response to this, even though it would have been clear to any who considered it that it was highly unlikely that there had been no civilian casualties. The military did not venture any numbers on either enemy casualties or civilian casualties until a November 9th press conference.[108] Even careful observers of the prestige print press would have had difficulty figuring out what the human toll of the operation had truly been. Later, Grenadians would count 160 dead and 100 wounded. The Cubans suffered 71 killed and 57 wounded. These numbers would have come as a surprise to anyone who had watched coverage on TV, which Metcalf said showed that Urgent Fury "was going to be a marvelous, sterile operation."[109]

Finally, journalists, digging for more information in the months after the invasion, discovered that Urgent Fury had not been the smoothly run operation the Pentagon portrayed, but rather a case of military bungling and incompetence that would have had serious consequences had the U.S. faced a more capable opponent. The military, busy claiming credit for the brilliant victory Reagan had pronounced the Grenada operation, neglected to reveal several disturbing facts about its performance: Because of the surprise nature of the strike, accurate maps could not be created and U.S. troops were given tourist maps of Grenada, with the result that artillery strikes could not be called in with any accuracy. Army Rangers showed up a one of the medical school campuses to rescue students only to find out for the first time that most of the students were at another location, and did not find dozens of the students until days later. Had the Grenadian forces wanted to take students hostage as the Reagan administration said it feared, they would have had ample opportunity. In a pre-invasion maneuver, most of a special forces team drowned in rough seas. Once on the island, the various services could not communicate with each other due to incompatible radio equipment.[110] The military's combat performance in Grenada was so poor, moreover, that it became a centerpiece of efforts by the congressional Military Reform Caucus to push the military to update its strategy, tactics, procurement, and other activities. By the time these stories were reported, however, Reagan's victory in Grenada was cemented in the public mind; only prestige papers such as the *Times, Post,* or *Wall Street Journal* ran such stories following up on the invasion. For those who relied on television, Grenada dropped from the news before these facts became known.[111]

Press Reaction to Urgent Fury

The evolution of public affairs policy might have followed a different path had the press taken stronger steps to confront the government after the invasion. Although the press was furious with the public affairs system during Urgent Fury, it did little in practical terms to ensure that the next time would be better for journalists. The fact that the public approved highly of the invasion and seemed to support the government's restrictions on the press weakened the press's resolve to take on its toughest opponent. This inactivity helped set the terms of engagement for the development of post-Urgent Fury public affairs.

The driving element of journalists' outrage at the restrictions was the perception that denying access to the press was an assault on journalism's role in the political process and a violation of the public's "right to know" what its government was doing. Edward Joyce, president of CBS News, launched the press' rhetorical attack on the government's restrictive press policy:

> I am seriously concerned that we may indeed be witnessing the dawn of a new era of censorship, of manipulation of the press, of considering the media the handmaiden of government to spoon-feed the public with government-approved information. If the government is permitted to abrogate the First Amendment at will, to the detriment of not simply the press but the public as well, I am concerned that such action will be taken again and again and again, whenever a government wishes to keep the public in the dark.[112]

Another, less idealistic motivation behind the media's distress was the simple fact that it could not cover the biggest story of the moment. Predictably, the press gave a great deal of coverage to its own complaints about the public affairs situation in Grenada, the vast majority of it unfavorable to the administration and military. Nacos found, in fact, that on issues indirectly related to the invasion during the first two days, including the press ban and the War Powers Act debate, negative coverage of the administration ran with a greater than two-to-one space advantage over positive coverage.[113] In addition, all three major networks and major newspapers came out strongly against the treatment of the press in editorials. In the end, however, aside from sharp language in many editorials, the only resistance the press gave the government was to write letters of protest to the president and to the Defense Department.[114]

Things might have turned out much differently had a group called Reporters' Committee for Freedom of the Press and its ad-hoc committee of ten major news organizations decided to move forward with legal action in response to the administration's possible violations of the First Amendment.[115] They did not. Braestrup notes that the prevailing feeling was that it was not a good time politically to take the press' case to court. The public, highly supportive of the invasion, might have equated a legal challenge with an attack against the president. Arousing the public's ire was something that editors did not want to do given the media's concern with its current state of unpopularity in recent polls.[116] Further, First Amendment expert Floyd Abrams felt that the press could very well lose the case, despite its merits.[117] Instead the group decided to initiate negotiations with the Reagan administration to wrangle concessions on future wartime public affairs systems.[118] Unfortunately for the press, however, the subsequent negotiations went nowhere.[119]

PUBLIC AFFAIRS AFTER GRENADA

The Sidle Panel and the Creation of the Pool System

On November 6th in response to the hue and cry both from journalists and from lawmakers, Chairman of the Joint Chiefs of Staff General Vessey called for a panel to examine the military/media relationship and devise a better system for conducting public affairs in the future. He called on retired information officer Major General Winant Sidle, a public information officer in Vietnam, to lead the panel. Vessey appeared on the television news program "Meet the Press" to discuss the panel, which he said would establish guidelines acceptable by both government and the press for future conflicts.[120]

The panel met for five days in February of 1984, reading statements from the press as well as interviewing various journalists and public affairs officers.[121] Six months later, the panel released its report and Secretary of Defense Weinberger ordered Assistant Secretary for Public Affairs Michael Burch to take the necessary steps to implement the panel's recommendations.[122] The Sidle Panel report affirmed the basic principle of press access to the battlefield, given the necessities of operational security, and offered eight recommendations for improving the military/media relationship. In summary form, those eight points were:

1. That public affairs planning take place concurrently with operational planning.
2. When pools are necessary, they should be as big as is feasible and their life span should be as short as possible.
3. A standing list of journalists to make up a pool should be considered.
4. Voluntary compliance by media with security guidelines should be basic tenet of media access (as in Vietnam).
5. Public affairs planning should include sufficient equipment and qualified military personnel to help media cover operations adequately.
6. Planners should consider media communications requirements to ensure earliest feasible availability, and perhaps consider facilities dedicated to the media.
7. Planning should include provision for transportation in the theater of operations.
8. Understanding and cooperation between the military and the media should be improved through increased contact by officers with the press and press issues.

Unlike after Vietnam, after Grenada the military actively sought ways to improve public affairs. The military's initiative in repairing its public affairs system actually frightened some observers, who took the Sidle Panel as proof that the civilian leadership had ceded control over press issues to the military. Many believed that the matter of press access to battlezones was properly a matter for civilians to decide.

What these observers missed, however, was that Reagan administration officials had already settled the larger *political* question of press access to their satisfaction. Baker and Shultz made clear after the Grenada invasion that the administration was happy to keep the press on the sidelines. Baker, who claimed that he had not known about the restrictions in advance but approved of them, said he would approve them again in similar circumstances. Shultz was more openly negative towards the press in such situations, stating that, "These days, in the adversary journalism that's been developed, it seems as though the reporters are always against us and so they're always seeking to report something that's going to screw things up. And when you're trying to conduct a military operation you don't need that."[123] Reagan officials were clearly comfortable defending the political decision to exclude the press. The administration has simply left the military to implement the policy of limited access. Thus, rather than an intrusion into civilian responsibilities, the Grenada case is evidence of the comfortable arrangement between the Reagan administration and the military. Had the administration been concerned that the military would not deal appropriately with the press, it certainly could have taken action. It did not, and its failure to reaffirm the principle of press freedom to cover conflicts was a source of consternation to journalists and other observers.[124]

The Sidle report, aside from supporting the general principle of press access, never entered the realm of politics, and did not discuss the role of civilian political leaders in ensuring press coverage of conflicts. For an essentially in-house report, the panel provided a remarkably penetrating assessment of the obstacles within the military to effective public affairs planning. What the report failed to do, perhaps understandably, was to discuss *why* these obstacles existed.

Nonetheless, the report's recommendations provided the basic outline of a new public affairs system. In particular, two items would prove to be of decisive importance: the press pool as a permanent fixture of public affairs planning and the media's voluntary acceptance of pool groundrules in lieu of censorship.

First, the press pool was established as the option of choice for remote conflicts or those of such a nature (surprise attacks, etc.) as to require limiting press notification and access. The pool concept was an unpopular one with those representatives of the press who spoke before the panel. As the Sidle report notes, "Media representatives appearing before the panel were unanimous in being opposed to pools in general. However, they all also agreed that they would cooperate in pooling agreements if that were necessary for them to obtain early access to an operation."[125]

It seems clear that the press objected to the pool system on the constitutional or political level, afraid that to agree to such an arrangement would be to admit that the government had a right to limit press access. On the practical level, however, it is also clear that news organizations would not let abstract issues stand in their way of getting to a big story. If agreeing to a pool was the only way the press was likely to get to certain conflicts, that would be better than no coverage at all. The press representatives before the panel argued, and the panelists agreed, that the pool should only last as long as necessary before full coverage could begin. With this promise, the major news organizations were willing to strike the bargain on the pool. At any rate, no actions were taken to counter the implementation of the report's recommendations when they arrived in August of 1984.

The second issue of import was the panel's suggestion to rely on voluntary compliance with public affairs groundrules like the ones used in Vietnam. The press, of course, much preferred such a policy to one involving censorship. This recommendation, along with the reasonable tone of the panel's report in general, was probably important in enticing the press corps not to fight the administration too vigorously over the issue. By offering the press at least a partial return to the Vietnam-era system it enjoyed so much, the sting of the pool system may have been eased.

The long-term implications of the report were not evident when it was released. Although the panel had been asked to consider public affairs generally, in fact its recommendations aimed at making sure Grenada would not happen again.[126] The panel did not envision that the pool would be necessary at all times nor did it discuss making standard practice of limited press access to conflicts. Further, of course, no one could have been sure how the system would eventually work in practice.

And although the press was generally not excited to have to deal with a new set of rules regarding coverage of military actions, the tone of the report was not overly threatening.[127] By declaring support for the role of the press in informing the public during armed conflict, the panel eschewed the hard-line position of many in the military and elsewhere that the press would inevitably turn the public against U.S. actions and should therefore be heavily restricted in all situations during a conflict. Further, by recommending that the press comply voluntarily with security guidelines, rather than recommending any form of censorship, the panel also implicitly rejected the public arguments of military and civilian officials during Urgent Fury—that the media could not be trusted to maintain operational security and would endanger American troops.

Assistant Secretary of Defense (Public Affairs) Burch met with representatives of several major news organizations in October 1984 to work out arrangements for the media pool. Initial plans were for an eleven person pool, including wire and television reporters, but no daily newspaper representative. The plan was quickly changed to a twelve-person pool after print organizations protested at being left out. The pool system proposed by the Pentagon followed roughly the outlines of the Sidle Panel's recommendations; and the groundrules for the pool were copied directly from the guidelines drawn up in Vietnam.[128]

Institutionalizing the Pool System: 1984-1989

The pool was activated for its first test run to cover exercises in Central America in April 1985. Understandably the first run was not as smooth as anyone would have liked. In fact, by both military and media accounts the test proved a failure.[129] The military was concerned about leaks and the pool reporters felt that their stories took too long to be relayed by the military back home. The next test several months later was an easier one, covering exercises in Kentucky, which seemed to prompt few complaints from either side.

Undergoing refinement along the way, the pool system then saw action in Libya,[130] Honduras,[131] and the Persian Gulf.[132] In each case complaints by both the military and the press were limited, though opinions varied as to how useful the pools had been. The most extensive pool operation, the oil tanker reflagging operation in the Persian Gulf in 1987-88, seemed to give pool reporters the sense that the system could work.[133]

None of these deployments offered much of a challenge, however, to the pool arrangements. Each story would have been close to impossible for the press to cover without the pool. Not only was the action almost always in spots too dangerous for the media to venture without military protection, but gathering meaningful information about events without access to military resources would also have been exceedingly difficult. There was no good alternative, for example, to accepting a ride on U.S. naval ships during the reflagging operation. Perhaps more importantly, each of these stories was of relatively minor importance compared with the invasion of another nation. Thus, neither civilian leaders nor the press were threatened enough by events to worry too much about arrangements for press coverage.

Although the pool was not battle-tested until Panama, the years after Grenada did serve as a period during which the military institutionalized the new public affairs system. In order to fix the lessons of Grenada and the Sidle Panel's recommendations in its "bureaucratic brain," the military had to create standard procedures, test them, and refine them. By 1989 when Panama loomed around the corner, the military had firmly implanted the pool system in its institutional memory through repeated testing and drafting of the pool and its ground rules. This is not to say that by 1989 the military had implemented all of the Sidle Panel's recommendations—it had not. But the process had a critical outcome: by the time of the Panama invasion the military's reflex in a crisis would be to activate the pool.

CONCLUSIONS

The argument that the military engineered its public affairs policy in Grenada to compensate for its outrage at the press during Vietnam is simply not supported by the historical record. The administration and its relationship with the press set the tone for government/press relations during the crisis. The Reagan White House made great efforts to influence news coverage of its actions on a daily basis and Grenada proved to be no exception. The administration's traditional strategy, followed during the invasion, was to allow the department dealing with an issue to take the lead on public relations until the White House could claim success, garnering positive coverage for Reagan. And though we do not have definitive proof, the available evidence tells us that at a minimum administration officials gave the go-ahead for the press ban, while strongly suggesting that most likely it was the White House that made the critical decision to bar the press from Grenada.

The military, for its part, had few established procedures for public affairs before Grenada, and none that were workable in a crisis. There simply was no institutional response to Vietnam to limit press access to covering wars and no evidence in the planning for Urgent Fury to suggest an organized and conscious attempt to "do it right this time." In addition, the fact that the military looked to the press guidelines from Vietnam in order to plan for public affairs after Grenada makes it clear that the military had not so thoroughly rejected Vietnam public affairs as had been argued. Were the conventional explanations for the military's behavior correct, we certainly would not expect it to turn so quickly to Vietnam for guidance on how to deal with the press.

More important than Vietnam in explaining Grenada public affairs planning and implementation for the military's part were its organizational routines and professional interests. In the days and hours leading up to the invasion, the military was hampered by its lack of attention to public affairs planning. The complete lack of a contingency plan to deal with the media in a situation like Urgent Fury suggests that the military was far less motivated to fix its public affairs problems than many have assumed. And in making its last minute plans for Urgent Fury public affairs, the military showed that once a crisis erupts, public affairs may receive even less attention; the JIB set up on Barbados from many accounts was poorly run compared to past efforts. Then once the invasion was underway, the desire to maintain operational security, to take the opportunity to impress Congress and the public with its competence, and to keep the uglier side of war from public view, encouraged the military to implement the press ban, to restrict the press once it arrived on Grenada, to keep quiet about enemy and civilian casualties and operational miscues, and finally to trumpet victory and praise the troops.

The impact of the press ban on news gathering and subsequent press coverage itself was substantial. Numerous stories were delayed, there was no firsthand coverage of U.S. troops in combat, and what details of the invasion's progress were reported came straight from the government. Administration rationales dominated television and print coverage, and little independent analysis of events was possible. The impact of this dominance, in terms of public and congressional support, is impossible to know precisely. What is clear, however, is that the administration and the military kept to a minimum the chances that the press would report anything to challenge official reports or to show the public shocking sights of war.

Grenada also marked the birth of what can be called "DoD TV." The importance of not allowing U.S. casualties to be shown on television news was keenly felt in the administration, emphasized by the sensational coverage and public distress over the tragedy of the Marines in Beirut. Network television never made it to Grenada in time to cover the invasion itself. Meanwhile, the Pentagon supplied the footage—much delayed, full of happy, smiling students, and lacking any combat footage—completely sterile, as Admiral Metcalf later put it. The absence of independent television meant that the public did not see any of the events that left 29 dead and 152 wounded American soldiers. The importance of keeping casualties off television was not lost on the Reagan administration. Grenada marked the beginning of a trend away from the unrestricted and at times bloody coverage of Vietnam towards government-controlled television, a trend that reached its peak in the most recent conflict in the Gulf.

None of the administration's or the military's efforts would have been so successful in limiting press coverage of Urgent Fury, however, without assistance from a fortuitous combination of factors. The fact that the invasion was a surprise, the fact that no press corps was present on Grenada at the time of the invasion, that Grenada was an island and difficult for journalists to get to, and that the operation ended up being so quick and successful all supported the decision by the administration and later by Metcalf to keep the press out. Without this combination of elements, public affairs in Grenada could have been very different. At the least, the government would not have enjoyed the complete information monopoly that it did.

This monopoly was critical, in turn, because it was the very effectiveness of the ban on the press that led to the uproar over the restrictions and thus to the creation of the Sidle Panel. The panel focused on the operational shortcomings of Grenada public affairs, leaving the larger question of press access aside. Unwittingly, the panel's recommendations fostered the development of a system that would make a rerun of Grenada more likely, rather than less.

In agreeing to the pool concept the press, in hindsight, made a strategic error. No one guessed at the time that by accepting the system the press would effectively allow the government to determine what reporters would be able to cover during conflicts. By agreeing to limit their numbers and forego unilateral reporting, the press understood the bargain to be limited to the early stages of only those conflicts whose circumstances required the pool. The military also understood the plan in these terms. But as we will see in Panama, once the press pool has been activated during a conflict, it becomes easy for the government to change its mind, and much more difficult for the press to do anything about the situation.

Finally, the failure of the press to respond more vigorously, combined with the public's support of the restrictions on the press during the invasion, should have made it clear to anyone watching that the government had gained the upper hand in public affairs. For all the potential power of the media, the government had successfully restrained the fourth estate at a crucial moment and escaped any real backlash. Grenada was thus a precedent for similar actions in the future, marking the beginning of the trend towards greater government restriction of the press in time of war.

ENDNOTES

1. "An Off-the-Record War," *Newsweek*, November 7, 1983.
2. Cited in Mark Hertsgaard, *On Bended Knee: The Press and the Reagan Presidency* (New York: Schocken Books, 1988), p. 212.
3. Drew Middleton, "Barring the Press from the Battlefield," *New York Times Magazine*, 1984.
4. Robert Harris, *GOTCHA! The Media, the Government, and the Falklands Crisis* (London: Faber and Faber, 1983); Derrik Mercer, ed., *The Fog of War: The Media on the Battlefield* (London: Heinemann, 1987); Phillip Knightley, "The Falklands: How Britannia Ruled the News," *Columbia Journalism Review*, September/October, 1982, pp. 51-53; Edgar O'Ballance, "The Other Falklands Campaign," *Military Review*, Vol. 63, No. 1, January 1983; Arthur A. Humphries, "Two Routes to the Wrong Destination: Public Affairs in the South Atlantic War," *Naval War College Review*, June 1983; Peter Braestrup, "Background Paper," in *Battle Lines: Report of the Twentieth Century Fund Task Force on the Military and the Media* (New York: Priority Press, 1985), pp. 77-82; "Military vs. Press: Troubled History," *New York Times*, October 29, 1983; Jane

Sharkey, *Under Fire: Military Restrictions on the Press* (Washington, DC: The Center for Public Integrity, 1991), pp. 61-66.

5. "Jewel" stands for Joint Endeavor for Welfare, Education, and Labor.
6. The following description of US-Grenada relations relies on several accounts: Hugh O'Shaughnessy, *Grenada: An Eyewitness Account of the Invasion and the History that Provoked It* (London: Sphere Books, 1984); Burrowes, *Revolution and Rescue in Grenada* (Somewhere, Somebody Press, 1988); Robert Pastor, "The United States and the Grenada Revolution: Who Pushed First and Why?" in Jorge Heine, ed., *A Revolution Aborted: The Lessons of Grenada* (Pittsburgh, PA: University of Pittsburgh Press, 1990), pp. 181-214. K. Schoenhals and R. Melanson, *Revolution and Intervention in Grenada: The New Jewel Movement, The United States, and The Caribbean* (Boulder, CO: Westview Press, 1985). One can also find the basic outlines in *New York Times* or *Washington Post* coverage of the crisis, beginning October 26, 1983.
7. O' Shaughnessy, *An Eyewitness Account*, p. 105. For other accounts critical of U.S. policy toward Grenada before the invasion, see Burrowes, *Revolution and Rescue*, Schoenhals and Melanson, *Revolution and Intervention*; and Kenworthy, "Grenada as Theater."
8. Robert Pastor, "The US and Grenada: To Leap or Be Pushed?" Pastor makes use of PRG Central Committee documents captured during the invasion.
9. "Transcript of Reagan Speech," *New York Times*, March 24, 1983.
10. Mark Adkin, *Urgent Fury: The Battle for Grenada* (Lexington, MA: Lexington Books, 1989), p. 111.
11. Hooker, "Presidential Decisionmaking and Use of Force: Case Study Grenada," *Parameters*, Vol. 21, No. 2, Summer 1971, p. 64.
12. Ibid., p. 65
13. The National Security Council normally includes the Vice President, the Chairman of the Joint Chiefs, the Director of the CIA, and the National Security Adviser. Special Situation Groups also include specialists in the areas, such as Grenada, under consideration during a crisis. The SSG met in the afternoon after a morning meeting of the Crisis Pre-Planning Group. The CPG is made up of the lower-ranking officials with expertise in the affairs of various regions and is used to develop options for consideration at the SSG and NSC meetings. It was this group that wrote the background memorandum for the Vice President's preparation for the SSG.
14. Constantine Menges, *Inside the National Security Council* (New York: Touchstone, 1988), pp. 54-90.
15. "D-Day in Grenada," *Time*, November 7, 1983, p. 27.
16. A National Security Decision Directive is a file containing all the materials: intelligence reports, military readiness reports, maps, memos, etc.—upon which the president will base his decision and which he must sign to formally authorize an operation.

17. Bennet, "Anatomy of a 'Go' Decision," *Reader's Digest*, February 1984.
18. Adkin, *Urgent Fury*, p. 121.
19. Sharkey, *Under Fire*, p. 70; for similar arguments see Richard Cohen, "Hey!" *Washington Post*, November 13, 1983.
20. Winant Sidle, "Public Affairs," in *Vietnam: 10 Years Later* (Fort Benjamin Harrison, IN: Defense Information School, 1983), p. 85.
21. Clyde A. Hennies, *Public Affairs Training for the Army's Officer Corps: Need or Neglect?* (US Army War College, Carlisle Barracks, June 6, 1983), p. 5.
22. These other studies will be discussed in later chapters.
23. Jack A. Gottschalk, "'Consistent with Security,'. . . A History of American Military Press Censorship," *Communications and the Law*, pp. 50-52.
24. Braestrup, "Background Paper," pp. 94-95; *Sharkey, Under Fire*, pp. 81-82.
25. News Conference by Secretary of Defense Caspar W. Weinberger and General John W. Vessey, Jr., U.S. Army, Chairman, Joint Chiefs of Staff, at the Pentagon, October 26, 1983, p. 5.
26. Ibid., p. 5.
27. "Admiral Says It Was His Decision to Tether the Press," *New York Times*, October 31, 1983.
28. William Safire, "Us Against Them," October 30, 1983.
29. Hearings before Civil Liberties Subcommittee, p. 9.
30. Ibid., pp. 34-35.
31. William Safire, "Us Against Them," October 30, 1983.
32. "American Envoys Going to Grenada," *New York Times*, October 23, 1983; *The Washington Post* also reported Grenada's warnings, "Grenada Puts Military On Alert, Warns of US Threat to Invade," October 23, 1983; the *Times* followed up with "Grenada Radio Warns of Attack," October 24, 1983.
33. "Barbadian Leader Describes Disputes and Confusion in Arranging Invasion," *New York Times*, October 28, 1983.
34. "Grenada Was Told of Invasion Plan," *New York Times* (from UPI), November 7, 1983.
35. This section borrows heavily from Peter Braestrup's excellent chapters on Grenada in his "Background Paper," in *Report of the Twentieth Century Fund Task Force on the Military and the Media* and Jaqueline Sharkey's *Under Fire* (Washington DC: Center for Public Integrity, 1991). Both Braestrup and Sharkey conducted many interviews of key public affairs officers and journalists who covered the invasion. They are required reading for anyone interested in wartime public affairs.
36. Metcalf, "The Press and Grenada, 1983," in *Defence and The Media in Time of Limited War* (London: Frank Cass and Co., Ltd., 1992), p. 172.
37. Speakes, *Speaking Out*, p. 156; Hertsgaard, *On Bended Knee*, p. 216; David Burnahm, "Curbs on Grenada News Coverage Criticized in House Hearing," *New York Times*, November 3, 1983.

38. Braestrup, "Background Paper," pp. 94-95; and Sharkey, *Under Fire*, pp. 81-82.
39. Braestrup, "Background Paper," p. 95; Sharkey, *Under Fire*, p. 82.
40. Braestrup, "Background Paper," pp. 95-96.
41. Ibid., p. 96.
42. Ibid., p. 96.
43. For a discussion of the legal issues involved with media coverage of war, see Marshall Silverberg, "Constitutional Concerns in Denying the Press Access to Military Operations," in Loren B. Thompson, ed., *Defense Beat* (New York: Lexington Books, 1991), pp. 165-175.
44. Marjorie Hunter, "US Eases Restrictions on Coverage," *New York Times*, October 31, 1983.
45. Metcalf, "The Press and Grenada, 1983," p. 170. On Metcalf's controversial but effective methods of enforcing the press ban, see "Admiral Says It Was His Decision to Tether the Press," *New York Times*, October 31, 1983.
46. Braestrup, "Background Paper," pp. 96-99. Also, William E. Farrell, "U.S. Allows 15 Reporters to Go to Grenada for a Day," *New York Times*, October 28, 1983.
47. Braestrup, "Background Paper," p. 94.
48. Ibid., pp. 105-106.
49. "Excerpts From News Conference of Secretary of Defense," *New York Times*, October 27, 1983.
50. Cited in B. Drummond Ayers, "Defense Dept. Says the Marines and Rangers Quickly Achieved Initial Goals," *New York Times*, October 26, 1983.
51. Jonathan Friendly, "Reporting the News in a Communiqué War," *New York Times*, October 27, 1983.
52. Lou Cannon and David Hoffman, "Invasion Secrecy Creating a Furor," *Washington Post*, October 27, 1983.
53. Several informative books have been written on the Reagan Administration's dealings with the press. For an insider's view read Larry Speakes' book *Speaking Out: Inside the Reagan White House* (New York: Charles Scribner's Sons, 1988), which makes quite clear that the goal was to "beat the press." For a highly critical book (both of the press and the Reagan administration) see Mark Hertsgaard, *On Bended Knee: The Press and the Reagan Presidency* (New York: Schocken Books, 1988). A useful study of administration press office organization is John Maltese, *Spin Control: The White House Office of Communications and the Management of Presidential News* (Chapel Hill: University of North Carolina Press, 1992).
54. Hertsgaard, *On Bended Knee*, pp. 22-23.
55. Ibid., pp. 32-37
56. Speakes, *Speaking Out*, p. 217.
57. Ibid., pp 117-118.

58. Smith, *The Power Game*, pp. 416-419.
59. Quoted in Dom Bonafede, "Muzzling the Media," *National Journal*, July 12, 1986, p. 1719.
60. Floyd Abrams, "The New Effort to Control Information," *New York Times Magazine*, September 25, 1983; An article that places the Reagan administration's efforts in recent historical context is John Shattuck, "National Security a Decade After Watergate," *Democracy*, Winter 1983.
61. Ibid.; For a reaction from a journalist to the administration's efforts (written during the Grenada invasion) see William Safire, "Us Against Them," *New York Times*, October 30, 1983.
62. Congress held hearings on the administration's efforts to limit the free flow of information during the invasion. The hearings are an excellent collection of arguments against such actions. See Hearings before 98th Congress, First Session, House Committee of the Judiciary, Subcommittee on Courts, Civil Liberties, and the Administration of Justice, November 2, 1983.
63. Michael Deaver with Mickey Herskowitz, *Behind the Scenes* (New York: William Morrow, 1987), p. 144.
64. See, for example, Chris Hanson, "Gunsmoke and Sleeping Dogs: the Prez's Press at Midterm," in *Columbia Journalism Review*, May/June 1983, pp. 27-36.
65. W. Lance Bennett, *News: The Politics of Illusion* (New York: Longman, 1988), p. 90.
66. *America's Team, The Odd Couple*, p. 105.
67. Jonathan Friendly, "Weinberger Tied to Curb on Press," *New York Times*, November 13, 1983.
68. Drew Middleton, "The Military and the Media," *New York Times Magazine*, February 5, 1984, p. 69.
69. The *New York Times* spoke for many critics in an editorial denouncing the military's influence, "Grenada and Mount Suribachi," October 28, 1983.
70. *America's Team, The Odd Couple*, p. 104.
71. Hertsgaard, *On Bended Knee*, p. 214.
72. See Speakes, *Speaking Out*, pp. 151-155.
73. Ibid., p. 156.
74. Reporters' views of the Speakes episode are recounted in Braestrup, "Background Paper,"; and Geoff Mungham, "Grenada: News Blackout in the Caribbean," in Mercer, ed., *The Fog of War*, pp. 291-310.
75. The text of Reagan's address can be found in the *New York Times*, "Text of Reagan's Announcement of Invasion," October 26, 1983.
76. Francis X. Clines, "At Reagan Press Office, It's Avoid the Negative," *New York Times*, October 28, 1983.
77. H. W. Brands, "Decisions on American Armed Intervention: Lebanon, Dominican Republic, and Grenada," *Political Science Quarterly*, Vol. 102, No. 4, 1987, pp. 607-624.

78. Shultz, in fact, used this phrase six times in his news conference. See "Transcript of Shultz's News Conference on Why U.S. Acted," *New York Times*, October 26, 1983.
79. Cited in "Legality of Grenada Attack Disputed," *New York Times*, October 26, 1983.
80. Ibid.
81. Hedrick Smith, "Reagan Aide Says U.S. Invasion Forestalled Cuban Arms Buildup," *New York Times*, October 27, 1983.
82. "School's Chancellor Says Invasion Was Not Necessary to Save Lives," *New York Times*, October 26, 1983.
83. A spate of articles outlined these initial reactions: "U.S. Warned by Mrs. Thatcher," *New York Times*, October 26, 1983; "Soviet Assails Move by U.S. As 'Undisguised Banditry,'" *New York Times*, October 27, 1983; "Latins in U.N. Council Assail the U.S. on Invasion," *New York Times*, October 26, 1983; "Most O.A.S. Members Assail Action," *New York Times*, October 27, 1983; "Grenada Debate Continues at U.N." *New York Times*, October 27, 1983; "Allies Criticism of U.S. Raises Wider Questions," *New York Times*, October 27, 1983.
84. *New York Times*, October 26, 1983; After the invasion Robert Pastor testified before Congress that he thought the U.S. had arrived "just in time to prevent an orderly evacuation of U.S. citizens from Grenada." Kenworthy, "Grenada as Theater," *World Policy Journal*, p. 638.
85. Hedrick Smith, "Reagan Aide Says U.S. Invasion Forestalled Cuban Arms Buildup," *New York Times*, October 27, 1983.
86. Weinberger-Vessey press conference, October 26, 1983.
87. See Francis X. Clines, "At Reagan Press Office, It's Avoid the Negative," *New York Times*, October 28, 1983. For those interested in a closer look at administration efforts at diplomacy and the debate that surrounds the administration's justification of the intervention, a good place to begin is Robert J. Beck, "The 'McNeil Mission' and the Decision to Invade Grenada," *Naval War College Review*, 1991.
88. Fay S. Joyce, "First Evacuees Arrive in U.S. From Grenada," *New York Times*, October 27, 1983.
89. Speakes, *Speaking Out*, p. 160.
90. On the nature of Grenada's military ties to the Soviet Union, North Korea, and Cuba, see Robert Pastor, "Who Pushed First?" and Paul Seabury and Walter A. McDougall, eds., *The Grenada Papers* (San Francisco: Institute for Contemporary Studies, 1984).
91. "Transcript of Reagan's Televised Address," *New York Times*, October 27, 1983.
92. Anthony Lewis, "What Was He Hiding?" *New York Times*, October 31, 1983.
93. *New York Times*, "Poll Shows Support for Presence of US Troops in Lebanon and Grenada," *New York Times*, October 28, 1983; Richard

Whittle, "Questions, Praise Follow Grenada Invasion," *CQWR*, October 29, 1983, pp. 2221-2224; John Felton, "After the Invasion: Support Widens on the Hill," *CQWR*, November 12, 1983, pp. 2360-2361.

94. A complete list of content analysis efforts is found in footnote 7 in Chapter One.
95. Phil McCombs, "In Barbados, a Restless Press," *Washington Post*, October 29, 1983.
96. Braestrup, "Background Paper," pp. 96-100.
97. O'Shaughnessy, *Grenada: An Eyewitness Account*, pp. 204-205.
98. Considering the scale of the conflict in Grenada compared to Vietnam, the number of journalists who tried to cover Urgent Fury is staggering. Metcalf noted that there was a journalist for every eighteen U.S. troops. Braestrup, "Background Paper," and "Conference Report on US Military Operations and the Press."
99. Braestrup, "Background Paper," pp. 101-102.
100. Michael Kernan, "On TV, Picturing the Invasion," *Washington Post*, October 26, 1983.
101. Reporting in a Communiqué War," *New York Times*, October 26, 1983.
102. Nacos, *The Press, Presidents, and Crises*, pp. 165-167.
103. O'Shaughnessy, *Grenada: An Eyewitness Account*, pp. 214-217.
104. Shales, "Grenada: A Question of News Control."
105. Ibid.
106. Drummond B. Ayers, "U.S. Concedes Bombing Hospital in Grenada, Killing at Least 12," *New York Times*, November 1, 1983; and Rick Atkinson, "Estimates of Casualties in Grenada Rise," *Washington Post*, November 9, 1983.
107. "U.S. Officers Give Invasion Details," *New York Times*, November 9, 1983.
108. Stuart Taylor, Jr., "In Wake of Invasion, Much Official Misinformation by U.S. Comes to Light," *New York Times*, November 6, 1983; "U.S. Officers Give Invasion Details," *New York Times*, November 9, 1983; "Grenadians' Toll Put by U.S. at 21," *New York Times*, November 13, 1983.
109. Sharkey, *Under Fire*, p. 78. Admiral Metcalf made these remarks at a conference on military-media issues at Columbia University.
110. Stuart Taylor, Jr., "In the Wake of Invasion, Much Official Misinformation Comes to Light," *New York Times*, November 6, 1983; B. Drummond Ayers, "Grenada Invasion: A Series of Surprise," *New York Times*, November 14, 1983; John J. Fialka, "In Battle for Grenada, Command Mission Didn't Go As Planned," *Wall Street Journal*, November 15, 1983.
111. "In the Wake of the Invasion, Much Official Information Comes to Light," *New York Times*, November 6, 1983; "Grenada Invasion: A Series of Surprises," *New York Times*, November 14, 1983; "In Battle for Grenada, Command Mission Didn't Go As Planned," *Wall*

Street Journal, November 15, 1983; Richard Gabriel, "Scenes From An Invasion: How the US Military Stumbled to Victory in Grenada," *The Washington Monthly*, February 1986.

112. "Networks Take Censorship Complaints to Congress," *Broadcasting*, November 7, 1983, p. 36. The hearing was before the 98th Congress, House Judiciary Subcommittee on Courts, Civil Liberties, and the Administration of Justice, November 2, 1983.
113. Nacos, *The Press, Presidents, and Crises*, p. 170.
114. James E. Roper, "D.C. Press Corps 'Brawls' with White House," *Editor and Publisher*, November 5, 1983, pp. 11-13; and Andrew Radolf, "News Organizations Protest Grenada Restrictions," *Editor and Publisher*, November 5, 1983, pp. 14-15.
115. The committee carried out an in-depth study of the history and issues involved with press access to the battlefield. Some in the group, including the executive director, Jack Landau, wanted to move ahead with legal action. See "Reporters' Committee May Sue Government," *Editor and Publisher*, November 19, 1983, p. 16, and Landau's "Excluding the Press from the Grenada Invasion: A Violation of the Public's Constitutional Rights," *Editor and Publisher*, December 10, 1983, pp. 10-11, 22. The committee included the American Newspaper Publishers Association, American Society of Magazine Editors, American Society of Newspaper Editors, the Associated Press, Associated Press Managing Editors, National Association of Broadcasters, Radio-Television News Directors Association, Reporters Committee for Freedom of the Press, Society of Professional Journalists, and United Press International.
116. *Time* recorded the media's distress over its unpopularity and determines that it has resulted, in large part, from the media's behavior. See "Journalism in Crisis," 1983.
117. Braestrup, "Background Paper," pp. 127-128.
118. Jonathan Friendly, "Press Groups Ask Talks on Combat Coverage," *New York Times*, December 2, 1983; and "Accord Asked on Reporting of U.S. Military Operations," *New York Times*, January 11, 1984.
119. "News Organizations Seek a Meeting [with] Reagan on Censorship," *Editor and Publisher*, December 10, 1983, p. 23; "Media Organizations Take a Stand," *Editor and Publisher*, January 14, 1983, pp. 18-19; and John Consoli and Andrew Radolf, "Working with the White House," *Editor and Publisher*, January 21, 1984, pp. 9, 20.
120. See "Panel to Review Curb on the Press," *New York Times*, Nov. 7, 1983.
121. Vessey had planned to include both journalists and military officers on the Sidle Panel, as it became known. Working journalists refused to sit on the panel, however, thinking that participation would signal acceptance of Grenada as a precedent for public affairs. Thus, instead of sitting on the panel itself, journalists gave written testimony to the fourteen panelists for consideration.

122. The report, of course, made news. "Key Sections of Panel's Report on the Military and the Press," *New York Times*, August 24, 1984; Also see Statement of the Secretary of Defense, Caspar Weinberger, August 23, 1984, No. 450-84.
123. Baker's thoughts were revealed in Jonathan Friendly, "Weinberger Tied to Curb on Press," *New York Times*, November 13, 1983. Shultz's comment is cited in Margaret Shapiro, "Shultz Defends Press Ban," *Washington Post*, December 16, 1983.
124. See Bernard Weinraub, "U.S. Press Curbs: The Unanswered Questions," *New York Times*, October 29, 1983; and *Battle Lines*, p. 5-6.
125. Sidle Panel report, section 2.
126. In a letter to Weinberger accompanying the report, Sidle wrote, "You did not request our assessment of media handling of Grenada and we will not provide it. However, we do feel that had our recommendations been 'in place' and fully considered at the time of Grenada, there might have been no need to create our panel." See Braestrup, "Background Paper," p. 125.
127. See Charles Mohr, "The Continuing Battle Over Covering Wars," *New York Times*, September 14, 1984.
128. Richard Halloran, "Pentagon Forms War Press Pool; Newspaper Reporters Excluded," *New York Times*, October 11, 1984; Halloran, "Pentagon Plans to Add Newspaper As Member of Its War Press Pool," *New York Times*, October 12, 1984; and Halloran, "Pentagon Is Proposing Rules For the Press at Battlefields," *New York Times*, October 13, 1984.
129. Eleanor Randolph, "Defense News-Pool Test Described a Failure," *Washington Post*, April 27, 1985.
130. Philip Shenon, "Press Units Frustrated on Libya, But Few Blame Pentagon," *New York Times*, March 27, 1986; Eleanor Randolph, "The Networks' Libyan Fly-By," *Washington Post*, March 26, 1986, and George Garneau, "Cooperating With the Military: NBC Withheld Story About U.S. Plans to Bomb Libya," *Editor and Publisher*, November 21, 1987.
131. George Garneau, "New Press Pool Activated: American Reporters Accompany U.S. Troops Airlifted to Honduras as Sandinista-contra Battle Heats Up Along the Border," *Editor and Publisher*, March 26, 1988.
132. For more general assessments of the pool's experience between Grenada and Panama see Barry Willey, "Military-Media Relations Come of Age," *Parameters*, March 1989, pp. 76-84. Also, Jeffrey Carnes, "The Department of Defense Media Pool: Making the Media-Military Relationship Work," in Loren Thompson, ed., *Defense Beat*, 1991.
133. Mark Thompson, "With the Press Pool in the Persian Gulf," *Columbia Journalism Review*, November/December 1987, pp. 40-45; Tim Ahern, "White Smoke in the Persian Gulf," *Washington*

Journalism Review, Vol. 9, October 1987, p. 18; and Richard Pyle, "Covering a Mini-War: Sometimes the Pool Works," *Washington Journalism Review,* Vol. 10, July/August, 1987, pp. 14-17.

5

Pinning the Press Down in Panama

From the perspective of government press policy the invasion of Panama was essentially a rerun of Grenada, which made it even more clear that the White House, not the military, has been the prime force shaping restrictive press policies since Vietnam. Journalists and other observers once again laid blame for the restrictive press policies at the military's door. The military, however, came once again to the operation without a public affairs plan and existing military public affairs policy (crafted in the wake of Grenada) bore almost no relation to the policies of Just Cause. The main reason the military had no plan was because the White House did not want to follow the existing policy but instead chose to pursue a more restrictive one. Secretary of Defense Richard Cheney activated the pool even though the situation did not call for it and delayed the pool's call-up, knowing that these acts would cause journalists to miss the opening and most critical battles in Just Cause. As it turned out the press pool, designed by the military after Grenada as a way to get journalists to the earliest action in a conflict, proved a useful tool for senior civilian officials to control them with instead.

During the invasion the military's continued lack of preparedness for crisis time public affairs hampered the pool's functioning yet further. Poor logistics and insufficient communications equipment degraded the pool's ability to move about Panama and to report its stories to the United States. This would have been even more serious had the pool had much news to transmit. Unfortunately for the pool, the military shared the White House's distaste for battlefield press coverage and helped ensure that the pool had little news of interest—and no combat stories—to send home. But things were even worse for those journalists in Panama who were not part of the pool. The pool's activation allowed the military and the Bush Administration to justify restraints on the freedom of movement of journalists who were not in the pool. Thus, both those journalists in Panama City and those who traveled on their own to Panama once the invasion had begun found the U.S. military an obstacle to their newsgathering efforts.

The government's handling of the press during Just Cause again prompted press cries of foul play, though fewer than after Grenada. The administration offered a half-hearted apology and the military promised again to do better next time. The press once more accepted the government response rather than challenge its press policies in a more serious manner. Panama revealed how effective a government tool the pool would prove. This time the press could not say that it had been shut out entirely as in Grenada; it could only complain that a system it had accepted did not work as well as it was supposed to. Thus the press had left itself without a firm basis to challenge the government. Six months later the government's system for dealing with the press during the Gulf crisis emerged as a yet more highly refined version of what had been done in Panama.

BACKGROUND

General Manuel Noriega, head of the Panamanian Defense Forces (PDF), became the de facto military dictator of Panama in 1983, when he reneged on a powersharing arrangement with other senior military officers. The United States looked on Noriega with mixed feelings. On one hand, he was brutal to his political opponents and had become rich through his role in drug trafficking. On the other hand, Noriega had enjoyed a close relationship to the CIA and to the U.S. military since the 1960s, acting as an informant in the drug war and helping the Reagan administration in the 1980s to aid the contras in Nicaragua. For several years the U.S./Panama relationship remained uneasy but essentially stable.[1]

Eventually, however, Noriega became public enemy number one. In 1987 the Panamanian public was mobilized by charges leveled at Noriega by Colonel Roberto Diaz Herrera, former PDF second in command, of rigging the 1984 Panama elections, of corruption, and of plotting to kill Panama's former leader, General Omar Torrijos. Public protest and demonstrations lasted months. A public opinion poll showed that 75% of Panama wanted Noriega to step down. The United States began to reconsider its relationship with Noriega. The Senate passed a resolution calling for Noriega to step down. The Reagan administration, after much internal debate, cut off economic aid to Panama in July 1987 after Noriega supporters vandalized the U.S. embassy, but remained uncertain of how far to go in dealing with Noriega.[2]

Events soon dictated that the administration move more vigorously against the Panamanian leader. In February 1988 two U.S. grand juries indicted General Manuel Noriega on drug trafficking-related charges. After the indictments, the Reagan administration felt it had to escalate the pressure on Noriega, even though some at DEA and the Defense Department wanted to keep working with him. Thus, the administration encouraged Panama's president, Delvalle, to fire Noriega. Delvallc tried, but was thrown out of office by Noriega instead. Delvalle fled to Miami, where he was recognized as Panama's legitimate leader, and worked to force the United States to take harsher steps against Noriega. In April of 1988, the administration instituted full economic sanctions against Panama and attempted to negotiate with Noriega for his removal. Neither the sanctions nor the negotiations produced results, however, and Reagan was forced to back down during the 1988 election season.[3]

When Bush took over the presidency he inherited the Panama problem but faced even greater political difficulties dealing with Noriega. During the 1988 campaign Bush had broken from Reagan and staked out his own position on Panama, announcing that he would not deal with an indicted drug dealer. Although this move seemed to make good political sense given the country's mood and its desire to prosecute the "war on drugs," it in fact left Bush with yet fewer options for dealing with Noriega. Making matters worse for Bush was the fact that he had already dealt with Noriega—twice meeting him when Bush was the director of CIA. Thus during the 1988 campaign Bush was accused, despite his new stance, of having a cozy relationship with a known drug trafficker. Further, Noriega crowed that Bush would never move against him because he knew Bush's "secrets."[4]

Panama's own elections in May 1989 kept the Noriega issue at the top of the political agenda here in the United States.[5] Bush took the elections as an opportunity to put pressure on Noriega to step down, and gave ten million dollars of covert aid to the opposition coalition for its campaign. U.S. officials and other observers doubted that Noriega would accept the results of a fair election. Bush warned that "The United States will not recognize the results of a fraudulent election engineered simply to keep Noriega in power."[6] Former Presidents Jimmy Carter and Gerald Ford led an international team to monitor the fairness of the elections, and Bush sent his own congressional team of observers.

Noriega, however, had no intention of allowing a fair election to take place. His troops stuffed ballots, played games with voter registration, and harassed voters at polling areas. Exit polls indicated that despite Noriega's efforts the opposition had taken a three-to-one lead in the voting; even PDF troops were voting for the coalition led by Guillermo Endara, Guillermo Ford, and Ricardo Calderon.[7] Not impressed by the results, Noriega nullified the elections and installed his own candidate. Opposition candidates and their supporters took to the streets, demanding that Noriega and his government concede defeat, but on May 10 Noriega's Dignity Battalions (civilian paramilitary squads set up by Noriega) made a violent show of force, attacking and wounding opposition candidates.[8] Television cameras captured the scenes of violence on film, bringing the Panama problem into vivid focus. As *Newsweek* noted of television coverage from that day:

> The images seared viewers around the world: goons in red or blue T shirts, slicing like sharks through the crowd, viciously beating their victims with guns and tire irons. The helmeted police quietly watching. The silver-haired candidate, his face and shirt bloody, stumbling away from his attacker, pleading with a soldier, being thrown into a car and driven away.[9]

Bush could not ignore the images of violence or the charges of fraud made by Carter and other election monitors; the press had proclaimed that Panama had become his first major foreign policy test. Noriega's continued flaunting of U.S. efforts to oust him were beginning to become a serious political liability for Bush.[10] Bush condemned the election fraud and the violence, and ordered 1,900 U.S. troops to Panama to join the 10,000 already there. Though Bush took the action ostensibly to protect American citizens from violence, he refused to rule out the possibility of future military action. Raising the rhetorical decibel level, Bush announced, ". . .we will not be intimidated by the bullying tactics, brutal though they may be, of the dictator Noriega."[11]

Bush also ordered U.S. citizens to move onto U.S. military bases in Panama, recalled the U.S. ambassador, and announced that economic sanctions would continue.[12] In his statement of the measures, Bush also sent a veiled message to the Panamanian Defense Forces that an overthrow of Noriega would be welcome: "The crisis in Panama is a conflict between Noriega and the people of Panama. The United States stands with the Panamanian people. We share their hope that the Panamanian Defense Forces will stand with them and fulfill their constitutional obligation to defend democracy."[13] Meanwhile, Bush also conferred with Latin American leaders on measures to pressure Noriega.[14] Bush's tough stance on the elections proved popular, both with congress and the public. A Newsweek poll found that 73% had confidence in Bush's ability to handle the crisis, and 58% approved of his decision to send additional troops to Panama.[15]

On May 17 the Organization of American States condemned the elections, though in weaker terms than the Bush Administration had hoped. The OAS, however, could get no further in negotiations with Noriega than Bush had done. Noriega remained in power and appeared to be firmly in control despite the popular uprisings in the wake of the election.[16] The stalemate over the Panama situation frustrated Bush, who despite his highly publicized efforts appeared to be headed for a major foreign policy setback.[17] Tensions between Panama and the United States continued at a less visible level throughout the summer, as Noriega's forces harassed and even at times arrested U.S. citizens and military personnel.[18] The Bush Administration kept up the pressure, expanding economic sanctions in September and tying Noriega more closely to the drug trafficking trade.[19]

After a lull, Panama burst onto the political scene again with the October 3 coup attempt led by Major Moises Giroldi.[20] Giroldi had told the CIA in Panama of the coup and had asked for U.S. military assistance. He wanted the U.S. military to block off the roads from which Noriega's forces could reinforce him at the Comandancia (PDF headquarters). Uncertain whether the coup plot was real, and fearing U.S. casualties, the Bush Administration ordered its troops to block two of the necessary roads, but failed to barricade the road from the airport. It was from that direction that Noriega's troops in fact came, crushing the coup within the day.[21]

The failed coup was widely considered and reported as a failure for Bush.[22] Worse, however, was the administration's unsuccessful attempt to distance itself from the failure by initially denying any role in the coup. Marlin Fitzwater, White House spokesman, stated that "We did not take any action that would have constituted direct involvement."[23] Secretary of State James Baker and Secretary of Defense Richard Cheney also denied U.S. involvement. They had considered helping the plotters, they claimed, but decided against it because the coup might have been a setup by Noriega to embarrass Bush and out of uncertainty about the dangers to U.S. troops.[24] Reporters soon uncovered the truth. Not only did the administration learn of the coup ahead of time, it had also given military assistance to Giroldi and his forces.[25]

Incessant criticism and lengthy media analysis of Bush's foreign policy failure followed the coup attempt. Senator Jesse Helms labeled the administration "Keystone Kops," and even Bush officials, while defending their decision, acknowledged that their crisis management system had worked poorly. Critics charged that Bush had invited the PDF to overthrow Noriega, but had not developed any plans to aid rebels in the event that they did attempt a coup. Criticism continued as Noriega executed the officers involved in the coup.[26] In the wake of the crisis, the administration fashioned new plans to unseat Noriega and Bush announced that the United States might indeed use military force in the future, but took few public actions until December, when the shooting of an American Marine officer finally precipitated the U.S. invasion.

Lt. Robert Paz was killed by PDF soldiers as he and three other Marines sped away in their car from a roadblock near PDF headquarters in Panama City. The Marines claimed that they had merely been lost when the PDF troops opened fire. Aggravating the incident, PDF soldiers seized an American naval officer and his wife who had witnessed the scene. They held the Americans for hours while soldiers repeatedly kicked the officer and threatened his wife with sexual abuse.[27]

President Bush called the December 16 killing "an enormous outrage," and the administration stated that the incident reflected "a climate of aggression that has been developing that puts American lives at risk."[28] The press speculated about whether Bush would use military force, but both the Pentagon and the White House refused to discuss what the nature of the administration's response would be. Then, in the early morning of December 20, U.S. forces moved into Panama and "Just Cause" was underway.

Over 20,000 troops were involved in the mission to neutralize key PDF strongpoints, capture and hold airports, radio and television stations, and to capture Noriega. Although by the administration's account Bush did not make the final decision to invade until December 17, the night after the U.S. Marine was shot, the military had in fact been rehearsing Just Cause for several weeks. The plans for such a contingency had been redrawn after the October 3 coup which, according to an unnamed Pentagon official quoted in the *New York Times*, had created a "philosophical turnaround" in the White House and the Pentagon and encouraged serious thinking about the possible use of force.[29]

The complicated operation went quickly with relatively few U.S. casualties (23 dead, 324 wounded).[30] Within hours U.S. forces had eliminated the PDF as an effective fighting force and had taken control of most of Panama, causing considerable damage to Panamanian property and killing several hundred Panamanian troops.[31] By 7 a.m. Bush was able to claim in his television address to the nation that "Key military objectives have been achieved. Most organized resistance has been eliminated."[32] Despite the best efforts of special operations teams, however, Noriega escaped, only to turn up at the Vatican embassy two days later claiming asylum. A tense standoff ensued until Noriega finally gave himself up to the United States a week after the invasion had begun.[33]

The press, once again, found itself left behind. This time, instead of being shut out entirely, the press pool was activated too late, missing the early and critical hours of the operation, and never managed to find any combat to cover. In addition, the military kept the hundreds of journalists who flew to Panama on a chartered jet away from the action in a hangar at Howard Air Force Base. The military did not release the "unilateral" journalists until the fighting was over. Those correspondents already in Panama might have expected to have an easier time, but in fact found themselves hiding out in the Panama City Marriott Hotel trying to avoid being kidnapped by Panamanian forces or accidentally shot by U.S. forces. In sum, the press fared little better covering the invasion of Panama than it had done in Grenada.

THE BUSH ADMINISTRATION AND PRESS POLICY IN JUST CAUSE

The invasion of Panama provides powerful support for the argument that the White House, not the military, is the primary force behind increasingly restrictive wartime press policies. Though we still lack a complete record of White House decision making, we now have direct evidence in the form of a Pentagon initiated report in the wake of Panama in which Cheney revealed that he made the critical decisions that made it impossible for the press pool to cover the invasion. In addition Cheney and his Assistant Secretary of Defense for Public Affairs, Pete Williams, kept the military's public affairs team—already stationed in Panama—out of the planning loop until just before the invasion began. The military was thus left to implement the pool system without any preparation leaving it incapable of helping the pool do its job well.

Bush and the Press

The Bush White House team, like Reagan's, understood the importance of media coverage to the president's political fortunes and believed that managing the information reaching the public about Bush's actions was essential. Once again, the White House's daily approach to the art of news management served as a blueprint for dealing with the press during Just Cause and its media strategy, a combination of press restrictions and public relations, served a critical role in helping Bush to claim a political victory after the military victory. In particular the Bush administration benefitted from the absence of television images of war and the ability to control the images and information that the public would receive with regard to the invasion.

Though on the surface Bush's everyday approach to dealing with the press appeared less aggressive and more congenial than Reagan's, reporters soon began to note that despite his more accessible demeanor the Bush administration was far less open to the press than the Reagan White House had been. And when the Bush administration looked to dominate the media agenda, its tactics borrowed heavily from Reagan. As Newsweek's Thomas DeFrank writes:

> For all its apparent spontaneity and geniality, the Bush approach is no less calculating that the Reagan script. It is the product of a detailed, eyes only Fitzwater memorandum last December heavily embellished by the president's own hands-on-view of how to deal with the press. The Bush media plan aims to establish the aura of an engaged as well as engaging chief executive—and to reassert firmer control over White House coverage.

In fact it should not be surprising that the Bush program for dealing with the press borrowed from Reagan; after all, not only was Bush a member of the Reagan team, but Marlin Fitzwater, Bush's White House spokesman, had also served in the same post under Reagan during the last year of his presidency, and James Baker, one of the key media strategists in the Reagan White House, served as Bush's campaign manager and then as Secretary of State. Nor was Secretary of Defense Richard Cheney a stranger to dealing with the press at the highest levels, having served both as a member of Congress and as President Ford's Chief of Staff.

Cheney's views represent well the post-Vietnam White House perspective of the importance of the press and how to deal with it. Reflecting on his experiences there before he became Secretary of Defense, Cheney argued in an interview that the White House, in order to be effective, had to move aggressively to control the news:

> That means about half the time the White House press corp is going to be pissed off, and that's all right. You're not there to please them. You're there to run an effective presidency. And to do that, you have to be disciplined in what you convey to the country. The most powerful tool you have is the ability to use the symbolic aspects of the presidency to promote your goals and objectives. You're never going to get anywhere if you let someone step on

> your lead, or if you step on your lead yourself. You don't let the press set the agenda. The press is going to object to that. They like to set the agenda. They like to decide what is important and what isn't important. But if you let them do that, they're going to trash your presidency.

Administration Planning for the Press

After Grenada the Defense Department and the military services worked to establish the national media pool as the standard procedure for dealing with the press during military operations. The pool was called up on several exercises and in 1988 had accompanied the Persian Gulf reflagging operation. So far the pool had yet to be tested under extreme conditions; nevertheless, both the military and the press appeared to feel reasonably comfortable with the arrangement.

Panama press policy should in theory have followed the public affairs guidelines spelled out by the Sidle Panel in 1984. If necessary in cases where there were no journalists present or in which the operation otherwise demanded it, the press pool would be called up for action. In return for following certain ground rules, pool journalists would gain access to military operations in their earliest stages, accompanying troops and witnessing combat when possible. The ground rules were standard, flowing directly from those used in Vietnam. No discussion of future military operations was allowed, no pictures of dead or wounded were to be released until next of kin were notified, and other details that might give the enemy useful information were off-limits for reporting.

According to these policies, what should have happened in Just Cause? As Fred Hoffman notes in his study of Just Cause public affairs, the pool was not originally intended to be used in cases in which a large resident press corps was present and the action was close to the United States. Thus, following the letter of the Sidle Panel's recommendations, there should not have been a pool at all. Instead, something like the situation that prevailed in Vietnam should have been created, in which journalists were accredited to cover Just Cause by SouthCom (perhaps at Howard Air Force Base as they arrived) and then were then free to find their way to the action. But nothing like this happened. Instead the pool arrived too late to view the initial assault, and failed continually through the first few days to produce anything but news of secondary value. Stated policy did not match its implementation. Why not?

With President Bush's blessing, Secretary of Defense Richard Cheney took three actions that made covering the invasion more difficult for the press, each of which violated the spirit of the Sidle panel recommendations adopted by the Pentagon after Grenada. First, he decided that the press pool should be activated. According to public affairs policy, however, the pool was only to be used when an operation took place in a remote area without a resident press corps or the infrastructure to deal with the press. Panama clearly did not fit this description. Not only was there already a large contingent of American reporters in Panama City, but Panama was home to the headquarters of Southern Command and over 10,000 U.S. troops, with the capability of dealing effectively (at least in theory) with the press. Therefore, as originally envisioned, the pool was unnecessary. To make matters worse, Cheney decided to activate the pool in Washington. Although the pool normally would be called up in Washington to travel to a remote area of conflict, public affairs officers at Southern Command felt that a Panama-based pool would have been easier to work with from a logistical and security standpoint.[34] In addition, a Panama-based pool would obviously have included those journalists most familiar with Panama and the recent history of the U.S.-Panama tensions. Deploying the pool from Washington ensured that the most knowledgeable journalists would be largely shut out of reporting the invasion.

Cheney's second critical decision was to delay notifying the press pool members until 7:30 p.m. on Tuesday, with H-Hour set at 1:00 a.m. Wednesday. This ensured that the pool could not get to Panama in time to cover the initial phase of the operation, the very time period the pool was created to allow journalists to cover. Cheney admitted later that he did this with the understanding that it would mean the pool would arrive late. Cheney argued that the timing was the result of the need to maintain the "maximum security possible to avoid compromising the operation and to preserve the element of surprise."[35] Indeed, despite the tight secrecy imposed by Bush during the planning phase, news organizations were beginning to sense that something was about to happen. But the 7:30 timing meant that a leak about the pool's destination would at least not make the national evening news programs. Cheney took these actions despite the fact that a key purpose of the pool was to enable the Pentagon to call up a small group of reporters while maintaining operational security. The procedures for doing so were well established and had been practiced a number of times since Grenada. As Fred Hoffman notes, the pool could easily have been called up Tuesday afternoon instead, flown to Panama, briefed, and positioned to witness the initial attacks.[36]

Finally, Cheney and Williams kept the SouthCom public affairs team out of the loop until hours before the invasion and even then told SouthCom public affairs chief Colonel Ron Sconyers not to discuss the invasion with anyone, making it impossible for him to do more than minimal planing. Moreover, since Cheney's decision to call up the pool conflicted with established policy, the planning Sconyers did do was for naught, as he had assumed that journalists already in Panama would be accredited to cover the conflict. Learning of the press pool's imminent arrival only at 5 p.m. on Tuesday, Sconyers and his team had little time to prepare, a fact which would severely impair their ability to help the press do its job.

Turning Military Victory into Political Victory: Administration Public Relations During Just Cause

Just as in Grenada, the White House media strategy of controlling the press and shaping the news flow was as essential a part of the political victory to the Bush administration as the military victory. Like Reagan's team, the Bush administration knew the importance of controlling the message and of ensuring that television coverage in particular reveal only those images that would reflect positively on the president's policies. Though Bush was generally less successful than Reagan in creating positive coverage of his domestic agenda, Bush enjoyed stunning success in dominating the agenda during periods of international crisis.[37]

The administration's efforts to justify the invasion to the public began early. At 1:40 a.m. Marlin Fitzwater entered the White House news room to announce that, "The President has directed United States forces to execute at 1 a.m. this morning pre-planned missions in Panama to protect American lives, restore the democratic process, preserve the integrity of the Panama Canal treaties and apprehend Manuel Noriega." Fitzwater added that Bush was monitoring the situation from the White House.[38]

At 7 a.m. President Bush went on television to outline his rationale for the invasion and convince the public that it had been justified. Like Reagan had done in Grenada, Bush emphasized the "Americans in danger theme." Bush argued that "General Noriega's reckless threats and attacks upon Americans in Panama created an immanent danger to the 35,000 American citizens in Panama. As president, I have no higher obligation than to safeguard the lives of American citizens." And, "I took this action only after reaching the conclusion that every other avenue was closed and the lives of American citizens were in grave danger."[39]

With the press pool tied down the Bush Administration had almost all day Wednesday to set the tone of press coverage for the invasion. Senior officials repeated and buttressed his justification in their television press conferences throughout the day from their various vantage points. As *New York Times* television critic Walter Goodman wrote of their performance, "Nobody could miss the ordered official line: a carefully planned, perfectly executed, entirely successful action provoked by General Noriega."[40] They focused on the shooting of the U.S. Marine and tried to paint a picture of increasing harassment of Americans in Panama, directed by Noriega. At the State Department, James Baker tried to impress upon reporters the idea that the invasion marked simply the final step in a consistent foreign policy toward Panama.[41] At the Pentagon Cheney repeated Bush's rationale almost verbatim in his briefing to the press. Aiding in the effort to convince the public that an invasion made sense now when before it had not, Cheney argued that "Noriega had created an environment in which his troops felt free to terrorize and brutalize Americans who had every right to be in Panama. . ."[42]

Reporters and others questioned the administration's rationales and the legality of the U.S. action.[43] Baker defended the invasion's legal basis on the first day of the operation, citing the United States' right to self-defense under the OAS and UN charters. Although many scholars believed that the administration's legal arguments were extremely shaky, if not specious, neither Congress nor the public seemed inclined to split legal hairs on the issue.[44] And the media, having done their duty by raising the issue, did not pursue the matter in the absence of controversy, and in fact helped bolster Bush's position. The *New York Times* and most other major newspapers in the country ran editorials supporting the invasion and Bush's self-defense rationale.[45]

International condemnation of the invasion came swiftly and from expected places. The Soviet Union denounced the invasion as illegal and Latin American nations criticized it as another incidence of imperialist U.S. intervention in the region.[46] The OAS passed a resolution stating that the organization "deeply regretted" the U.S .action and called for an end to the fighting. European reaction was for the most part muted, but Prime Minister Margaret Thatcher announced her support for the move. And at the United Nations the United States failed to find much support; the Security Council only failed to vote to condemn the invasion as a result of a U.S. veto.[47]

For the most part the Bush Administration seemed to ignore international reactions, but the most memorable response to foreign pronouncements came from Bush himself. When asked what he thought of the Soviet Union's claim that the invasion violated international law, Bush said that he needed to let Gorbachev know that "if they kill an American Marine, that's real bad. And if they threaten and brutalize the wife of an American citizen, sexually threatening the lieutenant's wife while kicking him in the groin over and over again, then, Mr. Gorbachev, please understand, this President is going to do something about it."[48] Often repeated after it was first made, this comment helped Bush to dispel his wimp image and challenged would-be critics to take issue with his decision.

On the second day of the operation the administration began claiming success. Following the time-tested rule that a savvy president should claim credit by personally announcing his administration's successes, Bush announced on television that:

> This operation is not over, but it's pretty well wrapped up. And we've moved aggressively to neutralize the PDF, to provide a stable environment for the freely elected Endara Government. . . . It helps to insure the integrity of the Panama Canal and to create an environment that is safe for American citizens . . . General Noriega is no longer in power. He no longer commands the instruments of government or the forces of repression that he's used for so long to brutalize the Panamanian people.[49]

But without Noriega in hand, the administration could not fully convince congressional leaders that the invasion was successful. Although very few members of Congress debated whether or not the invasion was justified, almost all of them reserved final judgment of the action until Noriega was captured and it became clear that U.S. forces would not become bogged down in police duty or guerrilla warfare with Noriega loyalists.[50]

Thus the administration, although claiming that it had restored democracy to Panama, had to wait until Noriega appeared at the Vatican embassy to be assured of a political victory. And once Noriega had surrendered to U.S. forces, Bush appeared on television once more to claim victory:

> On Wednesday, December 20, I ordered US troops to Panama with four objectives: to safeguard the lives of American citizens; to help restore democracy; to protect the integrity of the Panama Canal treaty; and to bring General Manuel Noriega to justice. All of these objectives have now been achieved.[51]

The only mild threat to the carefully planned imagery of Just Cause had come on the second day of Just Cause as Bush met the press to discuss the operation. At the same time Bush was joking with reporters in Washington, the networks were also covering the arrival of coffins at Dover Air Force Base bearing the dead from Panama. Three networks used a split screen to show both the president laughing and the military honor guard unloading coffins from a plane. As Michael Oreskes of the *New York Times* noted "It was a powerful juxtaposition, and one that clashed with the Administration's effort to put the best face on a conflict that has so far been witnessed by a relatively small number of reporters."[52] Administration officials, unaware that both events would be covered live, were understandably furious. As media managers know, television pictures of a president laughing next to a solemn row of coffins cannot easily be displaced by words, no matter how sincere.[53]

Between the launching of the invasion and Noriega's surrender to U.S. forces two weeks later the administration offered few real details of the operation and avoided discussion of those facts which might have sullied the operation's cleancut and efficient image. While offering bland details from the Pentagon on the general progress of the operation, the administration did not broach the subject of Panamanian casualties, especially civilian casualties, of which there were a surprisingly high number, nor the subject of the displacement of thousands from their homes due to fires set at least in part by U.S. firepower and the destruction of vast amounts of property in the poorer areas of Panama located near the PDF headquarters. But with journalists unable to reach these areas to report, the administration did not need to comment. Journalists did not even know what questions to ask. And later, when news of these things finally did reach the United States, the invasion had already become a political success for Bush. Stories of Panama's problems were not really news.

With few independent sources of information, journalists had to rely almost entirely on the administration for news about the invasion and how well it was going. Due to the lack of television or other news of the invasion that might have diverted attention from official pronouncements or perhaps contradicted official assessments of the operation, the administration's justifications and claims of victory went without being seriously challenged. As Walter Goodman noted of the day on which Noriega sought asylum at the Vatican embassy:

> In the United States, a pride of the highest American officials went on television Wednesday to declare victory in what some phrasemaker had dubbed Operation Just Cause. Among those dozen points of light were the President, the Secretary of Defense, the Secretary of State, the chairman of the Joint Chiefs of Staff and other high-ranking officers. Lieut. Gen. Thomas W. Kelly of the Joint Chiefs gave the operation a 10 on the 1-to-10 scale. The slight static at news conferences by correspondents who had little information other than what they had been granted by the military could not compete with so formidable a chorus. . . . Whatever the problems in the field, the Administration seems to have won easily at home. The polls showed overwhelming support for the invasion even before the nation had had a chance to absorb it.[54]

Bush's actions and the invasion drew overwhelming popular and congressional support. Both aisles of Congress accepted the president's justifications for the invasion and supported his actions. *Congressional Quarterly Weekly Report* noted that "Whatever its eventual impact in Panama, one immediate result of the attack was to shore up Bush against widespread criticism, especially from Democrats, that he has been too cautious, even timid, to act decisively on the world stage."[55] Bush's public approval in the wake of the invasion gave him a political victory of great magnitude. Bush had succeeded in justifying the invasion to a large majority of the public, convincing them that the victory was substantial and the costs bearable.[56] With Noriega behind bars, Bush had finally come out on top and erased the "wimp" image that had long plagued him. As New York Times reporter R. W. Apple opined, "Whatever the other results of this roll of the dice in Panama, it has shown him as a man capable of bold action. . ."[57]

MILITARY PUBLIC AFFAIRS IN JUST CAUSE

As noted above, most of the pool's early failures are the direct result of civilian decisions. Had Cheney called up the pool earlier, it would have been in Panama and had the chance (at least in theory) to report on the important first skirmishes. The blame for the pool's continued poor functioning, however, must be laid at the military's doorstep for two reasons. First, the military again displayed the lack of high-level attention to wartime public affairs planning that was evident in Grenada. As a result, the military was incapable of dealing effectively with the media that showed up to report Just Cause. And second, above and beyond simple incompetence, the military did not seem inclined to let the pool to carry out its mission. The military's interests in garnering favorable coverage and avoiding the negative fallout that could result from battlefield stories led SouthCom public affairs escorts to severely limit journalists' access to the actual fighting.

Poor Planning Again Plagues Military Public Affairs

In many ways Panama public affairs were an echo of Urgent Fury. As Hoffman noted in his report,

> Some of the key problems that eventually burdened the pool had their genesis in overstress on secrecy and subsequent fumbles at the Pentagon and the Southern Command in November. As a consequence, about a month of possible planning time was lost and, when Operation Just Cause was mounted, *there was no public affairs plan.* (my emphasis)[58]

On November 13, 1989, SouthCom was informed by the Pentagon that an invasion of Panama was possible in the near future and that SouthCom should send a plan for public affairs to Washington. SouthCom faxed a minimally detailed outline of a plan to the Pentagon on November 22. Soon after it reached the Pentagon and began to circulate for comment, however, it was decided that for security reasons the plan should not be widely discussed. Lieutenant Commander Gregory Hartung, an officer in the Pentagon's public affairs Plans office, was told to "stick it in the safe and forget about it." Deputy Assistant Secretary of Defense Richard C. Brown of the Inter American Affairs office evidently gave the order for this action after discussing the plan at an interagency meeting. Brown noted in an interview that the plans could have compromised the mission given all that they revealed about the operations involved. Brown's office argued that they only meant for Public Affairs to be careful in planning, not that planning should stop. That, however, is what happened. While the public affairs plan languished in a vault, neither public affairs officers at the Pentagon nor at SouthCom questioned why public affairs planning was not moving ahead.[59] The failure to plan ahead taken with Williams' last minute notification of Sconyers that an invasion was imminent and that the pool would be called up from Washington ensured that matters would go from bad to worse once the pool got to Panama.[60]

SouthCom public affairs' difficulties with the pool reinforce the argument that public affairs remained a neglected mission area within the military. Though one might believe that not having public affairs plans in Grenada may have been an isolated incident of poor planning, the absence of such plans again in Panama reflects a deeper problem with public affairs. Hoffman's report of Just Cause public affairs makes clear that the military's wartime public affairs capabilities were inadequate. It is unlikely that any other specialty within the armed services suffers from such acute shortages of the equipment, personnel, and transportation to carry out its tasks. In addition, few units within the military would be tolerated if they performed as poorly as did the public affairs offices at SouthCom and the Pentagon during Just Cause.[61] As NBC Pentagon correspondent Fred Francis, a pool member, argued of the military's poor outing, "I don't believe it was deliberate. They just fucked up."[62]

Transportation was the biggest problem faced by SouthCom public affairs once the pool arrived. By the time Williams alerted Sconyers that the pool would be coming from Washington, it was too late for Sconyers to request a helicopter to transport the pool, and going by jeep was considered too dangerous. Thus, when the pool finally arrived four hours after the invasion had begun, expecting to head right out to cover the fighting, it was stranded at Howard Air Force Base. And after Sconyers had managed to commandeer a large enough helicopter to transport the sixteen-member pool, the helicopter was whisked away on a higher priority mission, stranding the journalists once again to watch television at Fort Clayton. *Dallas Morning News* reporter Kevin Merida noted, "We watched television, we got a cup of coffee. We actually watched a Bush news conference. We were right there with the viewer watching CNN."[63] The pool finally got moving at 10 a.m., nine hours after arriving.[64]

Inadequate and faulty communications equipment at both the Pentagon and SouthCom proved to be the next major difficulty. The fax machine at the Pentagon that was to receive pool reports malfunctioned. The problem was only discovered several hours after many reports had been sent, and everything had to be transmitted again. Due to the lack of dedicated telephone lines, still photographers suffered severe delays in transmitting their pictures, when Panamanian operators would pick up the lines, ruining the transmission and forcing pictures to be sent again. The only group to avoid these problems for the most part were the television reporters, thanks to the fact that Williams had allowed NBC's Fred Francis to bring along a one-ton satellite uplink dish to beam his reports home. These delays and miscues were inconveniences for the first day when the pool reporters were the only ones using the media center at SouthCom. On Thursday evening, however, SouthCom was overrun by hundreds of journalists who had flown in from the United States and the inconvenience turned into a nightmare.[65]

Adding injury to inconvenience, the military refused repeatedly to take the pool to cover the fighting as it occurred. SouthCom PAOs argued that the reason behind this was that they feared for journalists' safety, which could not be guaranteed in combat situations. The press corps, however, did not buy this argument. Several pool members argued that this was an attempt to make sure the press did not upset the public with battlefield coverage and to allow the military to put the most favorable spin on events. As pooler Steven Komarow argued, "Instead of being part of a military operation, we were brought in to view the spoils. The selections shown to us were designed for maximum propaganda impact."[66] Reporters in the pool were continually frustrated by their public affairs escorts, who kept taking them to places where fighting had taken place, rather than where it was ongoing. As Kevin Merida noted, "It was like forming a White House pool and then showing them an empty hall and saying, 'This is where the President spoke.'"[67] Instead of being taken to see combat, the pool was taken to Noriega's hideouts and to captured arms caches, similar to the pool's routine during Urgent Fury. Nor at first could reporters interview those who had taken part in the action. One author notes that "the pool was repeatedly rebuffed when it asked to interview senior commanders, wounded GIs, or front-line troops."[68]

As bad as the pool had it, however, the more than 250 journalists who arrived in Panama later on a chartered jet from the United States faced even tougher problems. First, of course, they had missed almost all of the important action taken by U.S. forces. And second, the military would not let any of them leave Howard Air Force Base, arguing again that it was too dangerous to let them move about the country. To top it off, the already understaffed SouthCom public affairs unit had not anticipated such a horde of journalists, and was simply unable to provide adequate information or services after their arrival.

Once again, journalists did not believe the military's argument that safety was the reason they were being held at the base. More likely, they reasoned, the military felt that as long as the press pool was covering the operation there was no reason to let other journalists move around and get in the way. Better that a few escorted reporters witness the invasion than hundreds of independent correspondents roaming the streets in search of a story. After the fighting had died down, those journalists who had stayed on at the base (many had simply gone home) were finally allowed to leave and go wherever they wanted to go. The story at that point, of course, was not combat but the continued search for Noriega and the impact of the invasion on the Panamanian public and their country. These were worthy stories, but they were not what most journalists had gone to Panama to cover.

In addition to organizational miscues and poor planning, the military's handling of the pool in Panama also likely stemmed from the desire to foster a positive image of the invasion and the military's role. As detailed in the next section, while public affairs escorts were keeping the pool from reporting anything of note, senior military officials with responsibility for keeping the public informed about the invasion were less than candid concerning several issues, and strove to paint a picture similar to the one the Bush Administration was offering. Military officials kept very quiet about casualties and how they occurred, especially among Panamanian civilians, lied about the Stealth fighter's maiden performance, and helped the Bush Administration to demonize Noriega for public consumption.[69] Such efforts were far more likely to succeed as long as the pool in Panama did not have access to any information which would contradict official claims. Without access to the invasion, the press could not challenge the military's pronouncements or even raise issues the military had neglected to mention. It was not until long after the invasion had faded from the front pages that stories appeared uncovering the government's miscues and misinformation.[70]

THE IMPACT OF GOVERNMENT MEDIA STRATEGY ON THE PRESS

Cheney's decisions and the military's subsequent handling of public affairs dictated that the press pool, rather than easing the way as promised, provided a tremendous obstacle to journalists trying to cover Just Cause. The tight control over the pool and other journalists meant that once again the press would have to rely on the administration for information on how the conflict was going, how the military had performed, and what Noriega and his forces were up to. This led again to press coverage that was devoid of combat footage, devoid of American casualties, and of anything else about battle which might have cost the administration public support. And again, the inability of journalists to corroborate administration and military pronouncements meant that the picture of the Panama invasion that the public received was far rosier than reality. As critic Eric Boehlert argued:

> Looking back, the White House must have been generally delighted with the coverage. Most of the highs were highlighted and the lows were subordinated. The first, albeit slightly restricted press pool pictures from Panama were nothing short of an Army recruiting film: helicopters silhouetting the sky; soldiers dodging through the foreign predawn streets, and the opposition's headquarters engulfed in flames. . . . Where, you may have wondered, were the hundreds of dead and thousands of injured? Where was the violence so many soldiers described?[71]

Much that otherwise undoubtedly would have been reported more thoroughly at the time took place behind the cover of government press restrictions and public relations. As with Grenada, it was not until months later that the story of what really happened in Panama was revealed in the press, after the invasion had stopped being big news and long after the revelations had lost the political impact they might have had if they had been uncovered at the time.

The government's media strategy made newsgathering a difficult prospect in Panama not only for the press pool, but for those journalists already in Panama City and for those who showed up after the invasion began. On the plus side for pool reporters, at least in theory, they were the first journalists to get to Panama and they had access to military personnel, relatively safe transportation, and communications facilities. Had Cheney not intervened, the pool might even have witnessed at least some of the opening moments of the fighting. Instead, the pool showed up late and found itself stuck with an unprepared and reluctant public affairs team with very limited independence and little ability to move about the country. The pool saw no real combat, faced military officers who were distrustful of the pool and journalists, and produced very little worthwhile copy for their efforts. Worse for the press, however, the pool not only failed to produce much in the way of noteworthy film, photos, or stories, the pool's very existence made things more difficult for other journalists who came to cover the invasion.

But where the government made things difficult for the pool, life was worse for those journalists already stationed in Panama City, most of whom were based at the Marriott Hotel. Theoretically their primary advantages were that they were close to the action and independent of military control, free to move about and report whatever the chaotic situation allowed. As CBS correspondent Juan Vasquez, one of those at the Marriott, noted, "those of us who were in Panama at the time of the invasion were able to file the only on-the-scene reports of the war not filtered through Pentagon handlers."[72] But this independence was limited. When reporters actually ventured outside to seek stories, they faced an uncooperative U.S. military—MPs detained several reporters for hours who had arrived at Howard Air Force Base seeking information.[73] U.S. roadblocks also kept reporters from pursuing stories at local hospitals and in the Chorrillo neighborhood, home of PDF headquarters and scene of the worst destruction. Moreover, their high visibility as journalists and attractiveness as potential hostages made following the story less appealing. Several journalists were kidnapped by PDF forces, although all were released unharmed in the end.[74] In addition to danger from opposing forces, journalists on their own found that the middle of the war zone is not the safest place to roam. Just Cause cost one unlucky Spanish journalist his life when U.S. soldiers mistook one of their own convoys for the enemy and hit the photographer in the ensuing crossfire. Faced with trouble on both sides of the conflict, most of the journalists at the hotel thus ended up filing reports from their rooms based on telephone calls and what they could see from the roof or from their windows.

The government saved its most restrictive welcome for the massive group of journalists who began arriving on the night of the December 21 once the military gave permission for their chartered jet to land at Howard Air Force Base. As noted, the military did not allow this group to leave the base despite the fact that the potentially worrisome story—U.S. forces in combat—was all but over. When they were finally released after all the scattered firefights had subsided, all that was left for this group was to seek the follow-up stories. Having already been beaten to the punch by both the pool and those journalists already in Panama, many journalists went straight home, frustrated by their inability to get past the military.

Television had a particularly tough time in Panama and fared little better in its efforts to cover Just Cause than it had in covering Urgent Fury. Coverage of the early hours of the invasion were especially unsatisfying for the networks, as their cameras missed almost all of the fighting. As television critic Tom Shales noted, "We seem to be at war. It's a little hard to tell. Since 1 a.m. Wednesday, when US forces invaded Panama, the networks have had precious little footage from the scene of the fighting. . . . At one point you had Jane Pauley and Deborah Norville on the screen alone discussing the situation in Panama and possible courses of action."[75] The first pool footage did not arrive until after 5 p.m. on the first day of the operation. Some footage from an independent television agency was available earlier, but as Broadcasting noted: ". . . for the most part, the pictures did not match the drama of the story. Throughout the night, viewers saw and heard the anchors reporting on developments. They were reading from wire copy or interviewing colleagues in Panama City by telephone."[76]

Both CNN and NBC did, however, manage to provide at least a small sample of action coverage. NBC caught on film the brief firefight between 82nd Airborne troops and PDF forces as the Americans came to rescue the journalists trapped at the Marriott Hotel. And CNN, by means of a hidden camera, revealed the chaos and looting on the streets of Panama City. In addition, CNN unleashed an innovative newsgathering technique during the invasion. CNN provided viewers in Panama with a toll-free phone number to call in and report what was going on in their neighborhoods. Many did, providing CNN with vivid details of the invasion, albeit of unverifiable accuracy.[77]

The result of the media's inability to cover the invasion firsthand and independently was, as in Grenada, press coverage that failed to give a clear picture of events as they happened, especially those issues that might have caused political problems for the president or the military. Issues the government preferred not to discuss—civilian casualties, military miscues, and destruction to civilian property, were difficult for the press to report on in any depth until the restrictions had been lifted, the dust had settled, and journalists were finally free to inspect the countryside at length and to find both Panamanian and American sources willing to discuss how the invasion had unraveled. Americans reading their newspapers and watching television news learned nothing accurate about these issues until weeks or in most cases months after the invasion.

The touchiest issue about which the American public learned least during the invasion was that of Panamanian civilian casualties. As in Grenada, the military was extremely reluctant to discuss the numbers of Panamanian civilians who had been killed as a result of the invasion, despite reports that suggested that as many as several thousand civilians may have been killed. It was not until three weeks after the invasion that the military announced a tentative total of roughly 200 civilians killed, without making clear where that figure had come from, even though many observers were highly skeptical about numbers so low given the ferocity of the invasion. As one journalist noted, ". . . even though the tally of military dead has been carefully maintained by the Southern Command, no firm new figure has emerged [of civilian casualties], nor has any American or Panamanian Government agency publicly assumed responsibility as the authority for information on Panamanian civilian deaths."[78] The government still had not offered a full accounting of civilian casualties ten months after the invasion despite the fact that by that point most reliable estimates had begun to center around the 300-700 range civilians dead.[79]

Government restrictions and overly rosy pronouncements also ensured that the press could not give an accurate account of the military's performance in Just Cause. The military and Bush administration gave little detail of the operation. What they did offer was often inaccurate or misleading. The best example of this was the Pentagon's claims for the performance of the F-117 stealth fighter, which flew its maiden combat missions in Just Cause. The fighter, hailed as a rousing success during the operation, was only later discovered to have been somewhat less than promised, and by then was only a footnote to the invasion for the inside pages of prestige newspapers.

Unveiled to the public for the first time after its secret development on the same day it was used to bomb targets in Panama, Secretary of Defense Cheney announced that the F-117 mission had been successful and that the two planes had dropped their bombs with "pinpoint accuracy." It was not until months after the invasion, in April of 1990, that the Pentagon finally admitted that the F-117 missions had not gone as planned and that pilot error had caused the bombs to miss their intended targets. The Pentagon's admission, it should be noted, came only after *New York Times* reporter Michael Gordon went to the intended target area and photographed the site, proving that the bomb craters were nowhere near where the military said they were supposed to be. In the wake of the embarrassment, Cheney initiated an inquiry to find out why he had not been given accurate information about the Stealth's performance. The inquiry found that the Air Force general in charge knew that the F-117s had missed their targets but had not passed on the information, claiming that he had not thought it merited mentioning.[80]

Such efforts to check up on military performance were impossible in most instances because most of the operation did not leave such easily verifiable footprints as bomb craters. Far more difficult to uncover, for example were reports that the military had suffered from a failure to maintain operational security. In fact, the press itself did not and could not have broken the story itself. Again, it was not until months after the invasion when admissions of mistakes carried less potential for damage that the government filled in the holes in its accounts of the battle. In December, Pentagon spokesman Pete Williams had stated that the Rangers assaulting the base at Rio Hato had not been fired upon by Panamanian troops because they had been stunned by the bombs dropped by the F-117s. Two-and-a-half months later, however, Lt. General Carl W. Stiner admitted that a security breach led directly to the death of one Ranger as he prepared to parachute from an aircraft and to increased numbers of injuries to other troops.[81]

Last, it took a *Newsweek* story based on a leak from "well-placed military sources" in June of 1990 to prompt the military to discuss the number of soldiers who had died as a result of friendly fire. The *Newsweek* story claimed that friendly fire was responsible for 9 of the 23 killed and 60% of the 347 wounded in the invasion. Soon after the *Newsweek* article appeared in print the Pentagon released its own report, claiming that only 2 of the 23 soldiers killed and only 19 of the 347 wounded were the result of U.S. military actions. Though no one can doubt the military's desire not to suffer casualties, especially at its own hands, its reluctance to discuss the issue fits the pattern of accentuating the positive and ignoring the potentially negative or distasteful. With the press unable to talk to almost anyone in command in Panama during the invasion, there was little chance that journalists would uncover any details about friendly-fire deaths or anything else.[82]

Press Reaction to Just Cause Public Affairs

Predictably, both journalists who had covered Just Cause and many who had watched it from afar fumed at the government's restrictions. Journalists heaped most of the blame on the military and its handling of the pool.[83] In addition to being guilty of incompetence, they charged, the military in Panama was extremely reluctant to aid the press and unexcited by the prospect of battlefield coverage from Panama.[84] As Kevin Merida argued, ". . . what happened in Panama seemed designed to render the American people blind and deaf to much of the U.S. troop activity. During the four days the pool was in operation, military officials either didn't understand or ignored our needs as journalists."[85]

The press experience in Just Cause destroyed any beliefs that the pool existed to get journalists to the battlefield. They now understood that the pool could and would be used against them. As Stanley Cloud, an editor at *Time* magazine, noted of the pool, "From the government's point of view, it's a way not so much of helping disseminate information but a way to control the press. This is a limited pool that makes individual initiative impossible. Pool members are completely at the mercy of the Pentagon."[86] Nor were journalists pleased that it appeared the military was using the pool as an excuse to restrict the movements of nonpool reporters.

Just Cause also prompted a good deal of handwringing among journalists about their performance. Many felt that, despite obstacles, the press failed to challenge official statements, failed to dig out the important stories in Panama, and failed to provide the public with a complete explanation of events.[87] Columnist Tom Wicker argued that "The more one looks into President Bush's invasion of Panama, the more one should—and the more one wonders why those of us in the press have been so uncritical about both the 'justification' and the consequences of this egregious misuse of US military power. The Army's own Southern Command had provided more essential information than many news organizations in this country."[88]

Despite their displeasure with how things had gone in Panama, however, journalists and their news organizations did little to improve their lot. Apart from seconding the conclusions of Fred Hoffman's scathing report of Just Cause public affairs operations, the press did nothing to challenge the Pentagon or the White House to run things differently the next time such a crisis appeared. Perhaps because the press could not claim to have been shut out as it was in Grenada, and because many felt that the press had covered the invasion so poorly, its post-invasion complaints carried less weight. In either case, Just Cause did not prompt news organizations to prepare for their next wartime engagement with the U.S. military.

PUBLIC AFFAIRS AFTER JUST CAUSE

SouthCom's disastrous dealings with the press during Just Cause prompted the Pentagon to call for an in-depth investigation of its public affairs planning and policies. To carry out the investigation the Pentagon called in Fred Hoffman, a Pentagon reporter and the most recent former Assistant Secretary of Defense for Public Affairs. After interviewing scores of officials and visiting Panama, Hoffman offered a blunt assessment of the military's public affairs performance. Castigating Cheney for delaying the pool out of an excessive concern for secrecy, he charged Williams with failing to plan and coordinate public affairs adequately for the crisis, and found that the Pentagon's standard operating procedures for dealing with the pool were out of touch with the necessities of dealing with the press during crisis.[89]

Several of the recommendations Hoffman offered to improve public affairs planning and the pool's functioning provide further evidence that the military's distaste for public affairs planning had not yet changed. Hoffman advised, for example, that the both the Chairman of the Joint Chiefs as well as the Joint Staff be involved in public affairs planning as soon as a military operation came under consideration. Neither Colin Powell nor the Joint Staff were aware of or involved with public affairs during Just Cause. Without such high level involvement, he argued, officers in the field were unlikely to take the press pool or public affairs seriously. Nor would public affairs plans be likely to be well integrated with operational planning.

Although the press hailed Hoffman's report and vented steam against Cheney and Williams, the direction of public affairs within the Pentagon did not change substantially. Williams, although noting that he was in basic agreement with several of Hoffman's recommendations, never committed himself to adopting any of them. This was in contrast to the period after Grenada when angry journalists and the Sidle Panel's report helped spur the Pentagon, with Secretary of Defense Weinberger's approval, to change its policies. Given Bush's popularity with the public in the wake of Just Cause, civilian officials had little to fear and little incentive to alter press policies.

Nonetheless, though civilian Pentagon officials did little in the wake of Just Cause, the Joint Chiefs did respond to Hoffman's report by issuing "Annex F: Planning Guidance—Public Affairs." The guidance did not depart radically from established procedures. Fred Hoffman had argued that it was the implementation of the pool that needed work, and that the concept itself was sound. The JCS intended for Annex F to reinforce in commanders' minds the points stressed by Hoffman in his report. Specifically, the Chiefs emphasized that CINCs [Commanders In Chief] should plan for public affairs concurrent to operational planning, that large numbers of media should be expected to show up for wars, and that CINCs should prepare to host the press pool if the Secretary of Defense called it into action.[90] In addition, the guidance spelled out in detail the various responsibilities of public affairs planners: conducting daily briefings, media accreditation, security review, establishing a Joint Information Bureau and public affairs field communications, setting forth media access guidelines, providing transportation and logistical support for the media, and so forth.

Like most official documents, the guidance said all the right things about how the military would treat journalists and information in future conflicts. Security review would never be used to avoid embarrassment but would only be used to protect operational security. The press pool would go with units to battle at the outset of hostilities, and public affairs would provide all the necessary transportation and communications for journalists in the theater.

Just as before Just Cause, however, policies and guidances did not determine future actions. What was written on paper did not match what happened. Between March 30 when the JCS issued their guidance and August 2 when Iraq invaded Kuwait, nothing more was done to ensure that commanders had gotten the message that public affairs planning needed to change. No guidance was offered on how one should go about making improvements. No follow up was taken to make sure that commanders understood that public affairs was being taken more seriously at the highest levels. As a result, the overall impact of the March 30 guidance was close to zero. And, as we shall see in Chapter Six, this guidance was virtually ignored as the Bush Administration and the military dealt with the media during Desert Shield and Desert Storm.

CONCLUSIONS

As in Urgent Fury, White House officials controlled the public affairs planning in Just Cause. By deciding to use a Washington-based pool and by causing the pool to miss the opening stages of the invasion, the administration ensured that the government would play the dominant role in providing information and images during Just Cause. Not only did the White House have an easier time in getting its messages and themes across to the public as a result of its decisions, its actions also allowed the military to indulge its own desires to restrict press access to the battlefield.

The White House, thanks in part to the restrictions on the press and the ease with which its officials filled the airwaves and front pages with their arguments and announcements, basked in success after the quick victory in Panama. Panama, however, like Grenada, raises questions about how much the public learns about such military actions through the media. Not only did Bush's justifications for the invasion fail to get critically examined for lack of information, but the administration and the military's statements about how the invasion progressed passed straight from journalists' notepads to the news without qualification because no journalist saw what had happened. Explanations of the performance of the troops, the Stealth fighter, and of Noriega's actions all had to be taken at face value. Even when many of these explanations turned out to include a significant amount of sugarcoating, the public's attention had long since moved to another topic. Stories detailing the problems caused by the invasion—20,000 homeless Panamanians, the burnt-out neighborhoods, and the civilian death toll—were thus buried in the inside pages. Had journalists gotten the information sooner, many of these stories would have been front page material with political implications for Bush and the military. A better strategy for avoiding such scrutiny would be hard to devise.

The lack of forewarning, poor planning as a result of its enduring institutional distaste for public affairs, and a deep-seated desire to shine for the public explain the military's handling of public affairs during Just Cause. Cheney's decision to keep SouthCom public affairs in the dark about the invasion and the press pool determined that the military's public affairs efforts would be lackluster at best. All evidence suggests that had Cheney alerted SouthCom earlier and allowed Sconyers to prepare for the press according to the military's established policies, things would have run much more smoothly. Journalists in Panama would have been accredited to cover the conflict and would likely have had far greater access to the battlefield, to information, and would have undoubtedly received superior technical support from the military.

Despite this deciding factor, however, the fact that the military also failed to draft a more detailed contingency plan for dealing with the press in a potential invasion adds weight to the argument that public affairs is a neglected mission within the military. This neglect, as I have noted, is understandable to a degree. When a crisis is fast approaching in which soldiers may be sent into harm's way, other issues press harder on a commander's mind than how things should be explained to the press. This neglect also strengthens the argument that military public affairs since Vietnam have less to do with that war than with organizational realities and the course of recent history. If the military still believed that the media may cost the United States victory and yet did not have an effective public affairs planning process more than fifteen years after Vietnam, then we must seriously question whether current policies are the result of a rationally planned institutional response to the public affairs problems of the 1960s.

The military, which had done a poor job by even its own standards in planning for public affairs, then followed the administration's lead during Just Cause by not allowing the press pool to carry out its intended mission. The pool's short history in Panama strongly suggests that the military purposely kept the press pool from witnessing battle of out self-interest, and not out of an interest for journalists' safety as often claimed. The press did not report the destruction and death that the U.S. military inflicted in Panama. Despite confidence that such actions were necessary the military believes that it will benefit by keeping the public's awareness of those things to a minimum. In addition, keeping the press pool in limbo allowed senior military officers in Washington to tell the public without challenge that the military had done a fantastic job in

Panama, omitting any errors, lapses in judgment, or setbacks that might have tarnished the military's image.

Finally, journalists learned two things about the press pool and war coverage from Just Cause. First, they learned that the press pool was in effect a trade-off not between independence and access, as they had assumed (and been told), but a trade-off between independence and personal safety. A journalist in Panama could have one, but not both (in neither case did a journalist get much access). Just Cause reemphasized that covering a military operation can be extremely dangerous for the press if it does not have the military's help. Those journalists in the pool may not have seen much, but neither did the journalists holed up in the Marriott, many of whom were kidnapped and shot at for their efforts. The uncomfortable truth about war coverage for journalists is that they are often forced to choose between dodging bullets in a strange land and settling for a less than Pulitzer-quality story written from a relatively safe place. As noted, after Just Cause the press did little to press for major changes in the pool system. Whether conscious or not, this is a bow to the fact that even though the military reneged on giving the pool the type of access it desired, journalists very often need the military's help to cover a war effectively. If the pool was sometimes going to be the only way to get to the story, news organizations were not ready to stand on pride and announce that they would rather miss the story than submit to government control.

The second thing journalists learned was that the pool's presence in a situation was likely to mean very limited access to the action not only for the pool, but for any journalists the military could physically keep under control. As discussed above, an unexpected side effect of press pool was that the military felt comfortable restraining unilateral reporters because public affairs officers thought the pool was the limit of their obligation to allow press coverage of the operation. This expansion of the pool concept worried journalists, who had slowly begun to realize that the military was not so interested in making the pool work as it was in making sure the press did not cause headaches. And worse for the press, the military had the resources and nominal authority to restrict press movements on and near the battlefield until ordered to stop by civilian authorities. As no such order was forthcoming in Panama (nor did anyone really expect a president or secretary of defense to send more journalists to the front of any battle), the press had little alternative but to put up with the military's policies. It would not be a matter of who was right in an argument over access, it would be a matter of who had the power to enforce their will. In Panama and, as we will see, most of the Gulf War, it was clearly the military who had this power.

ENDNOTES

1. There is a large amount of material analyzing Noriega's rise to power and his close contacts with the U.S. government over the years: John Dinges, *Our Man in Panama: The Shrewd Rise and Brutal Fall of Manuel Noriega* (New York: Random House, 1990); Kevin Buckley, *Panama: The Whole Story* (New York: Simon & Schuster, 1991); R. M. Koster and Guillermo Sanchez, *In the Time of Tyrants: Panama, 1968-1990* (New York: W. W. Norton & Co., 1990); John Weeks and Phil Gunson, *Panama: Made in the USA* (London: Latin America Bureau, 1991); John Weeks and Andrew Zimbalist, *Panama at the Crossroads: Economic Development and Political Change* (Berkeley: University of California Press, 1991); Frederick Kempe, *Divorcing the Dictator: America's Bungled Affair with Noriega* (New York: G. P. Putnam's Sons, 1990); Margaret Scranton, *The Noriega Years: US-Panamanian Relations, 1981-1990* (Boulder: Lynne Rienner Publishers, 1991).
2. Linda Robinson, "Dwindling Options in Panama," *Foreign Affairs*, Winter 1989/90, p. 191; Buckley, *Panama*, pp. 78-101; Dinges, *Our Man in Panama*, pp. 230-283; Kempe, *Divorcing the Dictator*, pp. 212-235.
3. Buckley, *Panama*, pp. 111-144; Kempe, *Divorcing the Dictator*, pp. 236-331.
4. Buckley, *Panama*, pp. 146-156; Kempe, *Divorcing the Dictator*, pp. 332-349.
5. Buckley, *Panama*, pp. 169-184; Dinges, *Our Man in Panama*, pp. 304-305; Kempe, *Divorcing the Dictator*, pp. 350-357.
6. Bernard Weinraub, "Bush Warns Panama on Election Fraud," *New York Times*, May 3, 1989; Robert Pear, "Bush Says Noriega Will Commit Fraud in Panama Election," *New York Times*, April 28, 1989; Lindsey Gruson, "Noriega Is Rigging Election, Independent Monitors Assert," *New York Times*, April 29, 1989
7. Lindsey Gruson, "Charges of Fraud Mar Panama Vote," *New York Times*, May 8, 1989.
8. Lindsey Gruson, "3 Top Opponents of Noriega Assaulted in Street Melee; Disputed Election Nullified," *New York Times*, May 11, 1989; Kempe, *Divorcing the Dictator*, pp. 357-362
9. "A Test of Wills," *Newsweek*, May 22, 1989, p. 34
10. Carter appeared on ABC's "Nightline" to discuss the election; see "Lindsey Gruson, "Noriega Stealing Election, Carter Says," *New York Times*, May 8, 1989. The press began to bill the crisis almost as a personal contest between Bush and Noriega; see, for example, "A Test of Wills," *Newsweek*, May 22, 1989, pp. 34-39; "Transcript of Bush's News Conference on the Panama Vote," *New York Times*, May 10, 1989; R. W. Apple, Jr., "Bush's Trap On Panama," *New York Times*, May 11, 1989.

11. Bernard Weinraub, "Denouncing Fraud, Bush Bolsters Force in Panama," *New York Times*, May 12, 1989.
12. Bernard Weinraub, "Bush Urges Effort to Press Noriega to Quit as Leader," *New York Times*, May 10, 1989; Robert Pear, "Bush Condemns Attack on Panama Opposition," *New York Times*, May 11, 1989; Bernard Weinraub, "Denouncing Fraud; Bush Bolsters Force in Panama," *New York Times*, May 12, 1989.
13. Bernard Weinraub, "Denouncing Fraud, Bush Bolsters Force in Panama," *New York Times*, May 12, 1989; Bernard E. Trainor, "Bush's Latin Gamble: Hoping Panamanian Armed Forces Will Oust Noriega," *New York Times*, May 17, 1989
14. Richard Halloran, "U. S. Steps Up Its Anti-Noriega Drive," *New York Times*, May 13, 1989; Robert Pear, "US Looks to Latins on Noriega," *New York Times*, May 16, 1989; R. W. Apple, Jr., "The Capital," *New York Times*, May 17, 1989.
15. "A Test of Wills," *Newsweek*, May 22, 1989, p. 37.
16. Robert Pear, "Hemispheric Group Asks Noriega to Yield Power," *New York Times*, May 18, 1989; Robert Pear, "Latin Envoys Report No Progress In Their Effort to Dislodge Noriega," *New York Times*, June 20, 1989; Lindsey Gruson, "Noriega Rejects Bush's Demand That He Quit, Calling It Meddling," *New York Times*, May 18, 1989; "Noriega Celebrates," *Newsweek*, May 29, 1989.
17. Bernard Weinraub, "US Sees Failure on Noriega Policy," *New York Times*, July 29, 1989.
18. Robert Pear, "Military Arrests Exacerbate US-Panamanian Relations," *New York Times*, August 10, 1989.
19. Robert Pear, "US Renews Attack on Noriega, Offering Evidence of Ties to Drugs," *New York Times*, September 1, 1989; "US Expands Its Sanctions Against Panama," *New York Times*, September 13, 1989; Kempe, *Divorcing the Dictator*, pp. 362-368.
20. Buckley, *Panama*, pp. 197-208; Dinges, *Our Man in Panama*, pp. 305-306; Kempe, *Divorcing the Dictator*, pp. 369-397.
21. Andrew Rosenthal, "Noriega Officers Try Coup and Fail; US Knew of Plot," *New York Times*, October 4, 1989. Elaine Sciolino, "Once Again, A Survivor," *New York Times*, October 4, 1989, For the best description of the Bush foreign policy team at work during the coup period, see Bob Woodward, *The Commanders* (New York: Pocket Star Books, 1992), pp. 91-103.
22. Buckley, *Panama*, pp. 209-218; Woodward, *Commanders*, pp. 99-103.
23. Stephen Engelberg, "US Had Indications Coup Would Be Attempted," *New York Times*, October 4, 1989.
24. Andrew Rosenthal, "US Considered Aid to Panama Rebels," *New York Times*, October 5, 1989.
25. Stephen Engelberg, "Bush Aides Admit A US Role in Coup, And Bad Handling," *New York Times*, October 6, 1989.
26. The following is a sampling of the voluminous criticism of Bush following the coup: George Will, "The Unserious Presidency,"

Washington Post, October 12, 1989; Bernard Weinraub, "White House to Study Handling of Panama Crisis," *New York Times*, October 6, 1989; Stephen Engelberg, "Bush Aide and Senator Clash Over Failed Coup in Panama," *New York Times*, October 9, 1989; Maureen Dowd, "Bush, Under Fire, Defends Role in Panama Crisis," *New York Times*, October 7, 1989; "Panama Crisis: Disarray Hindered White House," *New York Times*, October 8, 1989; Frederick Kempe, "How the Inexperience of American Officials Helped Doom Coup," *Wall Street Journal*, October 6, 1989; R. W. Apple, Jr., "Bush and Panama: Chance Lost, Perhaps to Hesitancy," *New York Times*, October 8, 1989; Elaine Sciolino, "Panama Jinx," *New York Times*, October 8, 1989; "On Panama: Luck and Incompetence," *New York Times*, October 8, 1989; William Safire, "The Man With No Plan," *New York Times*, October 9, 1989; Tom Wicker, "'Covert' Means Fiasco," *New York Times*, October 10, 1989; Stephen Engelberg, "Furor Over Panama: It's Helms vs. White House," *New York Times*, October 12, 1989.

27. "Excerpts From US Account of Officer's Death in Panama," *New York Times*, December 18, 1989; Thomas L. Friedman, "Panama Shooting Condemned by US," *New York Times*, December 18, 1989. A thorough and very careful account of the shooting incident, questioning official stories in places, is John Roos, "Did President Bush Jump the Gun in Ordering the Invasion of Panama?" *Armed Forces Journal International*, September, 1992, pp. 10-14.
28. Andrew Rosenthal, "President Calls Panama Slaying A Great Outrage," *New York Times*, December 19, 1989.
29. Michael Gordon and Andrew Rosenthal, "U. S. Invasion: Many Weeks of Rehearsals," *New York Times*, December 24, 1989; on the planning see Woodward, *Commanders*, pp. 103-119.
30. Those interested in the military operation should see Flanagan, *The Battle for Panama: Inside Operation Just Cause* (Washington: Brassey's, 1993).
31. The question of how many Panamanians, military and civilian, were killed during Just Cause became a matter of heated debate. This issue is discussed below.
32. President Bush's address to the nation, December 20, 1989.
33. Kempe, *Divorcing the Dictator*, pp. 398-417.
34. Col. Ron Sconyers, Chief of Public Affairs, Southern Command, notes this in his after action report. Cited in the Hoffman Report, p. 7.
35. Hoffman Report, p. 7.
36. Ibid., p. 9.
37. This observation is made in Robert Lichter and Richard E. Noyes, "In the Media Spotlight: Bush at Midpoint," *The American Enterprise*, January/February 1991, pp. 49-53.
38. Woodward, *Commanders*, p. 161; Michael Gordon, "US. Troops Move In Panama in Effort to Seize Noriega; Gunfire is Heard in Capital," *New York Times*, December 20, 1989.

39. President Bush's address to the nation, December 20, 1989 (CQWR, 12-23, p. 3534).
40. Walter Goodman, "From the Early Show to the Late Show, It's All Panama," December 21, 1989.
41. "Excerpts From Statement by Baker on U.S. Policy," *New York Times*, December 21, 1989.
42. "Excerpts From Briefings on U.S. Military Action in Panama," "Cheney's Reasons for Why the U.S. Struck Now," *New York Times*.
43. "Excerpt from Baker," *New York Times*. See also Susan Rasky, "Administration Says International Agreements Support Its Action," *New York Times*, December 21, 1989.
44. Saul Landau, "Imperialism, Bush-Style," *New York Times*, December 22, 1989; Charles Maechling, Jr., "Washington's Illegal Invasion," *Foreign Policy*, Summer 1990, pp. 113-131.
45. Gilbert Cranberg, "A Flimsy Story And A Compliant Press," *Washington Journalism Review*, March 1990; An example is, "Why the Invasion Was Justified," *New York Times*, December 21, 1989.
46. Francis X. Clines, "Soviet Union Condemns Strike but Says East-West Issues Aren't Involved," *New York Times*, December 21, 1989; James Brooke, "U. S. Denounced by Nations Touchy About Intervention," *New York Times*, December 21, 1989; *New York Times*, "American Nations Assail US Action," December 23, 1989.
47. Paul Lewis, "U. S. Finding Scant Support for Action in Panama," *New York Times*, December 22, 1989; Paul Lewis, "Security Council Condemnation of Invasion Vetoed," *New York Times*, December 24, 1989.
48. "Excerpts From Bush's News Conference on Central America," *New York Times*, December 22, 1989
49. Ibid.
50. R. W. Apple, Jr., "Big Obstacles to Victory," *New York Times*, December 22, 1989; Thomas L. Friedman, "Congress Generally Supports Attack, but Many Fear Consequences," *New York Times*, December 21, 1989.
51. "Text of Bush Announcement On the General's Surrender," *New York Times*, January 4, 1990.
52. Michael Oreskes, "Selling of a Military Strike: Coffins Arriving as Bush Speaks," *New York Times*, December 22, 1989,
53. Jeremy Gerard, "President Complains About TV's Use of Split Images," *New York Times*, January 6, 1990.
54. Walter Goodman, "The Television Has Become a Weapon in Panama and Rumania," *New York Times*, December 26, 1989.
55. Pat Towell and John Felton, "Invasion, Noriega Ouster Win Support on Capitol Hill," *CQWR*, December 23, 1989, p. 3533. Bush had been criticized both for the failed coup in Panama and for not moving quickly to do more about the collapse of communism in Eastern Europe.

56. Michael Oreskes, "President Wins Bipartisan Praise For Solution of Crisis Over Noriega," *New York Times*, January 5, 1990.
57. R. W. Apple, "War: A Presidential Rite of Passage," *New York Times*, December 21, 1989.
58. Hoffman Report, p. 4. For the military's report, which mirrors Hoffman in all important respects, see United States Southern Command Public Affairs After Action Report, "Operation Just Cause."
59. Hoffman Report, p. 5.
60. Ibid., pp. 5-6
61. This is meant in no way to disparage those individual public affairs officers at SouthCom or the Pentagon. On the contrary, the problems with public affairs stem from organizational, not individual, failings.
62. Chris Hanson, "Wading Around in the Panama Pool," *Columbia Journalism Review*, March/April 1990, p. 19.
63. Sharkey, *Under Fire*, p. 94.
64. Hoffman Report, pp. 11-12.
65. US Southern Command Public Affairs After Action Report, pp. 14-21.
66. Steven Komarow, "Pooling Around in Panama," *Washington Journalism Review*, March 1990, p. 49.
67. Stanley Cloud, "How Reporters Missed the War," *Time*, January 8, 1990, p. 61
68. Christopher Hanson, "Wading Around in the Panama Pool," p. 19.
69. Jaqueline Sharkey, *Under Fire*, pp. 95-102; Hanson, "Wading Around in the Panama Pool," pp. 19-20; Komarow, "Pooling Around in Panama," p. 49 It is educational to read newspaper coverage of official statements about these issues and compare it with what actually happened as revealed gradually long after the fact.
70. See, for example, "Inside the Invasion," *Newsweek*, June 25, 1990; David E. Pitt, "The Invasion's Civilian Toll: Still No Official Count," *New York Times*, January 10, 1990; Stephen Engelberg, "Congressman Criticizes Use of Stealth Plane in Panama," Michael Gordon, "Panama Alerted to Attack, General Says," *New York Times*, February 27, 1990; Larry Rohter, "Panama and US Strive To Settle on Death Toll," *New York Times*, April 1, 1990; Michael Gordon, "Stealth's Panama Mission Reported Marred by Error," *New York Times*, April 4, 1990; Michael Gordon, "Inquiry Into Stealth's Performance In Panama Is Ordered by Cheney," *New York Times*, April 11, 1990; Eric Schmitt, "Army Says US Fire Killed 2 GI's in Panama Invasion," *New York Times*, June 19, 1990; Michael Gordon, "Report Says General Knew Of Stealth Fighter's Failure," *New York Times*, July 2, 1990; Mark Uhlig, "In Panama, Counting The Invasion Dead Is a Matter of Dispute," *New York Times*, October 28, 1990; Charles Rangel, "The Pentagon Pictures," *New York Times*, December 20, 1990. An exception to the delayed exami-

nation of U.S. performance was Bernard Trainor, "Flaws in Panama Attack," *New York Times*, December 31, 1989.

71. Boehlert, "The Pool in Panama," *Columbia Journalism Review*, May/June 1990, p. 43.
72. Juan Vasquez, "Panama: Live From the Marriott!" *Washington Journalism Review*, March, 1990, p. 47.
73. Ibid., p. 46.
74. Lindsey Gruson, "Threats and Dark Streets For Reporters in Captivity," *New York Times*, December 21, 1989; Thomas Friedman, "At Least One American Is Being Held," *New York Times*, December 22, 1989; Donatella Lorch, "TV Producer, Freed, Says Panama Captors Did Not Harm Him Physically," *New York Times*, December 25, 1989; Jonathan Meyersohn, "A Pawn of War," *The New York Times Magazine*, January 21, 1990.
75. Tom Shales, "From Panama: Phone-in War," *Washington Post*, December 22, 1989.
75. "Media Go to War: Piecing Together the Panama Story," *Broadcasting*, December 25, 1989.
77. "Media Go to War," p. 26; Tom Shales, "Phone-in War."
78. "The Invasion's Civilian Toll: Still No Official Count," *New York Times*, January 10, 1990.
79. See "Panama and US Strive To Settle on Death Toll," *New York Times*, April 1, 1990; "In Panama, Counting the Invasion Dead Is a Matter of Dispute," *New York Times*, October 28, 1990.
80. "Stealth's Panama Mission Reported Marred by Error," *New York Times*, April 4, 1990; "Inquiry Into Stealth's Performance Is Ordered by Cheney," *New York Times*, April 11, 1990; "Report Says General Knew of Stealth Fighter's Failure," *New York Times*, July 2, 1990.
81. "Panama Alerted to Attack, General Says," *New York Times*, February 27, 1990.
82. "Army Says US Fire Killed 2 GI's in Panama Invasion," *New York Times*, June 19, 1990; "Inside the Invasion," *Newsweek*, June 25, 1990.
83. Michael Specter, "Second-Hand News Coverage Blamed on Military," *Washington Post*, December 22, 1989; Jon Sawyer, "Press Frustrated in Panama," *St. Louis Post-Dispatch*, January 25, 1990; James Warren, "In 1st Battlefield Test, Media Pool Misses Mark," *Chicago Tribune*, January 7, 1990; Stanley Cloud, "How Reporters Missed the War," *Time*, January 8, 1990.
84. Fred Francis, NBC Pentagon correspondent and member of the pool, championed the incompetence argument along with Fred Hoffman. Also see William Boot, "Wading Around in the Panama Pool."
85. Kevin Merida, "The Panama Press Pool Fiasco; The Military Let Journalists Do Everything Except Cover the News," *Washington Post*, January 7, 1990.
86. Quoted in Michael Specter, "Panama: Firsthand Coverage and Secondhand Diplomacy; News Organizations Struggle With 'Pool' Format," *Washington Post*, December 21, 1989.

87. Richard Harwood, "A Pool in Panama," *Washington Post*, January 14, 1990; Colman McCarthy, "Lock Stepping Media & Military," *Washington Post*, December 31, 1989; Gilbert Cranberg, "A Flimsy Story and a Compliant Press," *Washington Journalism Review*, March 1990
88. Tom Wicker, "Panama and the Press," *New York Times*, April 19, 1990.
89. Hoffman Report, pp. 1-3.
90. Joint Operational Planning manual, Volume II, pp. II-339 to II-373, JCS Pub 5-02.2, March 30, 1990. Reprinted in US Congress, Senate, Hearings, *Pentagon Rules on Media Access to The Persian Gulf War*, 102nd Congress, 1st Session, February 20, 1991.

6

Persian Gulf Press Policy

The Gulf War was both the most widely covered war in history and the one in which the U.S. government imposed the greatest restrictions on the press short of outright censorship. In the wake of the war the conventional wisdom for these restrictions also hit its zenith among journalists and other observers. The opinion that the military was still getting revenge for Vietnam was all but unanimous. *New York Times* columnist Anthony Lewis restated this view in a column soon after the war, "The military, breaking with with long American tradition, barred correspondents from the front, except for small, controlled pools." Military correspondent Christopher Hanson's emphasis on the Vietnam revenge aspect was also typical, "The American gods of war were still bitter that journalists had had the temerity to report sensitive information about U.S. operation in Vietnam (no victory in sight, the My Lai massacre, soldiers' drug addiction, etc.)." Conservative military/media analyst Peter Braestrup's comments lent further weight to the conventional wisdom as he observed that "The military are learning, too, with some of the stupid censorship things they're doing. A lot of the military are living a myth—that TV news had a decisive effect on public support for the war in Vietnam."[1]

Once again, however, the conventional wisdom is wrong. The White House, not the military, laid the groundwork for the Gulf press system. Moreover, this seeming paradox of massive media coverage and extreme restrictions on journalists was neither a mystery nor a coincidence. The restrictions came precisely because the press would come in unprecedented numbers and wield greater potential than ever to make or break the crisis for the White House and military. In the media-saturated environment of a global military crisis that would put a permanent stamp on George Bush's presidency the White House faced pressing incentives to control the press and manage news coverage. Over a thousand journalists descended on Saudi Arabia determined to cover every aspect of the war in the desert, while hundreds more lay in wait in capitals around the world to report presidential missteps, miscues, and mistakes. Not only did the press come out in record numbers, it also brought with it a greater technological capability to report breaking events live from the battlefield, from behind enemy lines, and from the home front to viewers and listeners around the world. This increased the likelihood that journalists might broadcast the sorts of scenes that many believed would turn the public against war. Moreover, the White House did not expect the press to treat its policies kindly; officials knew that the press would focus on controversy and failures rather than successes. The press' anger over its experience in Panama had put a point on reporters' determination to get to the battlefield this time.

The White House thus had good reason to believe that without some control over press coverage of the crisis, its tasks of leading the international coalition facing Iraq and building public support for war would be far more difficult, if not impossible, to carry out. The transformation of American politics into a media dominated realm was by now obvious; no president could go to war without a strategy for managing the news to his advantage and keeping the press from unraveling his policies and successes. The comparison between Lyndon Johnson's and George Bush's approach to the press illustrates just how much the government/press relationship had changed since Vietnam. Whereas Lyndon Johnson helped choose targets for bombing and left the details of Vietnam press matters largely to the military, George Bush let the military decide where the bombs would fall and instead helped choose which military officers would give the daily televised briefings to the press. As this chapter will illustrate, by crafting a restrictive policy for the press on the battlefield and through sophisticated use of public relations, Bush and his officials managed with great success to ensure favorable press coverage of the administration's actions during Desert Shield and Desert Storm.

The military faced this unprecedented media onslaught at ground level where once again poor planning and the logistical nightmares of dealing with so many journalists surpassed its limited public affairs capabilities. The media's technology raised parochial fears of what the public might think about its troops if television showed too much combat, and the institutional cultures of the press and the military clashed to produce tension and mutual recrimination. The military was horrified to watch over 2,000 correspondents and media personnel show up in Saudi Arabia to cover the war with their cellular phones, laptop computers, and television cameras. The military, with its traditional lack of attention to public affairs, found itself incapable of dealing efficiently with so many reporters. If so many journalists were allowed to roam free and unattended the threat to operational security, in military eyes, would skyrocket. More importantly, commanders were not thrilled about the prospect of journalists prowling around their units looking for stories that might make the military look bad in the public eye. Thus, though not responsible for their initiation, the military happily implemented the White House's plans for restricting the press, and at times added its own unofficial twists to make life more difficult for journalists in the Gulf.

The press found covering Desert Storm an uphill battle. With the administration and military keeping tight control over information about the crisis and imposing multiple restrictions on access to the battlefield and the troops, journalists found it difficult to offer alternative perspectives on events; the official line dominated. Reporters bemoaned the heavy focus on official statements but proved unable to overcome the restrictions. The Gulf War revealed in stark terms that the nature of the press industry makes it almost impossible for the press to confront the government with a unified message. As a consequence of this failing, the government was able to maintain the restrictions it had imposed on journalists despite the fact that the press was extremely unhappy with them, and despite the fact that the press enjoys a critical role in politics. The resulting coverage was, from the administration's view, quite favorable and certainly less threatening to public support for the conflict than would likely have been the case otherwise. The power of the press, though greater than ever, is in fact not one that can be easily harnessed at will by journalists.

Background[2]

On August 2, 1990, Iraqi tanks rolled into Kuwait City. The bickering between Iraq and other Arab nations over oil production and with Kuwait over possession of the Rumalia oil field had ended in a rapid nighttime invasion. Iraq occupied Kuwait, installed a new government, and declared that Kuwait had been annexed as Iraq's nineteenth province. Within days, Iraq had massed thousands of troops near the border of Saudi Arabia, less than 300 miles from its capital, Riyadh. Iraq's power grab stunned and surprised the world, sending the Middle

East into panic and financial markets reeling as the price of oil jumped. World leaders quickly denounced the action, and the United Nations Security Council passed a resolution condemning the action and calling for the immediate and unconditional withdrawal of Iraqi forces from Kuwait.[3]

The next morning President George Bush and his senior officials met to discuss the invasion and assess its implications. The U.S. economy, already tilting toward recession, did not look like it could easily tolerate an oil shock, nor did the economies of the other industrialized nations. Worse, little stood in Iraq's way of threatening Saudi Arabia's vast oil fields to the south. No one knew what Saddam Hussein's intentions might be. There was also the matter of U.S. and other Western citizens now effectively trapped in Kuwait, unable to leave after Iraq sealed the borders. Bush had General Norman Schwarzkopf, Commander in Chief of U.S. Central Command, the command in charge of Middle East preparations, outline possible military options at a meeting of top advisers. Though the meeting ended without a firm decision about how the United States should deal with the situation, accounts indicate that Bush was already leaning toward a military response of some sort, at least to safeguard Saudi Arabia from attack.[4]

Bush's first steps were to label the invasion "naked aggression," to declare a U.S. trade embargo against Iraq, and to freeze $30 billion in Kuwaiti and Iraqi assets in U.S. banks. The administration then called on the UN to impose a worldwide economic embargo upon Iraq, which it did only days later.[5] Over the week following the invasion Bush lobbied world leaders for their support in isolating Iraq and to convince them that urgent action was necessary to keep Iraq in check.[6]

Bush quickly decided that the United States should dispatch forces to Saudi Arabia to deter Saddam Hussein from further adventurism. The administration publicly emphasized its concern about Hussein's intentions. Although Bush had initially announced that he had not foreseen sending troops to the Middle East, he executed an about-face and announced that he would support Saudi Arabia in "any way we possibly can" if requested.[7] And only days later on August 5, Bush went further, effectively declaring that U.S. policy would center on an Iraqi withdrawal from Kuwait: "I view very seriously our determination to reverse this aggression. . . . This will not stand. This will not stand, this aggression against Kuwait."[8] In response to Bush's claims Iraq stiffened its own resolve, and its government in Kuwait warned that Westerners in Kuwait would be held as "guests" if the international community acted against Iraq.[9]

As Bush staked out his position publicly, the administration worked behind the scenes with Saudi Arabia's King Fahd to convince him of the threat to his kingdom posed by Iraq and to persuade him to invite U.S. forces as a defensive buffer against Hussein's tanks. After meeting with Secretary of Defense Richard Cheney, Fahd agreed to accept a defensive force. U.S. military preparations, already underway in expectation of Fahd's approval, accelerated.[10]

On August 7 the Bush Administration announced that it had sent the first installment of troops and equipment to Saudi Arabia.[11] Then, in a televised address to the nation the next morning, Bush laid out the rationale behind his actions and their goals:

> Four simple principles guide our policy. First, we seek the immediate unconditional withdrawal of all Iraqi forces from Kuwait. Second, Kuwait's legitimate Government must be restored to replace the puppet regime. And third, my Administration, as has been the case with every President from President Roosevelt to President Reagan, is committed to the security and stability of the Persian Gulf. And fourth, I am determined to protect the lives of American citizens abroad.

Bush emphasized that the mission of U.S. forces in Saudi Arabia was defensive:

> America does not seek conflict. Nor do we seek to chart the destiny of other nations. But America will stand by her friends. The mission of our troops is wholly defensive. . . . They will not initiate hostilities but they will defend themselves, the Kingdom of Saudi Arabia and other friends in the Persian Gulf.[12]

Bush's decision to deploy troops to Saudi Arabia won broad support from Congress, the international community, and the public. A *New York Times*/CBS poll found that 61% supported the move, and Gallup polls indicated that roughly 80% approved of Bush's handling of the crisis.[13] Bush's support held even as the Pentagon revealed that the eventual number of troops in the Gulf would reach 100,000, not 50,000 as previously discussed. Bush was also bolstered by the speed with which the international embargo of Iraq took effect and the vote by the Arab League to send troops to be part of the coalition defenses.[14] Despite its rally to the President, however, much of the American public remained somewhat skeptical of Bush's actions. Many thought that the decision to send troops had been made hastily, and many simply did not understand where America's interests lay in involving itself in such a troubled region.[15]

Once the embargo had been installed, a tense waiting game ensued. As the U.S. military build-up grew, the inevitable scrutiny and criticism of Bush's policies also grew. Over the next several months, the political stakes for Bush rose as debate emerged over the costs and benefits of confronting Iraq in the desert. Questions arose over whether the United States should spend money and lives protecting nondemocratic nations like Kuwait and Saudi Arabia, and whether the United States might find itself in a never-ending commitment to the region. Doubts also percolated about exactly what motive lay behind the U.S. action. Many felt uncomfortable with the idea that the United States should be willing to expend American lives for oil and cheap gasoline.[16] Military and regional experts worried about various scenarios for ending the crisis. Would it be enough to have Iraq withdraw, or would Hussein's military forces have to be destroyed to bring stability to the region?

Turning up the heat on Saddam Hussein, Bush addressed a joint session of Congress on September 11. In that televised speech, Bush asked the public to give sanctions time to work, but sent a message to Iraq that the world community would not wait forever:

> I cannot predict just how long it will take to convince Iraq to withdraw from Kuwait. Sanctions will take time to have their full intended effect. We will continue to review all options with our allies, but let it be clear: We will not let this aggression stand.[17]

Though the administration was not prepared to spell out what these "options" might include, it was clear to all that offensive military action was now on the policy menu. Postwar accounts reveal that in addition to believing that Hussein was unlikely to yield to sanctions, Bush and his aides feared that sanctions would simply take too long for Bush to win a political victory even if they were successful in the end. Bush himself told *U.S. News and World Report* after the war that "I became convinced early on that, if diplomacy failed, we would indeed have to use force.[18]

Later in the speech, Bush warned Hussein that U.S. policy would not be swayed by Iraq's hostage taking. Bush also used the speech as an opportunity to remind the American public that the Gulf action was not a solo effort by the United States. The international community was arrayed in consensus against Iraq, argued Bush, and the United States had used the forum of the United Nations to coordinate Gulf policy. And finally, Bush also brought up a new rationale for opposing Iraq that would resound with the American public more than almost any other: curbing the spread of nuclear weapons, which Iraq was feared to be very close to developing.[19]

Rhetorical attacks and counterattacks by Bush and Hussein intensified after the September 11 speech. Bush carried the verbal fight into Iraq with a recorded message replayed on Iraqi television, warning Iraqis that because of Saddam Hussein Iraq found itself on the brink of a war that it would lose.[20] Bush then reiterated at a press conference that the United States was prepared to take further measures to ensure an Iraqi withdrawal. Hussein's Revolutionary Command Council responded by promising a long confrontation on Iraqi television:

> Everybody must realize that this battle will be the mother of all battles, and that God wanted us to wage the battle of liberating the nation and humanity, the battle of liberating Jerusalem and the holy shrines on the land of Iraq. . . . There is not a single chance for any retreat, for any retreat from waging the battle according to principles of honor and deep faith and determination to achieve victory.[21]

At the same time, Iraq bolstered its forces in Kuwait, digging in for the war that Bush was foreshadowing. Iraq also threatened that it would attack Israel and Saudi Arabia rather than be strangled by the international embargo: "We will never allow anybody, whoever he may be, to strangle the people of Iraq without having himself strangled."[22]

As the summer slipped into fall, it became clear that the crisis in the Gulf would not end soon. The economic sanctions had begun to bite, but seemed unlikely to force Hussein to withdraw from Kuwait or concede defeat in the near future. In late November CIA Director William Webster testified before Congress that his best estimate was that sanctions might take as long as six months to a year to make an impact.[23] But letting the stalemate with Iraq drag on carried even greater political risks for Bush. It became clear that such a large military force could not be sustained indefinitely in the desert without some sort of rotation policy, especially as the administration had called up thousands of reservists unaccustomed to long stints away from home. Morale in the desert was low because troops were uneasy about whether they would have to fight. Experts now also questioned how Bush could end the crisis successfully, and Congress warned Bush that he must get their approval for any military action.[24] Many, including administration officials, questioned how long the United States could hold together the coalition.[25] Reflecting these rising doubts, public support for Bush's handling of the crisis dipped through the early fall from giddy heights back to more mortal levels.[26]

Bush and his officials had feared from early on in the crisis that the public would not stand behind their Gulf policy if it dragged on far into the future. At a news conference Bush admitted: "If there is no open fighting and the deployment continues month after month with no end is sight, I'm not clear in my own mind on how long this kind of support holds up. . . . How long is too long? I think about those questions but I can't define it for you."[27] Thus, having first counseled patience to let the embargo against Iraq take effect, Bush and his officials began to increase the pressure on Iraq slowly, building on early hints about the use of military force if sanctions failed.[28] After the administration had floated the idea of military force for over a month, Secretary of State Baker departed for a whirlwind mission to assess the level of international support for a UN resolution that would authorize the use of force against Iraq if sanctions did not produce prompt results. Days later Bush finally made explicit that the United States would use military force if Iraq did not withdraw from Kuwait. And on November 8 Bush announced that he had ordered 200,000 more troops to the Gulf to give the coalition the option of taking offensive military action.[29]

As a result of the administration's careful program of hints preparing the public for such a move, Bush's announcement produced at first only a muted response from the public, a majority of whom already believed war was the likely outcome of the crisis. Bush argued that the new deployment would send a strong signal to Saddam Hussein that the world, but especially the United States, was serious about reversing Iraq's invasion.

Democrats in Congress, unlike the public at large, responded with sharp questions of Bush's decision. Congressional critics argued that Bush was rushing the nation toward war and that the public, though supportive of sanctions and the original deployment, did not understand why the current move, or war, was necessary.[30] Senator Sam Nunn (D-Georgia), chair of the Senate Armed Services Committee, voiced a cautionary note:

> The last thing we need is to have a war over there, a bloody war, and have American boys being sent and brought back in body bags and yet not have the American people behind them. . . . I think the president has a real obligation here . . . to explain why liberating Kuwait is in our vital interests, that is, an interest so important we're willing to spend thousands of American lives if necessary.[31]

Even Bush's own party in Congress wanted to make sure that Congress reviewed U.S. options in the Gulf before consenting to support the additional build-up, and that Bush not move ahead with such a momentous decision without congressional approval.[32] Senators Nunn and George Mitchell (D–Maine) announced that they would hold hearings in late November in an attempt to ascertain where the United States stood and what its goals in the Gulf should be.

As the administration struggled to explain its actions to the public, its efforts to get a UN resolution authorizing the use of force finally paid off on November 29. The resolution set a deadline of January 15, 1991 for Iraq to withdraw from Kuwait. If Iraq did not comply, the coalition arrayed against Iraq would be authorized to use "all necessary means" to eject Iraq from Kuwait. As the administration won support from the UN, congressional hearings raised the volume of domestic debate over Bush's Gulf policy. Many military and diplomatic experts argued for time to let sanctions take effect, including former Secretary of Defense James Schlesinger, and former Chiefs of the Joint Chiefs of Staff Admiral William Crowe and General David C. Jones.[33]

As the level of debate and worry grew among members of Congress, so did public fears about the possibility of war. To quell rising fears and to stifle criticism that he was rushing to war, Bush announced that he would send James Baker to Baghdad to find a peaceful solution to the crisis. Bush offered Iraq the chance to pick a date between December 15 and January 15 to meet with Baker, and invited Iraqi Foreign Minister Tariq Aziz to Washington for preliminary talks.[34] Although the move did give the President a respite from public criticism, by no means did it convince congressional critics that the administration was heading in the right direction. By the end of November Congress was divided along party lines, with Republicans supporting the President and Democrats arguing that Bush was not giving economic sanctions enough time to take effect.[35] The bipartisan consensus Bush had enjoyed at the outset of Desert Shield had evaporated. The public remained divided, too, with roughly equal proportions favoring war and continued sanctions should Iraq fail to retreat by the January 15 deadline.[36]

Easing Bush's political burdens somewhat, Saddam Hussein announced on December 6 that Iraq would release all of its Western "guests." Within a week the 900-plus Americans and 1,100 other hostages were safely home. With the hostage issue now settled, attention focused on the prospect of the talks with Iraq. After much haggling over acceptable dates, Iraq and the United States agreed to have Baker and Aziz meet in Geneva on January 9.[37]

The talks did not appear likely to change the course of the crisis. Iraq had shown no sign of willingness to retreat without compromise and had promised not to yield to American pressure. Bush had sent Baker to Geneva to meet Iraqi Foreign Minister Tariq Aziz with an inflexible portfolio. A Bush press release announced that there would be "No negotiations, no compromises. No attempts at face-saving, and no rewards for aggression."[38] When the talks failed to produce a peaceful solution, Baker announced that Iraq was completely inflexible, and that he saw no willingness to comply with the UN resolutions of the past months. Bush called the Iraqi position a "total rebuff."[39]

Under the shadow of the fast-approaching deadline, Congress began to debate the use of force the day after Baker's meeting in Geneva. Bush, confident that he now had support in Congress, had asked it on January 8 to authorize the use of force to deal with Iraq after January 15. Bush hoped that in so doing, Congress would amplify his message to Hussein that the coalition and the United States would not let the invasion stand. Such approval would also defend the administration from those who might claim the president had acted rashly. After impassioned debate on both sides of the issue, both the House and Senate voted to authorize Bush to use "all necessary means" to deal with Iraq should he determine that other means of resolving the crisis would not work. Practically speaking, as Speaker of the House Thomas Foley (D-Washington) noted, Congress had just voted a declaration of war. Americans waited for the last days before the deadline elapsed. A majority of the public believed that Bush had done all he could to avoid war, and now expected a long and costly war. Iraqi troops meanwhile dug in yet deeper, and Iraq's political leaders vowed to resist.[40]

At 7 p.m. Washington time on January 16, U.S. aircraft struck the first blow of Desert Storm against Iraqi targets in and around Baghdad. After announcing that the "liberation of Kuwait has begun," Bush manned the helm of a overwhelming thirty-eight-day air war to destroy Iraqi command and control sites, to eliminate its nuclear and chemical weapons facilities, and to destroy Iraqi tanks and heavy weapons. After weighing carefully the need to start the ground campaign, Bush gave Hussein another deadline. If Iraq did not withdraw its forces by noon on February 23, the ground war would begin. Iraq did not withdraw and the coalition launched a massive high-speed ground attack aimed at ejecting Iraqi forces from Kuwait and destroying much of Iraq's remaining military might. Desert Storm was spectacularly successful from the Allied view, with few American casualties, and Bush declared victory and ordered a cease-fire after only 100 hours.[41]

The media who had flocked to Saudi Arabia to cover the war found themselves almost as much at the mercy of the U.S. military as were Iraqi forces. Reporters were unable to move about on their own, accompanied at all times by public affairs escorts, and limited in their access to troops and the battlefield. After failing throughout the war to provide the public with a firsthand view of what was happening, the press lamented that it had been defeated again.

THE BUSH ADMINISTRATION AND DESERT STORM

The Bush Administration and Press Policy in Desert Shield/Desert Storm

Once again the White House dominated the process of press policy making. In fact, Bush Administration officials were not only the chief architects of press policy in the Persian Gulf, they also dictated its implementation to an unparalleled degree throughout the crisis in pursuit of both national interests and political interests. Secretary of Defense Richard Cheney and Assistant Secretary of Defense (Public Affairs) Pete Williams kept the press unaware of their plans for dealing with the press in the event that the crisis evolved into war throughout the fall even as they created policies both at odds with and far more restrictive than existing military public affairs policy. Throughout the crisis the White House directed the military's dealings with the press and used the information monopoly that resulted from the press curbs to bolster its public relations efforts and prevent press coverage from damaging either national or presidential political interests.

The increased power and importance of the press in politics and the policy making process loomed large during Desert Shield/Desert Storm, making it imperative for the Bush Administration to influence press coverage when possible to ensure support for its actions. The media's importance stemmed from several factors. The sheer number of journalists covering the crisis in both the United States and the Gulf (not to mention other foreign capitals) meant that the press covered every aspect of crisis and picked up on every maneuver and decision, analyzing it and picking it apart. News flew instantly from one capital to another where its impact was felt immediately, demanding a quick response. With the whole world watching, every leader, especially Bush, had to choose his words carefully. Bush had to speak to both domestic and foreign audiences, attempting to reassure allies, dampen criticism from critics, intimidate Saddam Hussein into capitulating, and increase his popular support all at one press conference. Press coverage became even more critical in administration eyes because of the vast audiences tuning in to television to get news of the crisis and later the war's progress. It is one thing to wage a policy debate in private, or when it only shows up on the inside pages of the newspaper. But polls revealed that most of America was glued to the television set for war news. Bush's announcement of war to the nation on January 16 was watched by the largest American audience in history; over 120 million people tuned in.[42] This intense scrutiny of every Bush word and deed raised the stakes for the administration to influence news coverage. For all these reasons, the Bush Administration found it imperative to think strategically about the media in an attempt to ensure positive responses from the large audiences both at home and abroad.

The adversarial nature of the government/press relationship also made managing both news from Washington and from the battlefield important to the administration. Administration officials had little confidence that the press would give Bush the benefit of the doubt in assessing his actions, as their decisions to restrict the press during Just Cause had already made clear. They knew that the press would jump on administration mistakes, point out its weaknesses, and challenge the rationales behind every action. Bush officials must have also feared that the relationship between the administration and the press had suffered during Just Cause as a result of press policy there.

The lack of consensus in Congress and the division in public over the wisdom of Bush's Gulf policy further encouraged the administration to make strenuous efforts to dominate the news agenda. Few would have challenged a strong U.S. response had the Iraqi invasion been bankrolled and supported by the Soviet Union ten years earlier. But in the foreign policy climate of 1990-91, it was not clear to many that the situation demanded the loss of American lives. Without the Cold War or even the "Americans in danger" theme to frame the crisis, the administration needed to work harder through the media to convince both public and Congress that the use of military force was necessary in January. And because the rationales the administration did use were less familiar to the public, and less persuasive, than containing communism or protecting American lives, the administration was forced to repeat them more frequently, and to defend their legitimacy in the face of criticism from other political leaders and foreign policy experts.

The explosion of media technologies represented the fourth trend influencing administration press relations during Desert Shield/Storm. Satellite phones and fly-away satellite dishes, cellular phones, e-mail, and fax machines brought frightening possibilities of live television coverage from Baghdad and near instantaneous print reports from the front. The potential lack of control over images and news emanating from the desert encouraged the Administration to make sure that correspondents never got the opportunity to deploy these technologies when they could endanger administration political interests. As it was, even the immediacy of restricted press coverage forced day-to-day responses from the administration to press coverage. An entire news cycle, for example, was taken up in analysis and administration response to the film footage of the U.S. bombing of an air raid shelter in Baghdad that killed several hundred civilians. Critics of the war were given powerful ammunition to question military tactics—

hadn't the administration been boasting of a humane air campaign with precision targeting and without civilian casualties? Had television not been there and reported the vivid news so quickly, it is unlikely that such a frenzy would have occurred, and the Administration would not have faced such intense questioning of its aims and actions. It was this power that the administration thus sought to curb.

Finally, the White House's reliance on public relations as a basic tool of governing during peacetime intensified during crisis and war. As the previous decade or so had shown, when presidential political incentives intensify, so do White House efforts to influence, and control when possible, the press and its coverage of administration actions. Thus, in the Gulf War, a president already steeped in the art of managing the news to steer a course through political seas turned again to media strategy to gain advantage over his foes and critics, and to cement political victory in the end. The success of restrictive press policies in Grenada and Panama, in addition to the White House's more general reliance on media strategy most likely led the Bush administration to the conclusion that their public relations efforts would be strengthened by tight control over the press in Saudi Arabia. With less information and less television coverage of the war, the media would not be able to disrupt the administration's messages to the public. Tough talk in Washington was thus matched with tough press curbs in the Persian Gulf.

Indeed, according to Cheney, two broad principles guided the planning: First, military needs should outweigh the media's "rights" to cover the war. This meant that ensuring operational security and military convenience would be placed above ensuring press access to the battlefield and information. Second, the government must at all costs maintain its credibility with the public, which meant, in Cheney's words, ". . . don't get out there making claims you can't back up."[43] Cheney and other top officials also argued that the policies were necessary to preserve operational security in an environment where communications technology allowed information to spread worldwide almost instantly. As Colin Powell noted, "[If a commander] in Desert Shield sat around in his tent and mused with a few CNN guys and pool guys and other guys, it's in 105 capitals a minute later."[44]

What Cheney did not reveal at the time, however, were the political motives that lay behind the press system and what officials hoped to accomplish by instituting a restrictive public affairs system in the Gulf. Arguing that military needs took precedence in planning over journalists' rights allows an official to cover his actions under the rubric of national security. Touchier to discuss is the more accurate observation that the Gulf public affairs system placed *political needs* above journalists' rights. A public affairs system that controlled access and information in the Gulf would help the administration sell its messages to the public more efficiently, unsullied by the media chatter that would be produced by hundreds of journalists running free in the desert. And more important, of course, a restrictive press system would mean that Bush would not be so likely to face televised pictures of "the down and dirty side of war," as television critic Walter Goodman has called it. With the media bottled up, no one could challenge the administration or the military on how the war was going, and so forth. The public, hoped the administration, would thus be more likely to hear and accept administration views rather than those of critics and thus be more supportive of the war. As Cheney admitted several years after the war.

> I felt it was very important to provide a lot of information, as accurate as we could to the public, but I emphasize, to the public, not necessarily to the press. . . . And I felt it was important to manage the information flow—not to distort it, but to make certain that we got a lot of information out there so that people knew what we were doing. . . . The information function was extraordinarily important. I did not have a lot of confidence that I could leave that to the press. . . . This is a free society, and the free press is an important part of that. But if I rely as secretary on the press to be the filter through which all information goes—about why we're going to send 500,000 kids off to the Gulf and may take heavy casualties——then I can't be at all confident that my side of the story's going to be told or that the policy's going to be carefully explained and that people are going to understand what it's all about.[45]

Devising the System while Keeping the Press in the Dark

After a discussion among senior Bush officials of past military operations in which the government had handled the press poorly, President Bush gave Secretary of Defense Richard Cheney primary responsibility for devising the military's public affairs system in the Gulf. Cheney in turn delegated much of the legwork to Pete Williams.[46] The first military planning document to deal with the media in Desert Shield was drawn up on August 14 by Captain Ron Wildermuth, USN. This memo, entitled Annex Foxtrot to denote that it dealt with public affairs, was based on a series of missives from Cheney and Williams.[47] Though many would later point to this memo as evidence that the military was responsible for imposing press restrictions, in fact it came from Cheney and Williams. General Schwarzkopf later testified to their primacy in press matters:

> When we were trying to hammer out the rules, at the very beginning of Desert Shield, they were not our rules. A lot of that stuff was OSD-imposed. They were sent to us, and we would try and put the theater spin on the thing and send it back to them. They were the ones approving it. But we were the ones getting, quote, the blame, end quote, for lack of a better word. But it really was an OSD-forged policy, and a Pete Williams forged policy, and one that was dictated by Washington, D.C. I think you'll see that it's very clear that the policy—all policies, with regard to dealing with the press—comes straight from OSD Public Affairs.[48]

This memo, which provided much of the basic form for Desert Storm arrangements, remained unaltered in its essentials throughout the crisis. At that early date, it was ordered that journalists would be escorted by military officers at all times and that their copy would undergo security review. Thus, only days into the crisis, plans for restricting press access to the battlefield and thus to potentially damaging information proceeded apace. Wildermuth's memo echoed closely Cheney's two guiding principles as well as those he did not state publicly. The press policy outlined in Annex Foxtrot certainly held "national interest" concerns above those of journalists' but, perhaps more importantly, the curbs it outlined would also dampen the press threat to the White House politically by making it difficult for the press to get close to the action.

Civilian officials, then, continued to play a central role in shaping military public affairs policy throughout Desert Shield, and in particular in shaping the arrangements for the media should the crisis escalate into war. Adding to Annex Foxtrot's restrictions, both Cheney and Williams made clear in later interviews and in their own writing that the decision to limit battlefield coverage to pools was approved by civilian officials in the fall of 1990 as it became more clear that war was in the offing and that a media circus was going to be there to cover it.[49] Administration officials defended the need for pools as the only practical way to deal with the huge volume of media people. As Cheney argued, "There's a huge gaggle of reporters out there, and the press has absolutely no capacity to police itself. There was no way we were ever going to put 100 percent of the reporters who wanted to go cover the war out with the troops."[50] Williams echoed this tone in a postwar assessment of press policy: "The US and international press corps went from zero on 2 August, to 17 on the first pool, to 800 by December, and to nearly 1400 just before the ground war started. Most of the reporters, the good ones anyway, wanted to be out where the action is. But with hundreds of fiercely independent reporters seeking to join up with combat units, we concluded that when the combat started, we'd have no choice but to rely on pools."[51]

Both the administration and the military knew that escorts, security review, and press pools would not sit well with the media. Had the military simply announced its public affairs policy in the form it ultimately took, the press might well have protested long and loud enough to force changes. It was thus necessary to craft the policy in secret, to let the details out slowly, and to act obligingly when news organizations complained about the restrictions so that their protests would never reach the critical pitch that might force an embarrassing about face of policy. The job of providing cover by keeping the press in the dark and unsuspecting of what was to come fell to Pete Williams.

Williams' first task was to reassure media chiefs in Washington that they would be able to get enough reporters into Saudi Arabia to cover fighting if it broke out, and that they would not have to operate under onerous Saudi-driven restrictions. Saudi Arabia is an extremely closed society, and before the crisis did not even allow journalists to station themselves there. The Saudis were concerned at the outbreak of the crisis that they would be flooded with journalists from the United States and other Western countries who would stir up trouble in their conservative, religious nation. Pentagon officials at first used this discomfort to explain both why the press pool had not been immediately activated to accompany the deployment and the restrictions placed on the pool once it finally did arrive on August 13. Cheney claimed at a press conference, "Saudi Arabia's a sovereign nation. They have their own rules and regulations and requirements and they establish the ground rules under which people have access to cover activities inside the kingdom. That's not something that we have control over."[52] Later, Cheney noted that "What you [a journalist] mean by free and unrestricted reporting might be different than what the Saudis think is free and unrestricted. . . . I think we have to respect their culture, just as they respect ours. . . . In the final analysis, they'll make the decision, but obviously we will be advocates for the concept that there should be significant coverage of US forces in Saudi Arabia available to the American people."[53]

On August 22, several news organizations, upset with the restrictions on the pool, and with the fact that the Saudis would not issue more visas for additional journalists to enter Saudi Arabia to report the American build-up, faxed Bush at his vacation home in Kennebunkport to demand help in getting the Saudis to loosen up.[54] On October 9, Michael Getler, an editor at the *Washington Post*, wrote to tell Pete Williams that if fighting broke out, American news organizations would need to send many more journalists and other personnel to the Gulf to be able to cover the war effectively. Getler and others worried that the Saudis would close their commercial airspace once the war started and they would have no way to get their reporters in to cover the story.[55]

Williams moved quickly to stem the rising media fears. Of course, the restrictions on the pool had already been articulated secretly in Wildermuth's Annex Foxtrot, but Pentagon officials found it more convenient not to mention this. Instead, Williams met with thirteen bureau chiefs from the major news organizations on October 25 to offer them enough concessions to convince them that the Pentagon and the administration were on their side. Williams acceded without hesitation to Getler's request that a military transport plane be provided to take additional media personnel to the Gulf in the event of war. He also assured them that the appropriate visas would be made available to their people at that time.[56] Williams also used the meeting to let the news chiefs know how press policy was shaping up. He made only vague references to pool coverage, and reassured his audience that pools in no way precluded independent coverage. He also noted that the Pentagon was not considering censorship. Williams made no mention, of course, of Annex Foxtrot. By providing access to Saudi Arabia, clearly the news organizations' number one concern, Williams had forestalled debate over exactly how journalists would do their jobs once they got there. By all accounts, the news chiefs left the meeting believing that Williams' intentions were benign, and without any clue of how press policy would ultimately restrict their operations. And, as John MacArthur argued, "In any event, Pete Williams had more candy in his suitcase; there would be more come-ons, more enticements, more rewards, more obfuscation, and, of course, more meetings and memoranda."[57]

Then on December 14 Williams dropped the first bomb on the media, issuing a memorandum to news organizations that spelled out the press groundrules in the event of hostilities:

> All interviews with service members will be on the record. Security at the source is the policy. In the event of hostilities, media products will be subject to security review prior to release. . . . You must remain with your military escort at all times, until released, and follow instructions regarding your activities. These instructions are intended only to facilitate troop movement, ensure safety, and maintain operational security.[58]

Williams elaborated on the groundrules, noting that the Pentagon's press plan would be a three-phased affair and that pool would be the primary method used to cover the war. First, two eighteen-member pools would be formed and would practice deploying with the troops while covering the crisis. Second, once war looked immanent, the pools would either be deployed forward with the troops or positioned such that they could move forward as soon as possible. Only in phase three would the pools disband and open coverage begin. And even in phase three, the memo stated, reporters would continue to operate under a public affairs escort.[59]

In their two previous meetings, Williams had not revealed that pools would play the unprecedented role of prime vehicle for press access to the battlefield. Nor had he ever mentioned the concept of "security review." Williams had in fact given the press the opposite impression: that he was working to ensure journalists' freedom of movement and that there would be no censorship of media reports. To reassure any who might have been upset by the memo, Williams reiterated the Pentagon's offer of a C-141 transport aircraft to take journalists to Saudi Arabia and also made sure to call for media comments and questions about the draft, suggesting that revision was possible. Williams gave the press the impression that the Pentagon and the media organizations were negotiating, when in fact they were not. Cheney's original edicts and the secret Annex Foxtrot continued to guide public affairs planning. Williams was simply staving off media outrage until it was too late to produce results. With some help from the fact that the media cared more about getting a spot in a pool than what the pool would see and report, Williams succeeded.[60]

A final meeting between Williams and roughly fifty media executives took place on January 4, as the UN deadline loomed and war seemed inevitable. Though the executives were unhappy with the current groundrules and guidelines, Williams was not there to negotiate. Despite his assurances that he welcomed comments, he did not offer to amend the offending restrictions. It was only in the wake of this meeting that news executives finally realized they were not part of the public affairs planning process, despite their numerous meetings with Williams. The January 4 meeting produced another Williams memorandum that made clear that escorts, pools, and security review were there to stay.[61] In a final memo a week later Williams thanked the press corps for its comments, said he understood their concerns, and announced that the public affairs plan had been put into effect without major changes from the January 4 meeting.[62] A day later the air war started; it was too late for the press to undo the Pentagon's planning. In their rush to get their people to the Gulf and into pools, the only way they could count on being able to report at least some of the action—their number one goal after all—they had been forced to comply with the Pentagon's rules and guidelines before fully realizing the impact they would have. And once the war was underway, complaining about the arrangements had to take a second place to the difficult task of simply covering breaking events in a complex environment. Williams' thorough job of stringing the media along throughout the fall was thus critical in paving the way for strict government control of the press in the desert.

Controlling Press Policy Implementation: From Press Controls to Public Relations Coups

Perhaps the most telling evidence of the White House's domination of wartime press policy was the extent to which the White House, through Cheney and Williams, maintained strict control over the military's implementation of the press policy they had laid down. That the White House felt the need to supervise the military's dealings with the press even after outlining a policy in great detail provides powerful evidence that the press has become far too important a variable during crisis and war to be left to the military. As Richard Cheney later noted,

> But it was so important, especially in connection with the Gulf conflict, where the possibility existed of a long-term, sustained kind of operation where the stakes were enormous, I felt that it was important to try to manage that relationship in a way so the press didn't screw us—if I can put it in those terms.

The Bush Administration thus wanted to curb the press and manage the news not only to ensure that it did not do damage to the national interest but also in order to avoid potential press criticism and thereby ensure a political victory for the president.

The Administration wasted no time preparing for its communication efforts once the war began, as the *Washington Post*'s Ann Devroy reported:

> The day after the United States went to war against Iraq, the White House press secretary Marlin Fitzwater put in place a communications system aimed at presenting the administration's view of the day's developments in a series of daily briefings, coordinated beforehand by phone, that would progress from the battlefield, to the Pentagon, to the White House and State Department.[63]

As discussed in previous chapters, even under normal peacetime conditions White Houses now consider the creation of a "line of the day" and the system to propagate it a routine necessity. The reasoning behind such a system is clear. Discrepancies in statements or policy disagreements among departments could divert the media's focus from administration successes and official messages and fuel negative coverage. But during Desert Storm, with the press firmly restricted and relying heavily on official pronouncements for its news source, the potential impact of a single, focused message coming from the administration would increase manyfold. The administration could shape the news simply be deciding what subject to focus on (Patriot Missile a Big Success, Air War Devastating but Accurate, Saddam Is Evil, etc.) and by having spokesmen throughout the administration reiterate its central themes.[64] Journalists, with almost no access to the battlefield or to independent sources of information in the Gulf about the war, had little choice but to incorporate official statements as the main thrust in their coverage of events. Most observers, including administration and military officials, believe that the system emerged as a great success.[65]

The structured daily briefing system was doubly effective as a consequence of the White House's strenuous efforts to control the military's dealings with the press. Not only did the White House coordinate daily themes to be emphasized, the administration also maintained control over what Central Command officers told the press by maintaining "information release authority" on key political and military issues. This meant that the Williams' office in the Pentagon would tell Central Command when they had the authority to discuss certain topics with the press. As General Schwarzkopf revealed several years after the war, "Before the Gulf War, there was a very controversial decision made under Colin Powell. Most of the CINCs objected to it, me included. It said that the principal, number one person who would control everything having to do with the media was Pete Williams, and that Washington would call all the shots, in theater, on how the media was dealt with." Cheney's revelation that he bore primary responsibility for press matters, as well as common sense, makes it clear that Pete Williams was not the final authority in Washington on directing the military's relations with the press. Far more likely, though we cannot know for sure in the absence of direct evidence, is that Cheney provided the broad guidance with input from the White House where needed and Williams dealt with the day-to-day details.

Much of Washington's public affairs guidance told Desert Shield/Storm commanders exactly what to say to the press on subjects like the use of nuclear weapons, casualties, reserve forces, and presidential intentions. In many cases Williams' office told commanders what to say in response to particular questions journalists might ask, such as whether the United States would use nuclear weapons in retaliation to a chemical attack by Iraq.[66] Each order served to strengthen the administration's voice and reduce the flow of information to the press that had not been approved by civilian leaders.

Schwarzkopf offers two examples of how tight civilian control over public affairs was during the conflict:

> So a lot of times, things that were blamed on the people in the theater had been directed straight from Washington for—let's face it—

> principally political reasons, probably. . . . I'll give you a very good example. At one point, we all got told that we couldn't deal with the press any more. This started, I think, about the end of November. From then until the war started, we were just told: "You cannot talk to the press any more. None of your generals can talk to the press any more."
>
> Another very good example was cruise missiles. We fired a lot of cruise missiles at the beginning of the overall strategic air campaign, and we were showing selective footage of cruise missile firing. Colin Powell called me and said, "These cruise missiles cost—I forget how much money—every time you fire one. Let's put a lid on firing cruise missiles. Let's stop. I'm sure it wasn't Colin's decision alone. It came from the Department of Defense. I said, "Fine, we can work around it." So we restructured the strategic bombing campaign, and we finally stopped using the cruise missiles. But we had a lot of footage on cruise missiles. Suddenly, unbeknownst to me, a whole bunch of cruise-missile footage starts being broadcast to the United States. I said, "Wait a minute. We're trying to de-emphasize cruise missiles. We're trying to stop firing cruise missiles, and here the drum is being beat on cruise missiles. Where is this coming from? Well, I came to find out that that footage was down in one of our media centers someplace. And Pete Williams had called up, found out it was there, and demanded it be sent directly to him. It was sent directly to him and it was shown in the Pentagon. And the theater commander and Colin Powell are sitting here, and it just goes, shoo, right around them and out the other door. Then Colin calls me up and says, "Damn it, what is this cruise missile stuff doing on the air?" I said, "It beats the hell out of me. I will find out." But that sort of thing happened.[67]

The great control over the access of the press to the battlefield and military information as well as its tight control over what the military told the press allowed the administration to shape news and, more importantly perhaps, to ensure that there would be few if any upsetting or violent television images beamed into American living rooms. Critics, or would-be critics of the war, received very little ammunition from the media with which to attack the president or to criticize his handling of the war.

Scooping the media and trumpeting successes to the public without competition or analysis from skeptical journalists proved to be a major benefit of the government's system. By providing critical war news directly to the public, the administration and military enhanced their own credibility, made the most of their successes, downplayed their mistakes, and lessened the impact of the press on its policies. In one such instance, Malcolm Browne, a veteran war correspondent for the *New York Times,* discovered from F-117 pilots the fact that they had just destroyed Iraqi plants and laboratories thought to be part of nuclear weapons production. But before Browne could dispatch what would clearly be a front-page story, given concern over Iraq's nuclear capabilities, he was asked to withhold the news for reasons of military security. He agreed, only to be scooped that evening as General Schwarzkopf himself made the announcement that the facilities had been destroyed.[68]

A second way in which the administration's oversight of the daily briefings paid off resulted from the decision to have only the most senior officers meet the press.[69] The public responded much better to their expertise and confident professionalism than to lower-ranking officers who often looked uncertain or harassed by journalists. In particular, General Colin Powell, Chairman of the Joint Chiefs of Staff, proved to be a huge asset to the administration. His briefings from the Pentagon went a long way to establishing administration and military credibility during the war. He was aided, as one commentator points out, by his command of endless amounts of data and technical information about the war effort to which no one in the press was privy. There was little opening to challenge Powell on his pronouncements. Delivered in his confident and forthright manner, Powell's briefings helped the administration argue that it was sharing all the information with the public that it could.[70]

The fact that so many military briefings were televised further weakened the media's stance with respect to the government and military. The public became disenchanted with reporters' rude and pointed questioning of high-ranking and highly credible military officers like General Powell or Lt. General Thomas Kelly. Worse for the press, journalists repeatedly revealed themselves to be woefully ignorant of military affairs, often asking questions that would clearly endanger operational security if answered. A survey by the Times Mirror Center for the People and the Press discovered that nearly 80% of the public approved of the restrictions on the press.[71] Perhaps the low point for the press came when Saturday Night Live, normally a sure bet to needle the government in its skits, did a number scoring journalists instead for their ignorance and apathy towards the war. ("General, can you tell me when we're going to attack?") The Saturday Night Live skit, it turned out, helped convince a nervous White House that its restrictions were in fact popular and could be safely continued.[72]

The White House's close control over administration statements also paid off in crisis situations, such as when the United States bombed what Iraq claimed was a civilian air raid shelter. CNN, led to the scene by Iraqi officials, was on hand with its cameras to record the aftermath of the U.S. bombing of a building in which roughly 400 Iraqi civilians were killed. Iraq claimed the building was an air raid shelter and the television footage of burnt bodies sent chills through the White House. Those were exactly the sort of images that could cost the president support for policies, administration officials believed, and it was important that they respond quickly to the incident. Fitzwater immediately wrote a statement for Bush lamenting civilian deaths but asserting that the building was a military command center and placing ultimate blame for the attack on Saddam Hussein. Fitzwater then quickly coordinated the administration response among officials at the State Department and the Pentagon before reading Bush's statement.[73] And at the Pentagon, officials revealed classified intelligence to prove the Iraqis were lying. Though the Pentagon normally refuses to reveal information about its intelligence gathering, the need to defuse a budding crisis sparked greater openness.[74, 75] By promptly moving to rebut Iraqi claims with a single, coordinated response, the White House managed to head off any groundswell of sympathy for the Iraqis and defuse a potential crisis for Bush. The administration's credibility also paid off. 81% of the American public believed the government's claim that the building had a military purpose and 79% felt the air war should continue despite civilian casualties.[76]

Finally, there is reason to believe that the administration credits a good deal of their success to the restrictive public affairs policy and their public relations efforts. Secretary of Defense Cheney argued that Gulf War coverage was "better coverage" than "any other war in history" and noted of the Pentagon's press policy, "I look at it as a model of how the Department ought to function."[77] One of the Pentagon's star briefers, Lt. General Thomas Kelly, agreed in a remark that almost everyone on both sides of the government/press divide would agree with:

> For the first time ever, the administration—the Department of Defense—was talking directly to the American people, using the vehicle of a press briefing, whereas in Vietnam, everything was filtered through the press. I think that was a major advantage for the government. The press, wittingly or unwittingly, between Riyadh and Washington, was giving us an hour-and-a-half a day to tell our story to the American people . . . the American people were getting their information from the government—not from the press. . . .[78]

Military Public Affairs in Desert Shield/Desert Storm: Implementing the Restrictions

The military's role in Gulf War press policy gives further evidence that the military, far from using the Gulf as an opportunity to take revenge on the press for Vietnam through instituting a restrictive public affairs plan, found itself as usual implementing policies drafted by the White House while suffering from its chronic inattention to public affairs. As civilians developed public affairs policy, the military was left to work out the details and to implement the policy handed down from the Pentagon. The military, not surprisingly, was for the most part in harmony with the White House on how to deal with the press. Despite paying polite respect to the right of the press to cover war in public, most senior military officers felt much more comfortable having the press under tighter rein than the JCS planning guidance written after Just Cause would have entailed. In tandem with a White House interested in curbing press access to the battlefield and limiting press impact on public opinion, the military's implementation of public affairs helped to make sure that the media would have a harder time than ever covering an American conflict.

Military Planning for Public Affairs

On the eve of Desert Storm in January, Williams finally made public the groundrules and guidelines that would comprise public affairs policy for the war. The groundrules covering what information could not be reported for reasons of operational security remained almost unchanged since Vietnam and more recent conflicts. A new category of "guidelines," however, broke almost completely from existing JCS policy guidance on public affairs and from the Sidle Panel's recommendations, which until then had been widely considered by military and press alike as the philosophical and practical basis for wartime public affairs policy. As in previous conflicts, journalists had to agree in advance to the Pentagon's groundrules and guidelines in order to receive the accreditation from the military that would allow them to join the press pools and cover the war.[79]

In a departure from Pentagon assurances and from existing policy, the press would cover Desert Storm exclusively from pools. As of January 12, plans called for two eighteen-member pools, consisting of reporters from television, newspapers, newsmagazines, and the wire services. One would cover the Army, one the Marines. No "unilateral" or independent coverage would be permitted. The military would detain and take back to Dhahran any journalist found within 100 miles of the war zone. The Saudis later strengthened this rule by making the punishment for unilateral reporting arrest and deportation.

In addition, the Pentagon required that journalists remain with their public affairs escorts at all times and "follow their instructions regarding your activities." According to Williams, the job of the escort was to help get journalists to the action, help them navigate the military, but not to hinder their reporting in any way. Although pools had always been led by a military escort, escorts in the Gulf were to accompany journalists on a much closer basis than had ever been the case in the past. As Williams told public affairs officers in Saudi Arabia, "Then each little component of that pool, each little gaggle of two or three or four reporters is gonna have an escort."[80] Williams noted that escorts should not try to accompany reporters continuously around the clock, but should try to be present when things were happening: ". . . if a television guy is doing a standup, and I were an escort officer I would want to hear what he's saying, I would want to stand behind the camera . . . somewhere out of the shot where I can hear what he's saying."[81] The purpose of this proximity, according to Williams, was to allow escorts to tell reporters immediately if they felt something in their story violated the reporting groundrules. But escorts were to have other duties as well, not made public to the press. As Williams told his charges, ". . . you're the one that keeps them out of areas where they shouldn't be." In other words, escorts would be expected to keep journalists away from those things the Pentagon and military services did not want to be splashed across television screens. This might include highly classified special operations equipment, as Williams pointed out, but as journalists feared, it could also include areas that for political reasons it would be easier for the military not to reveal to reporters, such as the battlefield itself.[82]

Finally, all pool reports would be subject to what the Pentagon called "security review." A public affairs escort would review all pool reports to make sure that they complied with the reporting groundrules outlined by Williams. The groundrules dictated that there be no reporting of troop locations, movements, future war plans, intelligence gathering operations, and so forth. If the military escort found that a news story did not violate any of the groundrules, he would send it on its way to the JIB in Dhahran, where it would be copied and made available to the press corps. If the escort determined, on the other hand, that a report did violate one of the groundrules, he was to discuss the matter with the journalist, pointing out his concerns. If the journalist agreed with the escort and modified the report to comply with the ground rules, the report could then make its way to Dhahran. If the journalist did not agree to change his or her copy, the escort would then flag the report for review by officers at the JIB and representatives of the press pools. If they could still not get a journalist to agree on the need for changes, the story would finally go to Williams in the Pentagon, who would discuss the matter with a bureau chief in Washington. If they still did not come to agreement, the decision to print in the end remained with the press. The security review process thus did not represent censorship in the traditional sense. The policy did not give the military the power to censor news stories, or to change reports in any way. It did, however, give the military the ability to review press reports before publication or broadcast for the first time since the Korean War.

Though the press learned for the first time in January what the public affairs policy would be, the military and its public affairs people in Saudi Arabia had known its outlines since August. Despite this foreknowledge, neither the Pentagon nor the military did much to ensure that the implementation of that policy would run smoothly. Those involved in every aspect of public affairs reached the same conclusion. General Schwarzkopf noted after the war that "One of the big problems with Desert Shield, originally, and Desert Storm was the fact that, once again, we had not dealt with this problem since the days of Grenada. Therefore, you do one of two things: You fall back on what you came up with after Grenada, or you have to invent a system right there on the spot."[83] Navy Captain Ron Wildermuth, Schwarzkopf's public affairs aide and the highest ranking PAO in the Gulf, agreed: "Something which became immediately obvious was that wartime public affairs training had not been emphasized adequately by any of the services or DoD for some time."[84] John J. Fialka, a reporter for the *Wall Street Journal*, rendered a more blunt assessment from the outside: "In theory, there had been plenty of time for the policy governing the details of combat coverage to be worked out. In fact, there was no coherent policy."[85]

The military's lack of attention to public affairs made itself immediately evident to Navy Captain Mike Sherman and his team of public affairs officers who accompanied the DoD National Media Pool to Dhahran on August 13. Sherman's mission was to set up the Joint Information Bureau (JIB), which would keep track of journalists covering the crisis and help them cover the units in the field. Finding himself without many basic items he would need to do his job, Sherman had to commandeer a computer from the hotel which was the JIB's headquarters, and had to scrounge fax and copier machines from other units in Saudi Arabia. Another JIB in Riyadh was also set up to provide the daily press briefings on the crisis and information for the press about Desert Shield and later Desert Storm.[86]

The Pentagon disbanded the seventeen-member pool after two weeks of activity which garnered mixed results. Many in the media felt that the pool had failed to produce any truly worthy reporting: others felt that the pool had done an admirable job.[87] By August 26 when the pool was disbanded, roughly 300 journalists had descended on Dhahran and were looking to cover the U.S. build-up.

The Pentagon moved to unilateral coverage, but the new system nonetheless restricted press access to the troops. Though not strictly a pool system because their reports were not shared, journalists could not visit military units by themselves or on their own initiative. Instead, they had to request visits to particular units and areas, which were then subject to military approval. Many requests were never fulfilled, and far more often journalists would end up traveling to spots that the military deemed newsworthy. Reporters had to sign up at the JIB for the very limited number of seats on the buses that would take them to cover the troops under military escort. A group of ten to twenty journalists would then visit a military installation, unit, or event, after which their escorts would bring them back to Dhahran. Rarely did journalists spend a night with the troops in the field, and in fact very few visits to ground forces were permitted. And no trips were allowed to the airbases from which the F-117 fighters or B-52 bombers operated.[88]

Making the entire process more difficult for everyone was the fact that the JIB was overwhelmed with having to deal with so many journalists. There were only sixteen public affairs staffers working twenty four hours a day trying to handle press requests, escort press junkets into the field, and keep track more generally of what was going on in the Gulf. The JIB had only four twenty-two seat buses to transport media personnel and equipment. Colonel Bill Mulvey, commander of the JIB in Dhahran from January onwards, argued that the maximum number of reporters the JIB could really handle with its equipment and personnel was about 200.[89] That number had already been surpassed by mid-August and the number of reporters in Dhahran just kept growing. Unfortunately for public affairs officers things did not improve for at least two reasons. First, the JIB simply never had enough trained public affairs officers to handle the influx of reporters, in large part because many were reserves who had to return home in December. Second, although Captain Sherman began immediately requesting more equipment (phones, faxes, etc.) and extra vehicles to ferry journalists out to the field, he received little response from Central Command. As time went by the JIB was thus forced to do more with relatively less.[90]

In October Central Command considered and rejected a plan to deploy two press pools to the front to live and work with the troops in anticipation of how things would work during war.[91] Doing so would have allowed both journalists and the military to accustom themselves to working together in crisis conditions, and would have allowed plenty of time to practice getting pool reports back to the JIB in a timely fashion. The decision not to deploy the pools in October thus wasted several months of valuable on-the-job training for both the military and the press. The opportunity to salvage a month of such training was lost later, in December, when the pools were finally created but were not allowed to spend extended periods of time out in the field.

To appreciate what this lack of preparation meant, however, one must first understand the context in which the Pentagon expected public affairs officers to carry out their tasks. Previous conflicts had seen only limited use of pools and escorts, and no use at all of security review. As noted above, current public affairs policy had departed radically from the existing JCS guidance published only months before the Iraqi invasion of Kuwait. Thus, none of the public affairs people had any real experience with these concepts, especially with respect to how they would function in a large-scale war in Saudi Arabia, an environment very different from Grenada or Panama. With respect to security review, one must recall that the military's long-moribund reserve censorship units had been disbanded in 1987, when it seemed clear that censorship was no longer likely to be employed. This meant that the military had neither a system nor the trained personnel to handle the enormous task of reviewing hundreds of news reports for security risks. Moreover, public affairs officers have never had censorship in their portfolios. The mission had always been considered a job for military intelligence, the branch most familiar with those things that should not become public knowledge. Despite these glaring deficiencies, and despite the fact that they had been apparent since early August, nothing was done to alleviate them.

A January 12 teleconference held by Williams with public affairs officers in the Gulf highlighted the near-total lack of serious planning and practice of the new public affairs policy during Desert Shield. Four days before Desert Storm was to begin, Williams was just beginning to elucidate the role of the escorts and to describe how the groundrules should be applied during security review. Comments and questions from public affairs officers in Saudi Arabia make it clear that they did not fully understand how to act in their new roles. As Steven Katz, who helped collate and analyze Desert Shield/Desert Storm public affairs documents for the Senate Governmental Affairs committee hearings, recounted:

> By the conclusion of the 2-1/2 hour teleconference, no reference was ever made to any supporting Public Affairs Guidance, or instructions for implementation, or interpretation by the military. When a high-ranking public affairs officer was later asked if the teleconference provided as little concrete direction as it appeared by listening to it later on tape, he responded curtly, "Yes, and I had to sit there and listen to the whole thing."[92]

Katz went on to note that

> A review of the Public Affairs Guidance issued by the Department of Defense, Central Command, and other authorities during Operation Desert Shield and Desert Storm reveals that there was more official guidance for planning the homecoming events and parades than instructions for implementing the ground rules for "security review" or "escorting" the media.[93]

The lack of attention paid to the details of escorting and security review suggests that no one anticipated the problems that arose, or at least their magnitude. It is also possible that worries did exist, but that no one was ready to admit them to Williams at such a late date. The result was that the military's public affairs team headed into Desert Storm with minimal preparation, minimal guidance, and minimal support from either Central Command or the Pentagon.

Desert Storm Public Affairs

Predictably, Desert Storm public affairs operations reflected the neglected status of public affairs within the military generally and during Desert Shield in particular. No part of the process worked as smoothly as officials had envisioned. Many public affairs officers were horrified by how poorly the system functioned during the ground war. At the same time, many of the military's professional judgments about the press influenced its interactions with reporters. Whereas the Army as a whole tended to push the press away, the Marines welcomed journalists, reflecting their contrasting professional interests in using the press. At the level of the individual commander and certainly with public affairs escorts a similar dynamic operated. In some cases officers hopeful of good publicity invited reporters to stay with their units. In other cases officers wary of the press refused to allow pools to cover their units. Likewise, many escorts aided reporters considerably, but many inhibited open reporting and tried to manage journalists' activities to prevent negative reporting of the military.

As the air war heated up, the public affairs system began to feel the strain. On January 17, as promised, the Pentagon delivered 126 more journalists and media personnel to Dhahran, ballooning the press corps there to over 700.[94] Under the current pool system, only the two eighteen-member pools existed to cover the hundreds of thousands of Army and Marine ground troops in the field. This left roughly 700 journalists in Dhahran frustrated and desperate to find some action. After repeated protests by the press, Central Command relented and expanded the pool system, adding eleven seven-member "quick reaction" pools to cover breaking events and another two of the larger pools to cover ground forces. Later five of the smaller pools were converted to coverage of the forces in the field, reflecting the press' abiding interest in covering those troops closest to where the action would be.[95]

With press access to the battlefield limited by the pools, public affairs escorts had to deal with those lucky reporters who had gotten a slot. The escorts' job entailed making sure the pool found its appropriate destinations in the desert, keeping reporters company to make sure they did not get in the way or go places they should not go, reviewing pool reports for security violations, and making sure that those reports got back to the JIB. Public affairs escorts, by most accounts, turned in a spotty performance on the whole, though there were occasional bright spots.

Officially, the Pentagon's public affairs policy dictated that escorts were not to interfere in any way with reporting. It became apparent quickly, however, that many escorts operated under a different interpretation of the rules. Many journalists complained that their escorts glared at the troops they were interviewing so much that enlisted personnel were scared to give honest answers to questions. On several occasions escorts were reported to have jumped in front of television cameras during interviews and demanded a halt to the filming when a subject came up they felt was inappropriate. Despite Pete Williams' assurances that such behavior was not condoned by Pentagon policy, and despite attempts by JIB leaders to put an end to the more hostile practices, escort officers in the field simply had too much autonomy for effective oversight from Dhahran.[96] Even Williams admitted after the war:

> We could have done a better job of helping reporters in the field. Judging from what I've heard from the reporters who went out on the pools, we had some outstanding escorts. But we must improve that process. Escort officers shouldn't throw themselves in front of the camera when one of the troops utters a forbidden word. . . . We need to teach public affairs personnel how to do their jobs so that reporters won't feel their interview subjects are intimidated.[97]

Worse, however, and more subtle because it less obviously ran counter to stated policy, was the fact that public affairs escorts determined where reporters could and could not go, often for reasons having nothing to do with operational security. It seems, in fact, that some escorts enjoyed simply being able to deny journalists' requests to witness certain events or talk to particular people. This, more than anything, made it difficult for journalists to do their jobs. If they could not get to the front where the fighting was taking place, or to some unit to interview troops fresh from combat, then journalists could not even begin the reporting process.[98]

Security review also proved problematic, though not for the reason the press had feared at the outset. Despite widespread media distaste for letting the military review their copy, security review never emerged as a system of true censorship. Aside from several instances in which commanders or public affairs escorts took it upon themselves to edit or censor press copy, most press reports made it to the United States unscathed.[99] Of 1,351 pool reports filed during Desert Storm, only five ended up at the Pentagon for a final review. Four of these were published unchanged and one editor agreed to make suggested changes to a story about military intelligence operations and strategy.[100]

The unforeseen problem with security review was instead one of speed, caused by a lack of training and sufficient resources for dealing with such a volume of material. As Katz notes, "... the lack of training and guidance resulted in numerous conflicts between reporters and escorts, subjective decisions and judgments, delays in transmission, and some interference with news gathering. Few Public Affairs Officers had any idea what their colleagues might have decided in a similar situation, elsewhere in the theater."[101] By flagging a report for review, escort officers in fact dealt many stories a death blow. Chances were good that the story would be worthless by the time it had been transmitted back to the JIB, reviewed by the overworked staff, and approved for release, especially during the ground war. Journalists decried any extra delays in getting their copy to their news desks, but by this point there was nothing the military could do. It had only so many public affairs officers to do the job.

But by far the weakest link in the military's public affairs setup was its inability to get reports back speedily to the JIB during the ground war. Even Richard Cheney's glowing report to Congress on the conduct of the war admitted that much work needed to be done to ensure that reports made it to the public on time. Trying to put the best face on the numbers did not help much: sixty-nine percent of pool reports made it back to the JIB in less than two days, and 10% took over three days.[102] As John J. Fialka noted,

> Worst of all we faced a jury-rigged system to get our copy, film, audio, and videotapes back. Civil War reporters, using the new high technology of the telegraph, were able to send reports of the Battle of Bull Run to New York in 24 hours.
>
> In this lightning war, more often than not, technology stopped at the edge of the battlefield. Accounts of major battles took three or four days to reach New York because of a haphazard military courier system aptly dubbed the "pony express." One reporter's copy took as long as two weeks to make the eight-hour drive from the battle-

> field to Dhahran. A news photographer's film took 36 days. A television correspondent's videotape of two stories never got back at all.[103]

Desert Storm undoubtedly provided a difficult environment for maintaining a steady flow of reports from the battlefield to the rear. The distances involved were massive, hundreds of miles in most cases, and the speed of the of the military's advance kept outstripping the accommodations public affairs had made to take pool reports from one station to the next on the way to Dhahran.

The biggest obstacle to getting reports back to the JIB, however, was not the rigorous conditions but simply the lack of planning and the corresponding lack of critical equipment and transportation, just as had been the case in Just Cause.[104] As Schwarzkopf's chief public affairs officer, Captain Ron Wildermuth later admitted, "much of the equipment requested for public affairs support was diverted to fill priority combat and combat support shortages. This left public affairs in the position of trying to lease vehicles and borrow critical office equipment."[105] Officers in Dhahran tried their best to improvise, but by their own account could not counter the effects of poor planning.[106]

Other Military Public Affairs Activities

While journalists struggled with the pool system, the military, like the White House, took advantage of the opportunity to advance its interests through briefings in Riyadh. The JIB in Riyadh held 98 briefings, 53 on the record, 45 on background. Over 100 briefings were given at the Pentagon. In each case, the military was able to provide or withhold information as it desired, always able to argue that something could not be discussed for security reasons, certain that reporters had little way of checking on the accuracy or context of the military's claims. Nor was the military anxious to have reporters checking the accuracy of its briefings. Barry Zorthian, chief of information in Vietnam from 1964 to 1968, used to tell reporters, "Don't take my word for it, go and see for yourselves." In contrast, at a news conference on January 23 General Colin Powell revealed little information in response to questions but instead offered this suggestion to the media: "Trust me." Powell's brief but revealing remark illustrates the role the military wanted the press to play during the war.[107]

Though reporters were not particularly happy with the amount of newsworthy information provided, the military certainly found the briefings an invaluable opportunity to polish its image with the public and put the most flattering gloss on the war's progress. One way in which the military did this with exceptional success was by providing television networks with its gun camera footage of smart bombs hitting their targets crisply and without causing collateral damage. Despite occasional grousing that they were never shown any footage in which a bomb missed its target, the networks never failed to use the dramatic film in their reports. The constant repetition of these shots seems to have made an indelible impression on the public. Michael Deaver, Reagan's chief television specialist, gave the military high marks for its efforts: "The Department of Defense has done an excellent job of managing the news in an almost classic way. . . . There's plenty of access to some things, and at least one visual a day. If you were going to hire a public relations firm to do the media relations for an international event, it couldn't be done any better than this is being done."[108]

Another way to take advantage of its control over access to the battlefield was the Pentagon's Hometown News Media Project. During Desert Shield this program paid for journalists to fly to Saudi Arabia to link up with their hometown units in the desert for ninety-six hours and then fly back home. Publicly the Pentagon argued that the rationale for the program was that it would keep the public in closer touch with units that might otherwise not receive media attention, and that small town papers could not afford to fly over to Saudi Arabia in the first place. Privately, however, officials admitted that the remarkable access given to these hometowners was a result of the realization that the stories they wrote would be highly supportive of the troops and of the operation. They would not have enough time to really dig for any news deeper than human interest pieces on how the troops were doing, and the fact that many of the reporters were from towns heavily intertwined with and dependent on the military for their livelihood ensured that no one was likely to bite the hand that fed them. The Hometown News Media Project offended other journalists in Saudi Arabia who had been unable to get out into the field at all. Many criticized the government's transparent attempt to trade access for public relations gains.[109]

Despite the military's poor planning, public affairs policy did what the White House and the military wanted it to do: It restricted press access to the battlefield, ensured that no troublesome television coverage beamed into American living rooms from the battlefield, and maintained operational security through review of press reports. Most important of all, it also secured the government's domination of information and allowed the administration to shape the news reaching the public about the war to a degree unprecedented in modern times. As it turned out, in fact, the military's incompetence at public affairs enhanced government control over the media. Administration officials often knew what would be news before journalists as a result of the press restrictions and delays they caused. This turned out to be especially true during the ground war, when the delay in getting press reports to Dhahran during allowed Schwarzkopf to scoop the press and give the public all the details of victory personally.

THE IMPACT OF GOVERNMENT MEDIA STRATEGY ON THE PRESS

The massive outpouring of news from the Persian Gulf during Desert Storm provides compelling evidence that government restrictions can make independent wartime reporting almost impossible and thus influence the shape of war news in ways favorable to the president. By limiting access to the battlefield, and thereby to military officers and their troops, the government forced the press to rely almost entirely on senior government sources for hard news about the conflict, especially the fighting. Once again the government ensured that there would be almost no press coverage of combat, particularly by television crews. The press was left to write combat stories based solely on interviews with those involved, without adding any detail or context gained from firsthand experience of the battles. Many journalists, unable to get near the real story, made do by writing fluff pieces about homesick troops or troops playing volleyball. In the hard news vacuum left by the media, the administration and military filled the airwaves and newspapers with their own optimistic versions of events, and with their own carefully chosen television pictures of combat. They, and not the press, had the upper hand in determining what would be front page news. Further, the restrictions left the press unable to verify rosy official statements, a fact that became clear after the war as journalists began to poke holes in the very statements they had reported as fact weeks or months before. Press coverage of the Gulf War never became an obstacle to the Bush Administration, and may well have helped it to bolster public support throughout the war.

The Impact of Restrictions on Newsgathering

There were essentially two options open to journalists wishing to cover Desert Storm. Given the circumstances, the restrictions, and the geography of Saudi Arabia, neither option thrilled reporters much. First, a journalist could accept the pool system and work out of Dhahran, watching televised briefings and culling pool reports until a slot in the pool opened. This route assured journalists material for a daily story, and a chance for better once they got a pool slot. On the downside, covering a war from a hotel is not most journalists' idea of a good time—the real story was out in the desert. And worse, being in a pool was no guarantee of a good story, because it meant letting the military dictate where to go and what to see.

The other option was to reject the pool system and "go unilateral," venturing out into the desert, evading media-hostile military types and looking for a unit that would agree to let a journalist do a story. Of the 1,400 or so journalists occupying Saudi Arabia by the ground war, only a handful chose to attempt unilateral reporting and for good reason. It was dangerous. Several journalists wound up hostages of the Iraqis, and many lost themselves repeatedly, often in less desirable areas like minefields. Even if a journalist did manage to locate a U.S. military unit, there was a good chance of being detained and sent back to Dhahran with the threat of deportation by the Saudis. Nonetheless, the attraction of traveling and reporting freely without an escort or having to submit copy to security review pulled strongly enough to tempt more and more journalists into the desert as time went on. Once the U.S. victory seemed immanent, scores of journalists broke ranks and jumped in their jeeps heading for Kuwait City to report its liberation.

The Pools

The pool system made it impossible for journalists to balance the access/autonomy equation to their satisfaction. A journalist could remain independent, free from escorts and security review, simply by reporting the war from the hotel and rejecting the pool. To do so, of course, meant that a journalist had zero access to the military, to its high-tech weaponry, or to the battlefield where the biggest story in the world was taking place. For most news organizations and most journalists, this was an unthinkable situation. Gaining access to the battlefield was a duty, not an option. The obvious (and safest) answer was to join the pool, thereby ensuring that a journalist would catch at least a small slice of the story firsthand. In a journalist's eyes, however, joining the pool meant sacrificing almost all independence. A journalist could not determine where to go, what to see, or how long to stay somewhere. In essence, according to reporters, the military became their assignment editor. Nor, quite often, could a journalist interview people or film a report without an escort officer staring over his shoulder and intimidating his subjects. And once he handed his report over for the final indignity of security review, he had to worry that if the story was negative his escort might make the war that much more difficult to cover in the future.[110] Under these circumstances, though being part of the pool was clearly preferable to sitting in Dhahran, no journalist could feel proud at having to submit so thoroughly to the military's rules.

The decision to work through the pools and surrender one's autonomy did not, however, guarantee access. In fact, the military's system made access so difficult for individual journalists to achieve that many declared it "censorship by access."[111] At the outset of Desert Storm there were only 36 pool slots for between 700-1000 journalists. By the beginning of the ground war there were One hundred ninety-two pool slots for over 1,400 journalists. 192 was indeed, as civilian and military officials hastened to point out, a far greater number than had ever covered a battle at one time before. But the pools did not always find themselves on the battlefield covering the troops. Only two were permanently assigned to cover Army and Marine units in the field. R. W. Apple, the *New York Times'* bureau chief in Dhahran, found that on any given day most pools were elsewhere. On February 12, he noted, only three of fifteen pools were in the field.[112] This amounted to a grievous lack of access for today's media, whose expectations far exceed those of journalists in earlier eras. And from the perspective of the individual journalist, in particular, the system looked very restrictive. The odds of a journalist being in one of the pools during the ground war were roughly one in seven at best, and not all of the pools were attached to ground units.

Getting into a pool, moreover, did not mean one got to stay in the pool. There were permanent slots for the larger news organizations, but the rest of the slots rotated among the remaining scores of organizations. Before the war, pool membership would rotate after a pool had carried out its mission, if it was a quick reaction pool, or after two weeks, if it was one of the larger combat pools. Journalists had their names on the very long list for pool slots and as slots opened would work their way up to the top. Once a journalist had had a turn in the pool, it could be weeks before he or she could get back in another pool, if at all. Access for the individual journalist was thus spotty at best. Many correspondents, especially from smaller or specialty media outlets, never managed to get into the pool.[113]

Adding considerably to the media's woes, journalists for the first time became their own jailers in the Gulf. At their own insistence, representatives of the press ran the pool system, laying down the rules for deciding which news organizations and journalists would get pool slots. Each medium had its own system for determining which reporters would go with the pools and how the pool product would be shared. The television pool, which included the three major networks and CNN, was run by a single representative named by the networks to assign reporters to the pools. The photography pool was run by five editors, one from each of the wire services and the three major newsmagazines.

These five men not only determined how the pool slots would be allocated but also which twenty photos (out of around 6,000) would make up the daily set of pool photos to be transmitted back to the United States. The print pool was both the largest and the least well coordinated of the pools. According to John Fialka, the *Wall Street Journal* correspondent who had the dubious honor of running the print pool for a time, the print pool wavered from democracy to dictatorship depending on who was in charge. Together, the decisions made by each of the media groups would coalesce into the pools covering the action.[114] Few were pleased by the results, as John J. Fialka relates:

> And we had a good, hard look at each other. Preparing the news is like making sausage: it is not necessarily a handsome process in the best conditions. But we found we had helped make a pool system that was geared for multiple failures. We had created rules that impeded coverage, and some of us were more intent on beggaring our competition than on participating in the creation of a large mosaic of reportage that was needed to make sense of this war as it swiftly unfolded. We were pack journalism forced into a girdle. When it came undone, so did we.[115]

Two facts ensured the infighting and frustration caused by this system. First, there were always far more correspondents waiting for spots than there were spots in the pool. Second, the more powerful news organizations cooperated to keep reporters from smaller organizations out the pools. The press had argued that it had to control pool membership in order to make sure that neither the Pentagon nor Saudi Arabia was allowed to keep certain reporters out of pools for political reasons. Though most members of the press corps agreed with this reasoning in theory, in practice things did not work so smoothly. The print press, for example, was dominated at the outset of the crisis by a group which came to be called the "Sacred Ten," national news organizations which had arrived in force early in the Gulf. These organizations worked with the Pentagon during Desert Shield to ensure that they would have permanent pool slots, leaving all others to fight over the remaining openings. Nevertheless, the group was continually unhappy with the pool rules because their organizations were still only allowed one combat pool slot, leaving them unable to deploy all of their journalistic talent to the field. As a result, they shamelessly used their position of power to ensure that their reporters would get choice pool slots in the field, relegating smaller publications to tours of Navy ships floating far away from the action.[116] The Sacred Ten's early arrival also meant that it set many of the rules under which journalists could get pool slots, a fact that they used to their competitive advantage. One widely discussed example of this was the failure of David Fulgham, a reporter for *Aviation Week and Space Technology*, to secure a print pool slot. Fulgham was shut out because *Time, Newsweek*, and *U.S. News and World Report* had declared early on that their correspondents would be the only ones from newsmagazines to get slots in the print pool.[117]

The media's bickering over who would cover the war added to the government's control. As Williams peddled version after version of the groundrules and guidelines, all most news executives could think about was whether or not they would be able to secure a pool slot.[118] They were not happy about the pool rules, but on the eve of war worrying about the rules took a back seat to making sure they would not lose out to their competition by getting shut out of the pool all together. The infighting over the pools prevented the media from acting collectively to pressure the government for greater access to the battlefield. Instead, as Fialka laments, a "beggar thy neighbor" system had emerged. The national news organizations with permanent spots in the pool did not want to endanger their access at the last moment just in the name of solidarity with their smaller colleagues. The organizations that came later to the Gulf decried the pool, but were happy enough as long as they could wangle elite pool status, as several large regional newspapers managed to do. Only the small and specialty media organizations continued to complain about the system's fundamental challenge to the media as a whole–the unprecedented fact that it did not allow all those who wanted to do so to cover the war. As a result, efforts to pressure the government into loosening the reporting curbs were hamstrung from the beginning.

Further, the media unintentionally created a stake for themselves in the running of the pool system during the war. Reporters were no longer as appreciative of their brothers' and sisters' efforts to evade the pool. Those working inside the system were in fact often loathe to permit others to profit by working outside it. This was especially true if unilaterals tried to report in an area in which a pool was already operating. Those in the pool felt that they were working at an unfair disadvantage compared to the unilaterals, who did not have to worry about escorts or security review. The tension came to a head during the battle of Khafji. Several reporters, having gotten word of a ground battle, set out on their own to find the action. Robert Fisk, a reporter for the *Independent*, a major London daily, was one of those unilaterals covering Khafji. When he bumped into the pool that had belatedly made it to the battle, Fisk reports that one of the pool reporters "responded with an obscenity and shouted: 'You'll prevent us from working. You're not allowed here. Get out. Go back to Dhahran.'"[119] Thus, an ironic form of peer pressure emerged. The press corps, which under different circumstances would have applauded and encouraged unilateral efforts, in fact discouraged reporters from going outside the system.[120]

Once journalists had managed to secure a pool slot, they were often unhappy to find that the access they had gained was only somewhat better than nothing. During Desert Shield, the military had reduced the interest and news value of pool visits to troops by rehearsing what the journalists were to see and report as news. Lucy Spiegel, a producer for CBS, described the typical sense of frustration:

> They would have already called ahead and everything was set up. You never really surprised anybody. . . . Like everything in the military, you had a mission to accomplish and that was to see, let's say, an air force base. You'd watch them take off and you'd watch them come down. You'd interview the crew and you'd go and watch them eat a meal and you'd talk to the CO, and you'd come home. . . . There will never be any journalist award given for that stretch. There were no great investigative stories. There couldn't be. You were too controlled. If you did go off the road and they found out about it, or you ran into somebody who reported you, you were brought in and your hands were slapped, . . .They'd yell at you: "You had no business being up there without an escort. You know better than that."[121]

During Desert Storm, things got little better. The travails of correspondents working under the baleful glare of escorts, the fickle and time-consuming security review process, and the outdated "pony express" courier system have been duly noted. But worst of all, reporters discovered that being in a combat pool did not mean that one would witness combat. On any given day during the air war, as noted, a majority of the pools was grounded in Dhahran. And during the ground war being in the pool often meant simply that one would get to ride well behind the front lines with an escort uninterested in taking a drive into the dangerous traffic near the front.

No precise numbers are available on this issue, but it appears from anecdotal evidence that a majority of the reporters who accompanied U.S. Army and Marine units during the ground war phase of Desert Storm did not see actual combat. Instead, they had to write war stories based solely on interviews with troops and commanders who had come back from the front lines to where the pools were located. Though there is nothing wrong with interviews—they are, of course, one of the journalist's primary tools—any journalist who failed to witness the battles he or she reported would have been devastated.

Christopher Hanson reports a typical example of the problem faced in trying to cover the war as it happened. Hanson was a member of a combat pool attached to the Army's VII Corps and accompanied its Second Armored Cavalry regiment, which would lead one of the critical attacks into Iraq. In return for being allowed to ride with the unit, Hanson had to agree to ride with a public affairs officer at all times. Hanson consented, but found himself riding well behind the action with the regimental headquarters detachment. When he asked his public affairs escort if they could break away and join an M-1 or Bradley Fighting Vehicle squadron, he was put off. From behind the lines Hanson lamented, "The regiment's heavy armor is battling the Republican Guards along a twenty-mile front, but from this distance I can make no sense of the action. What could have been my biggest story ever is playing itself out, and I'm missing it."[122] Hanson never did manage to witness combat during the brief offensive, but notes that even so his pool experience turned out to be more rewarding than most, and that many correspondents had wound up even further from combat than he.[123]

Unilaterals

As a result of the pool system's restrictions on access to battlefield, most reporters wound up covering the war from their hotel, heavily dependent on the military for information. As Kim Murphy of the *Los Angeles Times* remarked, "A friend took a picture of me the other day taking notes [from a military briefing] in front of a television set. That's what being a war correspondent has come to."[124] A few hardy souls, however, refused to bow to military restrictions or the dangers of the desert.

These hardy souls numbered in the dozens, cumulatively, but it appears that far fewer were actually active at any given time, with the peak coming as reporters rushed to cover the liberation of Kuwait City near the end of the war. The reasons for this were fairly simple. First, of course, it was dangerous. Wandering through the desert without cities or obvious landmarks to guide oneself would be difficult enough, but the real trick was to find a friendly military unit while not detouring through a minefield or into enemy territory. The sad fate of CBS correspondent Bob Simon and his crew stands testimony to the dangers. Simon and his crew were taken hostage by the Iraqis after getting lost near the Kuwaiti border and held until after the war. They were beaten and otherwise mistreated while American bombs fell all around, on one occasion nearly killing them. Several other journalists were also taken hostage during the war, and many more managed to escape similar fates only through blind luck.[125]

A second reason for not going unilateral for many organizations was the expense and the lack of available manpower. Not all news organizations could afford the extra equipment a reporter venturing outside the pool system would need. Nor did every organization have enough people in Dhahran to spare one or more people trekking around in the desert, only sporadically sending stories home. Third, the prospect of covering a military on the battlefield must have loomed as a daunting task for the vast majority of reporters in the Gulf who had no military experience themselves, and no experience covering war. Knowing who and what to look for, not to mention what to say about them once having found them, would simply have exceeded most reporters' limits of competence. Finally, of course, there was the threat of being detained, poorly treated (a few journalists were even beaten by U.S. military personnel), and possibly deported during the biggest story of the decade. The correspondents who did go unilateral came overwhelmingly from the national newspapers, wire services, the television networks, and the newsmagazines. These organizations had reporters available who had covered the military and covered wars around the world, and they had the sophisticated technologies that would allow their reporters to operate in the desert without aid from the military. But for most, the uncertain benefits of traveling alone simply did not outweigh the many risks.[126]

To report from outside the pool system and without access to communications facilities in Dhahran required both ingenuity and good old-fashioned high technology. The technology, though advanced in terms of war coverage, was already standard fare for peacetime media operations. Several reporters rented jeeps equipped with cellular telephones, which allowed them to phone reports straight into their editors without having to suffer the delays of the military's courier system. Several correspondents also faxed their reports in from a hotel in Hafar al Batin, a Saudi town sixty miles from the Iraqi border and far from where they were allowed to go under public affairs guidelines. The biggest consumer of advanced technology, unsurprisingly, was television. Television, because it depends so heavily on equipment that is both bulky and obvious, had a much harder time undertaking unilateral coverage. Getting cameras past roadblocks was a much more difficult endeavor than just getting oneself past as print reporters could do. And to transmit television footage from the desert required an enormous logistical support system. David Green of CBS noted of his three-vehicle caravan, "We had state-of-the-art equipment, seven boxes weighing about a ton. We had three generators, two satellite phones, two LORANs [navigation devices]. We had enough gas and enough water for from ten days to two weeks."[127] Due to television's outsized needs, its big unilateral adventure came only near the end of the war, when the networks raced each other to Kuwait City to be the first to beam back pictures of its celebrating citizens and the victorious Marines.

Once equipped with the necessary technological gadgetry, a reporter had to make sure he stayed free of the military's long reach. Most unilaterals, it seems, were caught at least once by the military. By mid-February, according to one count, over two dozen had been detained while attempting to cover the war from outside the pool system.[128] Nevertheless, many managed to evade the military for long stretches of time. Chris Hedges of the *New York Times*, for example, though detained briefly twice, reported independently for two months from the field. Hedges, who speaks Arabic, took refuge with Saudi families, dressed in military garb and painted his jeep to bluff his way through roadblocks, and bugged out whenever the military police showed up. For his efforts, he managed to spend much more time with troops preparing for war than most reporters in the pools.[129] In general, however, despite their creativity, the military's rigid press policy made it difficult for unilaterals to spend as much time as they wanted with units in the field, or to piece together a coherent picture of the conflict.

The high points of the unilaterals' contribution to the press corps's overall news gathering efforts were beating the pool to the battle of Khafji and later entering Kuwait City before the Marines. At Khafji, firsthand unilateral reporting clashed with official statements about the fighting, and eventually forced U.S. officials to recant. U.S. military officials claimed initially that Saudi and Qatari forces had done all of the fighting to eject Iraqi forces from the Saudi town. In fact, as unilaterals had discovered, the Marines had provided the critical tactical air strikes and heavy artillery support, without which Saudi forces would have had a much more difficult time. When reports, including footage from unilateral television crews, reached the United States, the military had to admit the Marines' role, which it had downplayed for the political purpose of praising the Saudis' efforts.[130] Later, in beating the pools and the Marines to Kuwait City, unilaterals mainly enjoyed being first, as there was little to report immediately except that the Iraqis had fled.[131]

Apart from these journalistic coups the gains from going unilateral came more from salvaging one's pride than from producing meaningful coverage of the war. Even Chris Hedges' praise for the unilaterals reveals their limited gains:

> The fine stories on the Egyptian forces filed by Forest Sawyer of ABC News and Tony Horwitz of *The Wall Street Journal*, for example, could only have been done by going outside the system. Managed information always has an unreal, stale quality. And while none of us broke scandals or uncovered gross abuses, we were able to present an uncensored picture of life at the front.[132]

What Hedges fails to mention, of course, is that no one cared about the Egyptian forces. And conspicuously absent from his notes is any discussion of the contribution of unilaterals to true combat coverage. This is not surprising, as unilaterals played almost no role in covering combat after Khafji. The "flavor of life at the front" stories were important, no doubt, to a complete picture of the conflict. But unilaterals were not able to seize victory where the rest of the press corps had failed. John Fialka realistically summarizes the unilaterals' contribution:

> But a study of the coverage of the war shows that, despite the life-risking chances that many of the unilaterals took, they could operate only at the fringes of this war. For the most part they could not answer the question that kept Americans glued to their television sets and devouring newspapers: What was going on in the battlefield? With few exceptions, the lead stories were drawn from pool reports or official briefings and not from unilaterals' accounts.[133]

Covering the War from Baghdad

There was one other way to cover the war—from Baghdad. This remained primarily the province of television and in particular of CNN and Peter Arnett throughout the war. Several major American newspapers with correspondents in Baghdad pulled them out as the UN deadline approached, fearing the risks were too great. After the war started, the Iraqis expelled all foreign correspondents except Arnett, leaving him alone with a large slice of the world's biggest story. Eventually the Iraqis allowed other television crews back in the country, but no one was as widely monitored, praised, or criticized for their war reporting as Arnett and CNN.

Reporting from Baghdad after it had suffered allied bombing was a technical challenge. CNN, for example, was only able to continue live reporting during the opening stages of the air war because it had secured months before from the Iraqi government a "four-wire" telephone link for $15,000 a month. The four-wire line allowed CNN to send a steady signal back to the United States even when local power lines in Baghdad had been cut by the bombing. This gave CNN its first big prize on the first night of the air war, when its competitors' broadcasts went up in smoke with the power lines, leaving Arnett and two colleagues with the only live (audio-only) reports from that dramatic scene. Arnett also made regular use throughout the war of an INMARSAT phone. The satellite phone was the size of a suitcase and was powered by a portable generator, and allowed CNN anchors in Atlanta to interview Arnett live.[134]

In addition to the technical hurdles, correspondents in Baghdad faced severe obstacles to getting the story. Reporting at the pleasure of the Iraqi government meant that they had neither autonomy nor access. They could go only where the Iraqis took them, report only on what the Iraqis let them, had to submit their copy to censorship, and were not allowed (for the most part) to broadcast live. The reporters had no access to Iraqi officials, or even in general to Iraqi citizens. They had no way to shed light either on crucial domestic political issues or on how the war was progressing on the Iraqi side. In short, the potential in Baghdad was quite limited.[135]

These limitations fueled debate among journalists over the usefulness of coverage from Iraq. As Richard Beeston of *The Times* (London), who covered the war from Iraq, noted, "It became harder for journalists to justify their work, when it consisted exclusively of one topic (civilian casualties), which served the interests of the Iraqi war effort but failed to address the central questions of the war, namely, Saddam's survivability, the morale of the Iraqi people and military and the country's fighting capability."[136] Reporters in the United States find it distasteful enough to allow the American government to take advantage of the press in this way and are always on guard against such situations. It is thus understandable that reporters would have had doubts.

Supporters of the media presence in Baghdad, on the other hand, pointed out that television reports from Iraq had revealed what otherwise would have been invisible to the public: the results of the ferocious allied bombing campaign. The graphic footage of the death of hundreds of Iraqi women and children at the Amiriya bunker/shelter, for example, revealed to the American public for the first time the other side of the air war–the fact that innocent people were dying. These pictures, argued some, were even more important given the U.S. government's efforts to portray the air war as a humane, high-tech way to wage war. Though the use of precision-guided munitions certainly made the bombing of Baghdad less destructive than past city bombing campaigns, CNN's presence reminded people that even so, war has a terrible human cost.[137]

CNN's war reporting helped cement its international reputation. But many Americans were outraged that an American news organization should be serving up enemy-approved reports from Baghdad. It was obvious to everyone that the Iraqis would not have let Arnett or other journalists stay if they had not believed doing so would aid the Iraqi cause. Also clear to CNN watchers was the Iraqi strategy: Show the American public enough Iraqi civilian casualties to turn it against the war.[138] CNN's participation in this strategy offended many politicians in Washington. Twenty-one members of the House wrote a letter to CNN saying as much. And Senator Alan K. Simpson (R-Wyoming) complained bitterly in public about CNN's presence in Baghdad and argued that Arnett "is what we used to call in my day a sympathizer."[139] Nor did CNN win many friends in the military. Colonel Harry G. Summers, the well-known author of *On Strategy*, noted in congressional testimony that reporting from the enemy capital during World War II would have been treason, and argued that CNN's reports were elements in Iraq's psychological warfare strategy. CNN's reports of captured allied pilots being forced by the Iraqis to criticize the war evoked a similar conclusion from General Schwarzkopf:

> And I didn't like the idea that I was seeing them [the pilots] on CNN. I will have to state that openly. I did resent, you know, CNN aiding and abetting an enemy who was violating the Geneva Convention by putting, you know, that's a clear violation of the Geneva Convention. Yet CNN was broadcasting them to the world; that bothers me.[140]

In hindsight it may be of some comfort to those upset with CNN to realize that Iraq's propaganda attempts backfired almost completely. Instead of turning the American public against the war, if anything they stiffened American's resolve to deal harshly with Hussein. A poll taken in the wake of the Amiriya bombing incident found that 79% of the public blamed Saddam Hussein and Iraq, not the U.S. military, for the civilian deaths.[141] And any sympathy Hussein might have generated by revealing the toll on his people was erased by his parading of captured pilots, obviously shaken and frightened, across American television screens.[142] Perhaps even more reassuring to some, CNN's reports managed not to turn the public against the war but rather against CNN itself. CNN's military analyst, retired Air Force Major General Perry Smith, recounts that CNN's coverage from Baghdad spurred thousands of angry letters from viewers who simply could not understand what Arnett was doing there.[143]

Regardless of its ultimate effect, CNN's reports from Baghdad reverberated in Washington with a potent resonance not generated by reports from the press pools in Saudi Arabia. Of the many reports that prompted administration concern, one instance deserves particular mention—the bombing of the bunker/shelter in Amiriya. Images of the hundreds of civilians killed who had been inside provided the first graphic evidence of the air war's human toll, precisely the sort of thing presidents and militaries hate to see on television. The media immediately seized on the incident to illustrate that the government's claims of precision bombing were exaggerated, and columnists began opining that too much more of such coverage could sap public support for the air war.[144] The administration agreed, and as a result stopped bombing urban command centers to prevent antiwar sentiment from growing in response to the deaths of any more Iraqi civilians. Given the importance attached by the military to destroying military buildings in and around Baghdad, this response was a remarkable example of the power of the press during wartime to affect the prosecution of a war.[145]

The Impact of Restrictions and Public Relations on Press Coverage[146]

The national interest camp could not have been happier about the coverage of Desert Storm, at least in terms of what the media was able to show of the actual fighting. The air war, as air wars usually are, was very difficult to cover except from air bases. Nothing of interest happens at air bases, of course, except that planes take off and land there. This was in fact the bulk of television's contribution to air war coverage—planes in the night taking off on bombing missions. Reporters, with one exception, never managed to accompany a bombing mission, and had no practical way to venture into Iraqi territory to find out what impact the bombing campaign was having. Except for CNN coverage from Baghdad during this time, press coverage was limited to recitations of military-provided statistics: how many sorties had flown that day, during the war to date, what the presumed success rate was of those missions, what targets had been struck, and the like. As a result, press coverage of the air war was bland, and quickly took a back seat to the military's other offering: gun-camera footage of precision guided bombs closing in on their targets, flying down air shafts and destroying them neatly. These images, not independent work by journalists, became the most memorable air war press coverage.

As limited as press coverage of the air war was, the clearest example of the effect of the reporting restrictions was coverage of the ground war. The lack of eyewitness newspaper accounts of combat and the complete absence of television evidence that a ground war was taking place made it clear that the government's press restrictions had succeeded for the third time in a decade in preventing the American public from seeing, hearing, or reading about the horrors of war while it was underway.[147] As Guy Gugliotta, a reporter for the Washington Post, complained:

> To hear the military officials tell it, yesterday was the biggest day of the war: the Iraqi Army was in full retreat; Marines were on the outskirts of Kuwait; U.S. Army tanks were fighting Iraq's Republican

> Guard; thousands of enemy soldiers were dropping their rifles, raising their hands and marching into allied custody.
>
> There are 142 combat pool reporters accompanying U.S. ground forces in Kuwait, Iraq, and Saudi Arabia. Yesterday, hardly any of them filed a dispatch that arrived in the United States in time for yesterday's evening news or today's morning newspaper. *And none provided a firsthand account of ground combat. By design or by default, the biggest day of the war was one of the most underreported days.*[148] (my emphasis)

Instead of vivid and moving press coverage of the first hours of the long awaited ground war, the American public got General Norman Schwarzkopf's famous briefings. Instead of independent assessments of how the ground war had gone, there was Schwarzkopf's personal assessment. Instead of graphic footage of tanks in the desert, viewers were greeted by Schwarzkopf's jowly face, flushed with excitement and success. Schwarzkopf, who had begged Cheney to relax his news blackout after it became clear that the war was a rout, went on television and told the nation and the world that the allies were cruising to victory, while journalists sat at his feet and took notes.[149]

The press' inability to offer compelling coverage of the war allowed the military to step in and take over as both news source and news provider. The military's ability to provide the public with information without sifting it through the usual filter of the adversarial press was for some the most important aspect of the government's success. As veteran press-watcher and White House media strategy guru David Gergen notes:

> The argument over pools, as important as it is, unfortunately misses the larger significance of what the military achieved in press management during the war: an unprecedented dominance over the pictures and words conveyed by the media. . . . In the Persian Gulf the military came ready to provide its own home videos, better than anything the press could concoct, and the pictures that burned their way into the public psyche were of precision-guided bombs moving in on their targets—perfect bull's-eyes, no blood, thank you. . . . The press simply could not compete.[150]

With the military scooping the press at its daily briefings and providing the most exciting television footage of the war, correspondents were left to write what were often called "hi-mom stories." CBS producer Lucy Spiegel listed some of the stories that journalists found themselves doing for lack of access to hard news:

> Arrival of troops; not enough mail; the weather: it's too hot, it's too cold; fill in the blank: the helicopter doesn't work, the gun won't work, too much sand, too much dirt, too much whatever; women are going to war; husbands and wives are going to war; should women be going to war?; making a reunion between the husbands and the wives or the wives and the husbands . . .[151]

These stories certainly are worth reading, but do nothing to add to a reader or viewer's knowledge of the real factors behind impending war and its outcome once underway. Nor, due to the military's escorts, were these stories even as revealing as they might otherwise have been. With troops so worried about the consequences should they say anything negative in front of an escort officer, most reporters believed that they were not often told how things really were among Desert Storm units.

Not even the media's most dreaded weapon—live television coverage—could operate effectively under the government's restrictions. Despite much discussion about CNN and the Gulf War being the first real-time war, the Gulf War was, in fact, a far cry from what people have predicted and feared from live television war coverage. The only thing remotely resembling live war coverage seen on television were the Patriot-Scud engagements over Israel and Saudi Arabia. They made dramatic television, but hardly could be said to mark new heights in war reporting. The most exciting live coverage was essentially a live telephone conversation played over television as Peter Arnett and company crouched in their Baghdad hotel room on the first night of the air war. This, too, had been done before, over the radio, by Edward R. Murrow during the bombing of London in World War II. To the dismay of the networks, few television crews came anywhere near the battlefield when it counted, and even fewer sent back material in time to be useful for the evening news.

Some press critics argued that even without the restrictions the press would have done a poor job in covering the war. Michael Massing argues that the press worked under the delusion that they could and should report the Gulf War as they had Vietnam. But Desert Storm, a large-scale high-intensity conventional war, demanded a different approach. Reporters, he argues, should have tried harder to gain perspective on the war by stepping away from the battlefield and analyzing the government's statements and actions.[152] Scott Armstrong argues that this weakness became evident during Desert Shield, ". . . American journalism, focused mostly on the parochial issues of invasion, hostages, and occupation, has by and large missed a chance to provide a meaningful context for the dramatic events."[153]

Peter Braestrup and several military commentators complain that today's media fared poorly in Desert Storm because they were largely unprepared for their task—coherently reporting a massive and complex political and military operation. Very few journalists have served in the military, only a small handful cover the Pentagon or military issues on a regular basis, and even fewer have spent any time in the field covering war. The result, say critics, was that the press could not make independent judgments of the military situation in the Gulf. Adding insult to injury, their ignorance of military affairs made journalists look foolish during briefings as they asked uninformed questions.[154] Jon Katz notes that television in particular suffered from an institutional lack of resources to comprehend and intelligently report the war: "Yet for years now the networks have been busily tossing onto the streets the very researchers, producers, commentators, and staff that could have helped carry out such a role. Instead we saw the sorry spectacle of network news hiring a squadron of generals to cover the war."[155] A more compassionate statement of this argument might be that, as Philip Knightley has argued, some wars simply transcend the ability of journalism to understand and explain on a day-by-day basis.[156] Either way, press coverage suffered, in the view of many, because journalists did not have the necessary tools to make sense of the war.

The ultimate test of how the government's restrictions affected reporting is to compare official statements reported by the press during the war with the facts as they came to be known after the war. In the case of the Gulf War, as in Grenada and Panama, revelations after the war indicate that the press' lack of independence and access allowed the government to mislead the press, whether purposely or not, by exaggerating its successes and omitting mention of failures and embarrassments. Even a reporter with the maximum possible access to the military found that truth could be scarce. *Washington Post* reporter Molly Moore, despite having accompanied Marine Commander Lt. General Walter Boomer throughout the war, argues that, "I learned more in the two weeks after the war than I learned during the entire war. . . . I think we're going to keep finding out things . . . nobody knew about at the time, in the ongoing reporting process. . . . The American public got only the military view of this war for the most part. There was not access to get independent information."[157]

The most common military half-truths of the war were its reports of the effectiveness of its various weapons. In the opening days of the air war, Lt. General Kelly asserted that 80% of allied sorties were successful. Later, when pressed, he admitted that it was difficult to assess the damage done by those missions, and the 80% figure meant only that 80% of the aircraft flew over their intended targets and dropped their payloads. It was only after the war, however, that the top officer of the Air Force, General Merrill McPeak, revealed that during the first ten days of the air war the weather had been so bad that on 40% of the missions pilots could not even see their primary targets.[158]

Other examples of exaggerated success were the Tomahawk cruise missile and the Patriot missile system. Though the Navy claimed a 98% effectiveness rating for the Tomahawk, it turned out that this meant only that 98% of the missiles were successfully launched. In fact, the Navy did not know how many missiles actually hit their intended targets when they were claiming this success rate, and only much later was it admitted that only 50% had struck their targets.[159] The Patriot missile's performance turned out to be a tangled web of misperceptions. The military initially claimed a near-perfect record of intercepting Scuds, and the administration touted the system widely. Later investigation by both independent scientists and the U.S. General Accounting Office, however, revealed that the method of rating the Patriot's success was simply to verify that a Patriot had been launched at an incoming Scud, without assessing whether the Patriot actually intercepted it. These investigations found that the Patriot's success was suspect, and eventually forced the military to back down further and further from their claims of success for the Patriot. Government investigators now argue that it is possible that the Patriot intercepted only one Scud throughout the war, hardly living up to its invincible image of Desert Storm.[160]

Journalists were also upset to discover that contrary to the Pentagon's carefully crafted impressions, the air war had not been nearly as "surgical" as they had been led to believe. Although all of the strike camera footage showed precision-guided bombs flying unerringly to their targets, only 9% of all the bombs dropped on Iraq and Iraqi forces were "smart bombs." The bulk of those dropped were unguided, many of them having been dropped on Iraqi troops from the B-52s that reporters were never allowed to go near during the war.[161]

More upsetting than inflated claims of performance, however, is an example that illustrates the very real potential for much more important issues to be hidden from the press during wartime. Patrick Sloyan of *Newsday* reported in September of 1991 on the use of U.S. tanks fitted with plows to bury Iraqi troops alive as U.S. forces breached Iraqi lines during the ground war. According to Sloyan's sources in the First Infantry Division (Mechanized), perhaps as many as a thousand Iraqis were buried alive by attacking U.S. units. Although there had been a press pool attached to the First, no pool journalists accompanied the units carrying out the operation, nor did the military volunteer the information to them. It was not until Sloyan got wind of the incident and investigated that it became public knowledge.[162] Clearly, such grim stories are not what either the military or the administration would have wanted to see in newspapers or on television news shows during the war. Sloyan's story would have been automatic front-page news. But the military delayed its publication for months by not mentioning the incident, by which point the story only made the inside pages, even in *Newsday*. Sloyan's story may be the first to appear only on the inside pages and yet win a Pulitzer Prize, as it did in April 1992. The fact that it took so long for such a remarkable incident to come to light suggests that the press simply does not even know where to begin asking questions about what happened during Desert Storm. There was so much journalists did not see or hear during the war that it is impossible to be sure whether or not there is more the public does not know about the war and how it was fought. Sloyan himself argued after the war that "If you look at what came over television for that period of time [the ground war], it had no bearing on what was going on."[163] Sloyan's story should serve not as an example of how the truth will eventually be revealed, but as an example of how well the government's restrictions worked in keeping the press from reporting any similar disturbing instances during the war when such revelations might have had some political impact on Bush or the military.

Taken in its entirety, press coverage emerged as a huge plus for the administration. Not only did the press fail to produce war-ending or even stomach-turning photographs, film, or reporting, the press in fact seemed to play the role of administration booster at key moments during the crisis. As Arthur Rowse notes of August 1990 television coverage, "One constant that could be observed in early coverage by all networks, however, was that the tone was favorable, if not downright solicitous, to the Bush Administration."[164] Newspaper editorials around the country also supported Bush and despite raising the occasional niggling issue, never seriously challenged Bush's decision to make war, his rationale for doing so, or his methods of making it.[165] In fact, say many, the press jumped on the war bandwagon so completely it helped Bush build support for war. Marvin Kalb, former CBS correspondent and current head of the Joan Shorenstein Barone Center for the Press, Politics, and Public Policy at Harvard University, argued that: "Even a sympathetic look at television coverage suggests that there is a certain whiff of jingoism on the airwaves and in print, that there is not enough detached, critical skepticism. When the boys go off to war, the press goes with them."[166]

Finally, postwar coverage of the Persian Gulf also supports the view that government restrictions in fact played a key role in subduing the influence of the press. The Bush Administration, eager to withdraw American troops from the Gulf quickly, was not inclined to aid the Kurds in their uprising against Saddam Hussein, despite having urged them to throw off Saddam's yoke. In the face of rising protests from media commentators about the inhumanity of leaving the Kurds to be killed and starved as they fled Iraq, the administration stood behind its policy of noninvolvement. In part this was because the administration believed that the public was happy with the military victory and did not want its troops stuck in the Middle East any longer than necessary. Armed with this public support, one White House aide argued, "A hundred Safire columns will not change the public's mind. There is no political downside to our policy."[167]

But as television cameras began to seek out the Kurdish refugee camps on the Iraq-Turkey border and showed horrible pictures of starving children and the victims of Hussein's brutal repression, the Bush Administration abruptly changed course. Less than two weeks from the first television reports of the Kurds—reports that never would have been broadcast during Desert Storm—the Bush Administration announced Operation Provide Comfort and the U.S. military began to set up encampments for the Kurds while deterring attacks on them by Iraqi forces. Postwar television coverage and the accompanying criticism on the domestic front forced the Bush Administration to reverse its policy 180 degrees, a feat previously unmatched by the media during Desert Shield and Desert Storm.[168] Whether the news media would have wielded such power during the war if allowed to report more freely cannot be known. But it is clear that under the prevailing restrictions their chances of doing so were small.

Press Reaction to Desert Storm

In the wake of its defeat in the Gulf, the press once again accused the government of breaching the public's trust by imposing tight controls on journalists. And once again, news executives fired off letters of protest to Secretary of Defense Richard Cheney. The press' party line, as enunciated in a letter to Cheney from the editors of fifteen major news organizations, ran as follows: "Virtually all news organizations agree that the flow of information to the public was blocked, impeded, or diminished by the policies and practices of the Department of Defense."[169] Many critics of the government's policy were more passionate and less polite, such as John R. MacArthur:

> If the Bush Administration's censorship by delay; censorship by direct intimidation of soldiers and interference with pool reporters doing interviews; censorship by outright arrest of unilateral reporters; censorship by preventing reporters from seeing anything interesting; and censorship of pool dispatches such as Bruni's is accepted as standard press relations, we are in great danger indeed.[170]

But unlike in the earlier instances, many in the press began to blame their own for at least some of the press' failings. Journalists, critics complained, were too unwilling to try to get around Pentagon restrictions, and accepted too readily the government's information monopoly in the Gulf. Worse, some claimed, many news organizations in effect helped the military to curb the press by shutting their smaller competitors out of the pools.[171] As Anthony Lewis of the *New York Times* wrote, "the control and the censorship, outrageous as they were, cannot excuse the compliant, unquestioning attitude of the American press. We glorified war and accepted its political premise, forsaking the independence and skepticism that justify freedom of the press."[172]

These harsh self appraisals, however, remained confined to professional journals and op-ed columns. Even before the war it was apparent that the vast majority of news organizations were less interested in vigorously challenging the government's press policy than they were in vigorously ensuring that they would have the most access possible given the situation in which they found themselves. When *The Nation* initiated a court challenge on January 10, 1991, suing the Pentagon for restricting access to the battlefield, no major American news organization joined the lawsuit, even to the extent of filing an *amicus curiae* brief. Just as in the wake of Grenada, most news organizations did not find it in their best interest to take on the government so directly. Once again, some feared that losing in court to the government could pave the way for tighter restrictions in the future. But in this case, it also seems that the major newspapers and television networks were unwilling to offend the government, and thereby risk losing their privileged seat at the war, for an uncertain legal victory which would come long after the war was over.[173]

After the war, the press, fragmented and competitive, moving on to other stories, proved again unable to improve its lot. Unable and perhaps unwilling to find a way to present a more united front to the Pentagon, a small group of news executives met to hammer out what they felt should be the guiding principles of wartime public affairs. They then sent a letter to Cheney arguing that the government must work with them to incorporate these principles into future policy. Cheney met with the group in September 1991, but waved off their central complaint that press coverage of the Gulf War had been poor as a result of the restrictions. Cheney could afford to be confident dealing bluntly with the press; polls showed that the public had overwhelmingly approved the military's restrictions on the press and had found press coverage quite satisfactory. Mirroring the manner in which he had dealt with the press during Desert Shield, Cheney directed Pete Williams to meet with press representatives to work out improvements to the system and to agree on the principles that should guide its creation and implementation. By January of 1992, a working committee of Pentagon and press representatives had agreed on all issues except the need for security review. But anyone who believed by this point that such discussions were a good indicator of how things would turn out during war would have had to have been asleep during the entire Gulf crisis. As we shall see in Chapter Six, future conflicts will certainly reveal subsequent rounds of the government/press struggle over the news.[174]

CONCLUSIONS

Even more directly than it had in Panama, the Bush Administration took the lead in imposing onerous restrictions on the press in the Gulf. Secretary of Defense Richard Cheney had primary responsibility for press policy. He, along with Pete Williams, laid down the principles and drafted the broad outlines of military public affairs policy, and oversaw the military's implementation of his efforts at a unprecedented level of detail. The administration's decisions both to restrict and to rely heavily on the press to sell its policies to the public stem from the same source: the transformation of the media's role in politics and the government/press relationship since Vietnam. With a press more adversarial, more pervasive, more technologically capable, and more central to American politics and public opinion formation than ever before, the administration believed that press coverage of the war would play a critical part in Bush's success or failure during the crisis. In the view of White House officials, it was imperative that they, and not the media, set the tone of that coverage. To allow journalists to have a free hand in reporting the war would have led to dilution of the president's message, would have forced the administration to answer more difficult questions and to respond to television coverage of bloody combat scenes and human suffering, all of which would weaken Bush's support and his chances for winning a big political victory.

The restrictions on the press in the Gulf War marked a modern peak in government control. Press access to the battlefield, to the machinery of war, and to the men and women who fought the war, was extremely constrained. Military officers kept a watchful eye on journalists to make sure they did not go anywhere they might find surprising or unwelcome news. The government's press policies kept most correspondents cooped up in Dhahran and Riyadh, covering the war from their hotel and from military briefings. The result of these restrictions was that the government enjoyed significant "information superiority" and considerable power to manage the news. Journalists, who could not challenge official statements or offer the public alternative information, were forced to report primarily whatever it was the government chose to reveal on a given day.

The administration took great advantage of its discovery that it controlled the public stage and that no one else was talking. Bush Administration officials fanned out across Washington and the world during the crisis to convince the public that their approach to confronting Iraq was the best course of action. Once the war was underway, they used the daily briefings to highlight and, at times, exaggerate, their successes, omitting mention of those issues less favorable to their policies that might threaten their public support. Without an independent press in the desert to challenge administration information and arguments, neither the public nor potential critics had much ammunition with which to attack its handling of the crisis or conflict.

The military, which received an undeserved lion's share of the blame for press restrictions, in fact showed again how little preparation for public affairs it had ever managed to carry out. The dominant characteristic of its public affairs performance was incompetence. The military once again let its policies be swept aside by events and White House interests—it did not devise Gulf War restrictions as revenge for Vietnam. None of the services were prepared to deal with the press in such a situation. The Gulf War should thus drive the final nail in the coffin of the argument that the military had long been plotting to avenge its Vietnam loss to the media. Those journalists who experienced the military's distaste for the press up close can, however, be forgiven that they overgeneralized from their own observations. Many officers, public affairs and others, did make life miserable for the press and undoubtedly some did so as a result of their perceptions of the press's role in Vietnam.

Overall, however, the military's public affairs policy in the Gulf was driven by civilian actions, not by military. The JCS guidance written after Panama was never consulted. And again, the military services improvised methods for implementing public affairs policies. That they erred in almost every instance against freedom of the press and in favor of their own parochial interests speaks less of a Vietnam hangover than a simple lack of preparedness and the universal desire to garner public sympathy and support for their actions.

The government's efforts to restrict the press succeeded in making an enormous impact on the character of press coverage. For the third time since Vietnam, the press failed to provide firsthand combat coverage, furnished few hard news pieces on tactics or strategy, broadcast almost no live coverage of any substance, and in general failed to convince viewers and readers that journalists had actually been witness to the events purported to take place. Journalists decried this coverage, arguing that it constrained the public's ability to judge the war for itself. Administration officials, on the other hand, continued to argue that Gulf War coverage was excellent, and that the public had heard and seen the full story of the conflict. They could do so knowing that the public, flush with the excitement of war, supported the government controls on the press and felt satisfied with the press coverage it received.

The press discovered to its dismay that things could get worse than they had been in either Grenada or Panama. It finally became clear to journalists during Desert Storm that the press faced two towering obstacles to getting the kind of access cum independence it wanted. First, the government obviously controlled those things to which access was desired: the troops, the bases, the tanks, and thus the battlefield itself. Why journalists did not fully understand this before is not entirely clear, but during Desert Storm it dawned on the press that if the military did not want journalists to speak with its troops, there was in fact very little the press could do about it. Second, the fundamental nature of the press—fragmented, competitive, unwilling to act collectively due to vastly differing interests—made it impossible for the press to oppose the government's restrictions effectively. Had the press been able to speak with one voice to the Pentagon, it undoubtedly would have been able to improve its lot, especially had news organizations been willing to play hardball and threaten the government with damning front-page stories if access were not forthcoming. Of course, no such act was possible for such a diverse group of independent and self-interested organizations. Instead, each organization tried to better its own position, often at the expense of others, under the system as it was already set up. Thus, for all practical purposes the government's tight control over the press went uncontested.

ENDNOTES

1. Hanson, "The Press Stands Alone," *Columbia Journalism Review*, March/April 1991; Anthony Lewis, "To See Ourselves. . . ." *New York Times*, May 6, 1991; Peter Braestrup interviewed in Richard Valeriani, "Talking Back to the Tube," *Columbia Journalism Review*, March/April 1991.
2. As with any international event of this magnitude, there exist innumerable accounts that cover the history of the Gulf crisis in varying degrees of detail. I rely primarily on only a small sample of them here. A solid chronicle, and especially excellent in terms of the ground war, is U.S. News and World Report, *Triumph Without Victory: The History of the Persian Gulf War* (New York: Times Books, 1992). For Bush administration decision making see Bob

Woodward, *The Commanders* (New York: Pocket Star Books, 1991). An excellent collection of historical, analytical, and editorial essays is Micah L. Sifry and Christopher Cerf, *The Gulf War Reader* (New York: Times Books, 1991). Also see Jean Edward Smith, *George Bush's War* (New York: Henry Holt & Co., 1992).

3. On the Iraqi invasion and world reaction, see U.S. News, *Triumph Without Victory*, pp. 7-27; Smith, *George Bush's War*, pp. 13-62; Matthew Wald, "Price of Oil Rises; Stocks in Retreat," *New York Times*, August 4, 1990; Paul Lewis, "UN Condemns Invasion With Threat to Punish Iraq," *New York Times*, August 3, 1990; Alan Riding, "West Europeans Join US in Condemning Invasion," *New York Times*, August 3, 1990.
4. U.S. News, *Triumph Without Victory*, pp. 27-39, 47-51; Woodward, *Commanders*, pp. 202-210.
5. Paul Lewis, "Washington Calls on UN To Impose Boycott on Iraq," *New York Times*, August 4, 1990.
6. R. W. Apple, "Invading Iraqis Seize Kuwait and Its Oil; US Condemns Attack, Urges United Action," *New York Times*, August 3, 1990; Clyde H. Farnsworth, "Bush, In Freezing Assets, Bars $30 Billion to Hussein," *New York Times*, August 3, 1990.
7. R. W. Apple, "Iraqis Mass on Saudi Frontier; Arabs Agree to Meet on Crisis; Bush Is Ready to Help if Asked," *New York Times*, August 4, 1990.
8. Thomas L. Friedman, "Bush, Hinting Force, Declares Iraqi Assault 'Will Not Stand'" *New York Times*, August 6, 1990.
9. John Kifner, "Proxy in Kuwait Issues Threat," *New York Times*, August 6, 1990.
10. U.S. News, Triumph Without Victory, pp. 76-86; Woodward, *Commanders*, pp. 245-256.
11. R. W. Apple, "US May Send Saudis a Force of 50,000; Iraq Proclaims Kuwait's Annexation," *New York Times*, August 9, 1990.
12. "Excerpts From Bush's Statement on US Defense of Saudis," *New York Times*, August 9, 1990.
13. Robert Reinhold, "Around US, a Cautious Chorus of Support," *New York Times*, August 9, 1990; Gallup Poll information is taken from John Mueller, *Policy and Opinion in the Gulf War* (Chicago: University of Chicago Press, 1994), p. 193. Mueller's book is the definitive compendium of poll data from the Gulf War as well as an excellent discussion of the link between opinion and policy.
14. John Kifner, "Arabs Vote to Send Troops to Help Saudis; Boycott of Iraqi Oil Is Reported Near 100%," *New York Times*, August 11, 1990; R. W. Apple, "US Says Its Troops in the Gulf Could Reach 100,000 in Months," *New York Times*, August 11, 1990; Michael Gordon, "In Just 2 Days, a Doubling of US Troop Estimates," *New York Times*, August 11, 1990; U.S. News and World Report, *Triumph Without Victory*, pp. 90-108.

15. Michael Oreskes, "Poll on Troop Move Shows Support, and Anxiety," *New York Times*, August 12, 1990.
16. Smith, *George Bush's War*, pp. 139-142; R. W. Apple, "Bush Facing Scrutiny by Congress on His Policy in the Persian Gulf," *New York Times*, August 28, 1990.
17. "Transcript of President's Address to Joint Session of Congress," *New York Times*, September 12, 1990.
18. U.S. News, *Triumph Without Victory*, pp. 172; Secretary of Defense Richard Cheney saw early on that Bush would not consider anything short of an Iraqi withdrawal a success. See Bob Woodward, *Commanders*, pp. 283-284.
19. "Transcript of President's Address to Joint Session of Congress," *New York Times*, September 12, 1990.
20. Andrew Rosenthal, "Bush Tapes a Message for Iraqi TV," *New York Times*, September 13, 1990.
21. Alan Cowell, "Leaders Bluntly Prime Iraq for 'Mother of All Battles,'" *New York Times*, September 22, 1990.
22. John F. Burns, "Iraqis Threaten to Attack Saudis and Israelis if Nation is 'Strangled' by Embargo," *New York Times*, September 24, 1990.
23. Michael Wines, "Head of CIA See Iraqis Weakening in 3 to 9 Months," *New York Times*, December 6, 1990; U.S. News and World Report, *Triumph Without Victory*, pp. 150-151.
24. Andrew Rosenthal, "Strains of Gulf Crisis," *New York Times*, September 24, 1990; Peter Steinfels, "Church Leaders Voice Doubts on US Gulf Policy," *New York Times*, October 12, 1990.
25. Woodward, *Commanders*, p. 341; Bush's approval on the Gulf was down to 61% by late October from its early peak of 80%. Mueller, *Policy and Opinion*, p. 193.
26. Michael Oreskes, "Economy and Mideast Standoff Bring a Drop in Bush's Standing," *New York Times*, October 14, 1990. A Times/CBS poll found that by mid October only 57% of the public approved of Bush's handling of the crisis. Also see Evelyn Nieves, "Thousands March in 16 Cities to Protest US Intervention in Gulf," *New York Times*, October 21, 1990.
27. Andrew Rosenthal, "Iraq Blockade Is Backed by Bush," *New York Times*, September 18, 1990.
28. Andrew Rosenthal, "Bush Seems to Toughen His Approach to War," *New York Times*, September 20, 1990; R. W. Apple, "Options for Bush," *New York Times*, September 27, 1990; Thomas L. Friedman, "US Pledges a Vigorous Response if Iraq Attacks Israel, Officials Say," *New York Times*, September 28, 1990; Andrew Rosenthal, "Sacking of Kuwait Is Pressuring US," *New York Times*, September 29, 1990; Judith Miller, "Kuwaitis Say US Doubts Embargo Will Get Iraq Out," *New York Times*, September 30, 1990; Andrew Rosenthal, "Weighing Balance Between War and Diplomacy," *New York Times*, October 7, 1990; Michael R. Gordon,

"US Is Considering Additional Forces to Confront Iraq," *New York Times*, October 24, 1990.

29. Thomas L. Friedman, "Bush and Baker Explicit in Threat to Use Force," *New York Times*, October 30, 1990. It is interesting to note that the Bush administration's preparation of the public and the media for this admission was so thorough that when Bush finally revealed that he would use force if necessary the story did not even make the front page.
30. Michael R. Gordon, "Democrats Press Bush to Put Off Combat with Iraq," *New York Times*, November 28, 1990; Smith, *George Bush's War*, pp. 204-220.
31. *Washington Post*, November 12, 1990.
32. The Gulf crisis and Bush's handling of it resurrected the war powers debate. See, for example, Anthony Lewis, "War and the President," *New York Times*, November 30, 1990; Martin Tolchin, "45 in House Sue to Ban Bush From Acting Alone," *New York Times*, November 21, 1990.
33. Michael R. Gordon, "2 Ex-Military Chiefs Urge Bush to Delay Gulf War," *New York Times*, November 29, 1990. Several former defense secretaries made similar pleas at a conference, see Michael R. Gordon, "Ex-Defense Secretaries Advise Patience in Gulf," *New York Times*, December 3, 1990.
34. R. W. Apple, "Bush Offers to Send Baker On a Peace Mission to Iraq, But Vows Resolve in a War," *New York Times*, December 1, 1990; U.S. News and World Report, *Triumph Without Victory*, pp. 184-185; Smith, *George Bush's War*, pp. 218-220; Woodward, *Commanders*, pp. 322-324.
35. R. W. Apple, "The Collapse of a Coalition," *New York Times*, December 6, 1990.
36. Michael Oreskes, "Poll Finds Americans Divided on Sanctions or Force in the Gulf," *New York Times*, December 14, 1990.
37. Andrew Rosenthal, "US Offers to Fly Baker to Geneva to Talk to Iraq," *New York Times*, January 4, 1991.
38. U.S. News and World *Report, Triumph Without Victory*, pp. 199-200.
39. Thomas L. Friedman, "Baker-Aziz Talks On Gulf Fail; Fears of War Rise; Bush Is Firm; Diplomatic Effort to Continue," *New York Times*, January 10, 1991; "Remarks by Baker at News Conference in Geneva on Standoff in the Gulf," *New York Times*, January 10, 1991; Andrew Rosenthal, "Bush, Noting a Hussein 'Stiff-Arm,' Finds Hope for Peace Waning," *New York Times*, January 10, 1991; Woodward, *Commanders*, pp. 350-351.
40. R. W. Apple, Jr., "Bush's Limited Victory," *New York Times*, January 13, 1991; Mueller, *Policy and Opinion*, pp. 237-241.
41. On the war see U.S. News and World Report, *Triumph Without Victory*; Michael Gordon and Bernard Trainor, *The Generals' War: The Inside Story of the Conflict in the Gulf* (Boston: Little, Brown,

1995); and Rick Atkinson, *Crusade: The Untold Story of the Persian Gulf War* (Boston: Houghton Mifflin, 1993).

42. Bill Carter, "Giant TV Audience for Bush's Speech," *New York Times*, January 18, 1991.
43. DeParle, "Long Series of Military Decisions Led to Gulf War News Censorship," *New York Times*, May 5, 1991.
44. Jason DeParle, "Long Series of Military Decisions Led to Gulf War News Censorship," *New York Times*, May 5, 1991. DeParle's two-part work on the Gulf press system is a critical document in tracing how that system came about. Interestingly, however, the title of this article does not match its contents. The most pertinent fact in the article is the fact that civilian officials had such influence on military public affairs policy. Also of note is the fact that DeParle bolsters the Vietnam hypothesis in several points, even while furnishing information that serves to minimize its importance. This is a result, I believe, of journalism's long reliance on the Vietnam hypothesis to explain military behavior and policy.
45. *America's Team, The Odd Couple*, p. 102
46. DeParle, "*Long Series . . .*"
47. Steven L. Katz, "Ground Zero: The Information War in the Persian Gulf," *Government Information Quarterly*, Vol. 9, No. 4, 1992, p. 388.
48. *America's Team*, p. 155
49. Cheney noted in his interim report to Congress on the conduct of the war that a public affairs team visited Saudi Arabia on October 6 and determined that given the likely nature of a war, open coverage of combat by journalists would be impractical, at least initially. The report was reprinted in US Congress, Senate, Committee on Governmental Affairs, hearing, *Pentagon Rules on Media Access to the Persian Gulf War*, 102nd Congress, 1st Session, February 20, 1990, pp. 774-777. (The hearing is cited hereafter as *Pentagon Rules on Media Access*.)
50. DeParle, "Long Series . . ."
51. Pete Williams, "The Press and the Persian Gulf War," *Parameters*, Autumn 1991, p. 6.
52. Michael Wines, "Press Left Out of Gulf Airlift," *New York Times*, August 9, 1990.
53. "Transcript of News Session by Bush and 2 Officials on Mideast," *New York Times*, August 23, 1990.
54. John R. MacArthur, *Second Front: Censorship and Propaganda in the Gulf War* (Berkeley: University of California Press, 1993, paperback edition), pp. 9-11; on press complaints, see Alex S. Jones, "News Organizations Angry at the Lack of a Press Pool," *New York Times*, August 10, 1990; *New York Times* editorial, "Getting Behind 'Desert Shield,'" August 11, 1990; Alex S. Jones, "News Executives See Pool Hamstrung by Rules of Coverage," *New York Times*, August 17, 1990; Michael R. Gordon, "Press Corps in the Desert: Lots of Sweat But Little News," *New York Times*, August 28, 1990.

55. MacArthur, *Second Front,* pp. 13-14.
56. Ibid., pp. 16-20.
57. Ibid., p. 24.
58. Williams' December 14, 1990 memorandum to bureau chiefs, reprinted in *Pentagon Rules on Media Access,* p. 559.
59. *Pentagon Rules on Media Access,* p. 558.
60. MacArthur, *Second Front,* pp. 26-29.
61. Williams January 7 memorandum to bureau chiefs, *Pentagon Rules on Media Access,* pp. 577-581; Neil A. Lewis, "Pentagon Adopts Gulf News Rules," *New York Times,* January 10, 1991; MacArthur, *Second Front,* pp. 29-36.
62. Williams' January 15 memorandum to bureau chiefs, *Pentagon Rules on Media Access,* pp. 636-638.
63. Ann Devroy, "Many Spokesmen, One US Position," *Washington Post,* February 14, 1991.
64. Gaylord Shaw, "President's Men 'Spin' War News," *Newsday,* January 23, 1991.
65. Jason DeParle, "Keeping the News in Step: Are the Pentagon's Gulf War Rules Here to Stay?" *New York Times,* May 6, 1991; Timothy Cook, "Domesticating a Crisis," in Bennett and Paletz, eds., *Taken by Storm,* esp. pp. 124-125; David L. Swanson and Rebecca A. Carrier, "Global Pictures, Local Stories: The Beginning of Desert Storm as Constructed by Television News Around the World," *Contributions to Military Studies,* Vol. 148, 1994, esp. p. 137; Sharkey, *Under Fire,* p. 129; E. J. Dionne, Jr., "Mission on the Home Front: Shaping Public Opinion," *Washington Post,* February 25, 1991; Howard Kurtz, "US Lets Some News Filter Through 'Blackout'," *Washington Post,* February 25, 1991.
66. All of the public affairs guidance of this nature is reprinted in *Pentagon Rules on Media Access,* pp. 339-548.
67. *America's Team,* pp. 154-155.
68. Malcolm W. Browne et al., "First Person: The Persian Gulf War," *Government Information Quarterly,* Vol. 9, No. 4, 1992, p. 424.
69. DeParle, "Long Series . . ."
70. Michael Wines, "Briefing by Powell: A Data-Filled Showcase," *New York Times,* January 24, 1991.
71. Howard Kurtz, "Media's Mixed Reviews," *Washington Post,* January 31, 1991.
72. Jason DeParle, "Long Series . . ."
73. Devroy, "Many Spokesmen . . ."
74. The enormous effort the administration expended to keep the incident from getting out of control was reflected in the number of stories which appeared in the paper recounting its reaction to Iraqi claims. R. W. Apple, Jr., "Commanders Deny Error On Target," *New York Times,* February 14, 1991; Alessandra Stanley, "Iraq Says US Killed Hundreds of Civilians at Shelter, But Allies Call It Military Post," *New York Times,* February 14, 1991; Andrew

Rosenthal, "Bush's Quandary," *New York Times*, February 14, 1991; Michael R. Gordon, "US Calls Target a Command Center," *New York Times*, February 14, 1991.

75. Alex S. Jones, "Process of News Reporting on Display," *New York Times*, February 15, 1991.
76. Mueller, *Policy and Opinion*, p. 318; Maureen Dowd, "Americans Back Continued Air Strikes," *New York Times*, February 15, 1991.
77. Jason DeParle, "Keeping the News in Step: Are the Pentagon's Gulf War Rules Here to Stay?" *New York Times*, May 6, 1991.
78. Cited in Sharkey, *Under Fire*, p. 129.
79. See Appendices for a copy of Desert Storm Ground Rules and Guidelines.
80. Williams telephone conference of January 12 with public affairs people at the Pentagon and in Saudi Arabia, p. 386 in *Pentagon Rules on Media Access*.
81. Ibid., p. 386.
82. See, for example, Sydney Schanberg, "Censoring for Political Security," *Washington Journalism Review*, March 1991.
83. *America's Team*, p. 154.
84. Ron Wildermuth, "The Military and the Media: They Can Both Win," *Government Information Quarterly*, Vol. 9, No. 4, 1992, p. 413.
85. John J. Fialka, *Hotel Warriors*, p. 4.
86. Sharkey, *Under Fire*, pp. 110-112.
87. Two favorable reports on the early pool are Frank Aukofer's notes in "First Person: The Persian Gulf War," *Government Information Quarterly*, Vol. 9, No. 4, 1992, p. 420; and Carl Rochelle, "The War and the Media: A Retrospective," National Press Club forum, March 19, 1991. Less favorable accounts include Alex S. Jones, "News Executives See Pool Hamstrung by Rules of Coverage," *New York Times*, August 17, 1990. It should be noted that at least part of the reason Aukofer and Rochelle praised the initial pool was probably because they were in it.
88. Michael R. Gordon, "The Press Corps in the Desert: Lots of Sweat but Little News," *New York Times*, August 28, 1990; Major Mark Hughes, USMC, "Words at War: Reflections of a Marine Public Affairs Officer in the Persian Gulf," *Government Information Quarterly*, Vol. 9, No. 4, 1992, pp. 440, 449; *Sharkey, Under Fire*, pp. 110-112; MacArthur, *Second Front*, pp. 164-172.
89. Sharkey, *Under Fire*, p. 128; Hughes, "Words at War," p. 440.
90. Sharkey, *Under Fire*, pp. 110-112.
91. Captain Ron E. Wildermuth, "They Can Both Win," p. 410.
92. Steven L. Katz, "Ground Zero: The Information War in the Persian Gulf," *Government Information Quarterly*, Vol. 9, No. 4, 1992, p. 395.
93. Katz, "Ground Zero," p. 398.
94. Pete Williams, "The Press and the Persian Gulf War," *Parameters*, Autumn 1991, pp. 5-6.

95. Debra Gersh, "Press Pools—The Military's View," *Editor and Publisher*, February 16, 1991; Debra Gersh, "Persian Gulf Press Pools Expanded," *Editor and Publisher*, February 23, 1991.
96. Fialka, pp. 12-14; Boot, "The Pool," pp. 24-27; M. Hughes, pp. 443-445.
97. Pete Williams, "The Press and the Persian Gulf War," p. 8.
98. Fialka, *Hotel Warriors*, pp. 12-14; Boot, "The Pool," pp. 24-27; Hughes, "Words at War," pp. 443-445; Ad Hoc Media Group, *Problems of News Coverage in the Persian Gulf War*, pp. 732-734.
99. For a discussion of the most widely discussed incident involving Frank Bruni, a reporter for the *Detroit Free Press*, see Malcolm Browne's section in "First Person: The Persian Gulf War," pp. 422-423.
100. Williams, "The Press and the Persian Gulf War," p. 6.
101. Katz, "Ground Zero," p. 399.
102. Richard Cheney, *Conduct of the Persian Gulf Conflict: An Interim Report to Congress*, July 1991, pp. 19-23.
103. Fialka, *Hotel Warriors*, p. 5.
104. Sharkey, *Under Fire*, pp. 132-133; Fialka, *Hotel Warriors*, pp. 12-19; Shotwell, "Fourth Estate," pp. 77-79; Hughes, "Words at War," pp. 453-456; Wildermuth, "They Can Both Win," pp. 416-417; Ad Hoc Media Group, *Problems of News Coverage in the Persian Gulf War*, pp. 734-735.
105. Wildermuth, "They Can Both Win," p. 414.
106. Sharkey, *Under Fire*, pp. 132-133; Fialka, *Hotel Warriors*, p. 17.
107. Andrew Rosenthal, "Pentagon Is Confident on War; But Says Iraqis Remain Potent; Sees No Imminent Land Attack," *New York Times*, January 24, 1991.
108. Quoted in Alex S. Jones, "Process of News Reporting on Display," *New York Times*, February 15, 1991.
109. Jason DeParle, "Long Series of Military Decisions Led to Gulf War News Censorship," *New York Times*, May 5, 1991; Debbie Nathan, "Just the Good News Please," *The Progressive*, February 1991, pp. 25-27.
110. John Balzar of the *Los Angeles Times* encountered this problem, for example. After viewing gun camera footage from an Apache helicopter attack that left many Iraqi soldiers dead from its 30mm cannons, Balzar wrote an article describing the attack. Afterwards, Balzar recounts, the military was far less cooperative. See MacArthur, *Second Front*, p. 163.
111. For example, Fialka, *Hotel Warriors*, p. 6.
112. R. W. Apple, Jr., "Pentagon Moves to Widen Reporters' Access to Gulf Ground Units," *New York Times*, February 13, 1991.
113. Sharkey, *Under Fire*, pp. 125-126.
114. Fialka, *Hotel Warriors*, pp. 36-44; The media's displeasure with the pool system was universal. Just two examples include William Boot, "The Pool," *Columbia Journalism Review*, May/June, 1991, pp. 24-27; *Problems of News Coverage in the Persian Gulf War*, compiled

by Ad Hoc Media Group, *Pentagon Rules on Media Access*, pp. 730-735.

115. Fialka, *Hotel Warriors*, p. 2.
116. Ibid., p. 39. The Sacred Ten included the *New York Times*, the *Wall Street Journal* (Fialka's paper), the *Washington Post*, the *Los Angeles Times, Associated Press, Reuters, United Press International, Time, Newsweek*, and *U.S. News and World Report*. The Sacred Ten eventually became sixteen, as the *Boston Globe, Chicago Tribune, Knight-Ridder, USA Today, Gannett News Service*, and *Cox Newspapers* worked their way into the inner sanctum.
117. Fialka, *Hotel Warriors*, p. 42.
118. This becomes very clear upon reading the correspondence between Pete Williams and various news executives in the months before the war. See *Pentagon Rules on Media Access*, pp. 550-650.
119. Robert Fisk, "Out of the Pools," *Mother Jones*, May/June, 1991, p. 58.
120. Even John Fialka, whose book best illustrates the dilemmas of the pool system, seems to have been upset at unilaterals for their "unfair" advantages in not having escorts and in being able to file their copy quickly and directly home. MacArthur also found this sentiment; see *Second Front*, pp. 180-184.
121. MacArthur, *Second Front*, pp. 166-167; also critical of Desert Shield coverage opportunities was James LeMoyne, "Pentagon's Strategy for the Press: Good News or No News," *New York Times*, February 17, 1991.
122. William Boot (Hanson's pen name), "The Pool," *Columbia Journalism Review*, May/June 1991, p. 26.
123. Ibid., p. 27. Other works back this conclusion. MacArthur, pp. 190-194.
124. Cited in William Boot, "The Press Stands Alone," *Columbia Journalism Review*, March/April, 1991, p. 23.
125. Bob Simon chronicles his ordeal in *Forty Days* (New York: Putnam, 1992).
126. Fialka, *Hotel Warriors*, pp. 56-57; Taylor, *War and the Media*, pp. 59-63.
127. Fialka, *Hotel Warriors*, pp. 49-50.
128. R. W. Apple, Jr., "Correspondents Protest Pool System," *New York Times*, February 12, 1991.
129. Chris Hedges, "The Unilaterals," *Columbia Journalism Review*, May/June 1991, pp. 27-29.
130. Philip M. Taylor, *War and the Media: Propaganda and Persuasion in the Gulf War* (Manchester: Manchester University Press, 1992), pp. 136-149.
131. Ibid., pp. 241-246.
132. Hedges, "The Unilaterals," p. 28.
133. Fialka, *Hotel Warriors*, p. 46.
134. Taylor, *War and the Media*, pp. 91-103.
135. Ibid., pp. 87-133.

136. Ibid., p. 123
137. Walter Goodman echoes this argument, "Arnett," *Columbia Journalism Review*, May/June 1991, pp. 29-31; also see Peter Applebome, "Carnage in Baghdad Erases Image of an Antiseptic War," *New York Times*, February 14, 1991; Anna Quindlen, "Hard News," *New York Times*, February 14, 1991.
138. Taylor, *War and the Media*, pp. 87-133; Michael Wines, "CNN Reports Allied Bombs Killed 24 Civilians in Iraqi Neighborhood," *New York Times*, January 26, 1991.
139. Robin Toner, "The Senator, the Press, and Crossed Swords," *New York Times*, February 12, 1991.
140. Taylor, *War and the Media*, p. 107.
141. Only 3% blamed the U.S. military in the poll. See Mueller, *Policy and Opinion*, p. 319.
142. On Iraq's mismanagement of the media, see P. M. Taylor, *Propaganda and Persuasion*, pp. 87-133.
143. Major General Perry M. Smith, *How CNN Fought the War* (New York: Carol Publishing Group, 1991), p. 32.
144. Alessandra Stanley, "Iraq Says US Killed Hundreds of Civilians at Shelter, But Allies Call It Military Post," *New York Times*, February 14, 1991; Andrew Rosenthal, "Bush's Quandary," *New York Times*, February 14, 1991; Peter Applebome, "Carnage in Baghdad Erases Image of Antiseptic War," *New York Times*, February 14, 1991.
145. Harry F. Noyes III, "Like It or Not, the Armed Forces Need the Media," *Army*, June 1992, p. 32
146. Press coverage of the Gulf crisis and Desert Storm is such a massive body of material that my discussion of it is necessarily limited. Many studies on every aspect of media coverage exist and many more are still being published at a rapid pace. A sample includes Barbara Zelizer, "CNN, the Gulf War, and Journalistic Practice," *Journal of Communication*, Vol. 42, No. 1, Winter 1992, pp. 66-81; Swanson and Carrier, "Global Stuff"; William Boot, "Operation Deep Think," *Columbia Journalism Review*, November/December 1990; Elihu Katz, "The End of Journalism? Notes on Watching the War," *Journal of Communication*, Vol. 42, No. 3, Summer 1992, pp. 5-13; Susan Jeffords and Lauren Rabinowitz, eds., *Seeing Through the Media: The Persian Gulf War* (New Brunswick: Rutgers University Press, 1994); Bradley S. Greenberg and Walter Gantz, eds., *Desert Storm and the Mass Media* (Cresskill, NJ: Hampton Press, 1993); Anna Banks, "Frontstage/Backstage: Loss of Control in Real-Time Coverage of the War in the Gulf," *Communication*, Vol. 13, 1992, pp. 111-119; Everette E. Dennis et al., *The Media at War: The Press and the Persian Gulf Conflict* (New York: Gannett Foundation Media Center, June 1991); Marie Gottschalk, "Operation Desert Cloud: The Media and the Gulf War," *World Policy Journal*, Vol. 9, No. 3, Summer 1992, pp. 449-486; Jon A. Krosnick and Laura A. Brannon, "The Media and the Foundations of Presidential Support: George

Bush and the Persian Gulf Conflict," *Journal of Social Issues*, Vol. 49, No. 4, 1993, pp. 167-182.

147. John J. Fialka, *Hotel Warriors*, pp. 55-66; Ad Hoc Media Group, *Problems of News Coverage in the Persian Gulf War*, reprinted in the *Pentagon Rules on Media Access*, pp. 732-735.
148. Guy Gugliotta, "Signs of Breakdown in Pool System," *Washington Post*, February 27, 1991.
149. R. W. Apple, Jr., "The General Tries Not to Seem Too Confident," *New York Times*, February 25, 1991; "Transcript of Briefing in Riyadh by the American Commander," *New York Times*, February 25, 1991; Richard L. Berke, "News from Gulf Is Good, and Cheney's Press Curbs Are Loosened," *New York Times*, February 25, 1991.
150. Though Gergen misses the pool's direct impact on the media's ability to find news to compete with in the first place, his statement is otherwise accurate. See David Gergen, "The Unfettered Presidency," in Joseph S. Nye, Jr. and Roger K. Smith, eds., *After the Storm: Lessons from the Gulf War* (Lanham, MD: Madison Books, 1992), p. 188.
151. Cited in MacArthur, *Second Front*, p. 167.
152. Michael Massing, "Another Front," *Columbia Journalism Review*, May/June 1991, pp. 23-24.
153. Scott Armstrong, "64 Questions in Search of an Answer," *Columbia Journalism Review*, November/December 1990, p. 23.
154. Peter Braestrup, "Censored," *The New Republic*, pp. 16-17; Bill Monroe, "How the Generals Outdid the Journalists," *Washington Journalism Review*, April 1991, p. 6.
155. Jon Katz, "Collateral Damage to Network News," *Columbia Journalism Review*, March/April 1991, p. 29.
156. Philip Knightley, "The Role of Journalists in Vietnam: A Feature Writer's Perspective," in Harrison Salisbury, ed., *Vietnam Reconsidered: Lessons From A War* (New York: Harper & Row, 1984), pp. 106-109.
157. MacArthur, *Second Front*, p. 159.
158. Sharkey, *Under Fire*, pp. 150-152.
159. Eric Arnett, "Awestruck Press Does Tomahawk PR," *The Bulletin of Atomic Scientists*, April 1991; Katz, "Ground Zero," p. 402.
160. Theodore A. Postol was the MIT scientist leading the charge against the Patriot system. See, for example, Theodore A. Postol, "Lessons of the Gulf War Experience with Patriot," *International Security*, Vol. 16, No. 3, Winter 1991/92, pp. 119-171; a journalistic account of the misinformation about Patriot is Patricia Axelrod, "Operation Desert Sham," *Penthouse*, November 1992.
161. Sharkey, *Under Fire*, pp. 150-152.
162. Patrick Sloyan, "Buried Alive–US Tanks Used Plows to Kill Thousands in Gulf War Trenches," *Newsday*, September 12, 1991.
163. *America's Team, The Odd Couple*, p. 165.

164. Arthur E. Rowse, "The Guns of August," *Columbia Journalism Review*, March/April 1991, p. 27. Rowse points out that even the conservative media watchdog group the Center for Media and Public Affairs found that 76% of all references to Bush during the first two weeks of the crisis were favorable. For a group that specializes in complaining about the opposite this finding seems all the more remarkable. Also finding an extremely uncritical press during the early months of Desert Shield are William A. Dorman and Steven Livingston, "News and Historical Content: The Establishing Phase of the Persian Gulf Policy Debate," in W. Lance Bennett and David L. Paletz, eds., *Taken by Storm: The Media, Public Opinion, and US Foreign Policy in the Gulf War* (Chicago: University of Chicago Press, 1994).
165. Everette E. Dennis et al., *The Media at War: The Press and the Persian Gulf Conflict* (New York: Gannett Foundation Media Center, Columbia University), pp. 51-64.
166. Marvin Kalb, "Late Night with the Gulf Crisis," *New York Times*, August 29, 1990; On the Media's Role in Building Support for War, see also Elihu Katz "The End of Journalism?"; and Paul Duke, "Censorship and the Press," reprinted in *Pentagon Rules on Media Access*, pp. 1233-1234.
167. Cited in Daniel Schorr, "Ten Days That Shook the White House," *Columbia Journalism Review*, July/August 1991, p. 22.
168. Schorr, "Ten Days," pp. 21-23.
169. "15 Top Journalists Object to Gulf War Curbs," *New York Times*, May 2, 1991.
170. MacArthur, *Second Front*, p. 192.
171. Bill Monroe, "How To Cover War: Forget the Pool," *Washington Journalism Review*, May 1991, p. 6; Frank A. Aukofer, "The Press Collaborators," *Nieman Reports*, Summer 1991, pp. 24-26.
172. Anthony Lewis, "To See Ourselves . . ." *New York Times*, May 6, 1991; this is also a major theme running throughout MacArthur's book.
173. MacArthur, *Second Front*, pp. 34-35; the court documents can be found in the *Pentagon Rules on Media Access*, pp. 1255-1545.
174. Sharkey, *Under Fire*, pp. 152-155; MacArthur, *Second Front*, pp. 199-202; *The Military and the Media: The Continuing Dialogue* (Chicago: Robert R. McCormick Tribune Foundation, September 19-21, 1993); *Reporting the Next War* (Chicago: Robert R. McCormick Tribune Foundation, April 23-24, 1992).

7

War in the Media Age

America now wages war in the what we might well call the "Media Age." Journalists in foreign capitals interviewing enemy leaders, presidential diplomacy via CNN, Pentagon films of guided missiles, and live television newscasts from the war zone have become as much a part of war as death and destruction. Even more important, they are all most people will ever know of war personally. News-hungry publics rely on the media to tell them how wars are going, how their troops are fighting, and how their political leaders are leading. News coverage of conflict shapes what the public thinks and feels about its military and its presidents in times of war. What makes the evening news, therefore, matters more to officials than ever before.

The findings from the cases prompt further questions. After summarizing the case against the conventional wisdom we must first ask why the conventional wisdom has dominated our thinking about wartime government/press affairs for so long. We must then answer questions raised by the success of Reagan and Bush in using the media to their advantage during conflict about the factors involved with such success. When and why will presidents be successful in restricting the press and managing the information reaching the public? When might they fail? In turn, we should also assess the implications of the new White House media strategy in time of war for U.S. foreign policy, for the government/press relationship, and for public opinion. In addition we might ask whether our experiences in recent conflicts have shed any light on the modern national interest/free press debate? Finally, we must consider the future of government media strategy, press responses to it, and the likely outcomes of the government/press struggle in future conflicts.

DEFLATING THE CONVENTIONAL WISDOM

The evidence presented here prompts a quick and thorough rejection of the conventional wisdom that has dominated thinking about wartime government/press relations since Vietnam. Almost every academic, journalistic, and military account to date cites Vietnam as the driving force and the military as the primary culprit behind press control from Grenada to the Gulf. But as each case here has illustrated, history does not support any of the conventional wisdom's central tenets. The evidence comes in two forms: First, the cases reveal numerous direct historical contradictions to the conventional wisdom's version of the evolution of military public affairs after Vietnam and the creation of press policies in post-Vietnam conflicts. Second, both the dominant role played by the White House in formulating and implementing press policies as well as officials' commentary on the issue make it clear than the White House understands and has adapted to the new power of the media by seeking greater control over the press in time of war.

The first stake in the heart of the conventional wisdom comes from an analysis of the military's public affairs development after Vietnam. Three central points emerge. First, Vietnam did not prompt innovation or change in military public affairs policies. Vietnam did wreak havoc on the military as an institution. And it did convince military officers, rightly or wrongly, that the press could play an enormous independent and negative role during war. Despite this, public affairs remained a stepchild mission within the military, which prefers to focus on the tasks associated with fighting wars than reporting them, and no major reforms were initiated in the wake of the war.

Second, current military public affairs policies owe more at any rate to post-Grenada reforms than to post-Vietnam reforms. The mechanics of public affairs in fact did not change at all until the Sidle Panel recommended changes in the wake of Urgent Fury. The panel's recommendations, furthermore, flowed from the peculiar and particular circumstances of the Grenada operation and borrowed from the public affairs guidelines in Vietnam. They were not a rejection of the Vietnam system, but of the Urgent Fury procedures. Thus, contrary to the conventional wisdom, Vietnam did not lead the military to public affairs innovations; critical changes in public affairs came not after 1973, but after 1983.

Third, the fact that the military came almost without any public affairs plans to both Grenada and Panama, and managed to fail to develop a sustainable press plan for the Gulf War despite the long lead time, reveals that the military, despite some modest reform efforts, has never developed a coherent plan to deal with the press at all, much less to do so in an aggressive and restrictive manner. If the military had responded to Vietnam by making plans to restrict the press in future conflicts as the conventional wisdom suggests, one would expect to have seen far more coordinated efforts to do so. Instead we have seen the opposite. This are hardly the actions of an institution actively seeking to avoid the press problems of Vietnam.

The second major blow to the conventional wisdom is struck by evidence from the cases illustrating that the White House, not the military, bears primary responsibility for creating and imposing press restrictions. White House management of press policy and specifically of military public affairs policy has become more overt over time. In Grenada, although many details of press policy making remain murky, the available evidence strongly suggests that White House concerns led to the press ban and that Secretary of Defense Caspar Weinberger gave the go ahead for the press lock-out from the island. Observers at the time also believed that it was Reagan's Chief of Staff James Baker who later gave the order to the military to lift the ban. Moreover, Admiral James Metcalf, the commander of the Urgent Fury task force who publicly took responsibility for instituting the press blackout, recanted in a speech a decade later, admitting that the order had "come from above."

In Panama civilian micromanagement of public affairs became more obvious as Secretary of Defense Richard Cheney made two decisions knowing that they would seriously hamper the media's ability to cover the fast-moving conflict. First, Cheney decided to call up the Washington, D. C. based press pool despite the fact that military public affairs policy would have dictated that a pool be created in Panama. This decision not only made it difficult for the military to plan for the press, it made covering the conflict almost impossible for those journalists already in Panama at the time by ensuring that the military would not help them. The second decision Cheney made was to call up and send the press pool to Panama too late to witness the critical opening battles.

Finally, in the Gulf War civilian control reached its modern zenith. President Bush gave Cheney the lead in crafting the restrictive press policies that the military would later implement. While the military made plans to implement the policy, Cheney and Williams provided cover by obscuring the aggressive nature of the restrictions in discussions with news organizations. Once the war had begun, Cheney and even Bush himself continued to make the major decisions dealing with press relations, from what military officials should tell the press about breaking events to which officers should do the Pentagon's daily briefing.

Though this evidence alone is enough to discredit the conventional wisdom, it takes on even greater persuasive power when combined with an analysis of how the political environment has changed since Vietnam as a result of the deterioration in the government/press relationship and the growth of media power. The new political environment facing presidents has taken shape as the press has become an ever more critical element of the American social and political system since Vietnam. The press today plays a central role in every political action taken, from running for office and announcing policy proposals, to passing judgment on elected leaders' performance. In doing so the press has superseded more traditional institutions in political life, such as political parties, community leaders, and the church. Not only has the press come to play a more central role in politics, journalists and officials now face each other more as adversaries than friendly rivals. What the press reports is more likely than ever to be critical of government actions, thereby making it considerably more difficult for officials to pursue their policy and political goals. Presidents thus believe with good reason that they must work harder to get their messages to the public and to ensure that they will not be buried in criticism from their opponents. The press now also wields technologies that enable it to gather more information and disseminate it almost instantaneously from the far reaches of the globe to American living rooms, forcing faster responses from government to breaking events and holding presidents responsible for happenings around the world. In the realm of foreign policy, the press plays a key role in aggravating the splits in elite opinion that have widened since Vietnam and the end of the Cold War, making it more difficult for presidents to build support for foreign adventures. Finally, the pressures of this new media-saturated political environment have pushed the White House to adopt increasingly sophisticated mechanisms for selling its messages to the public. Media strategy has taken a seat next to political strategy in the day-to-day business of governing America.

These trends, along with the lessons from Vietnam, have heightened presidential fears about the already dangerous connection between casualties and public opinion and given rise to the new White House approach to the press during war. Afraid that press coverage of the negative aspects of war, especially American suffering or death, could turn the public against even a conflict whose purpose people believed in, presidents have adopted a strategy aimed at minimizing the media's access to the battlefield and maximizing their control over the information which gets to the public about the conflict. This strategy, they hope, will obscure the human costs and the horrors of war while allowing

White House public relations efforts to justify the war, to convince the public that it was worthwhile, to forestall criticism of the president's handling of the conflict, and to ensure that the president receives a political victory and popular support in the wake of a military victory.

The accuracy of this explanation for White House actions is clear from the case studies: the new strategy starred in each of the three most recent American conflicts. In Grenada the press did not even make it near the battlefield until long after the fighting was over. No American casualties, dead or wounded, made the newspapers or television. Nor was the press able to investigate whether or not the invasion was truly necessary, despite the doubts many had at the time. The Reagan Administration and the military supplied all of the information about how the fighting went and used their information monopoly to keep criticism of the invasion to a minimum. It was not until much later, therefore, that the many military miscues committed during the operation came to light. Meanwhile, Reagan appeared on prime time television to announce a great victory over communism, thereby earning a boost in public support, putting the disaster of the Lebanon bombing behind him, and improving his reelection prospects. Reagan's media guru, Michael Deaver, later confirmed the importance of the new media strategy in his memoirs:

> I firmly believe that television has absolutely changed our military strategy, that we will never again fight a major ground war. Americans simply do not want to see mass killings on the TV screen in their living rooms—or wherever they keep their TV sets. You can strafe Libya for thirty minutes, but you can't do it day after day, and you can't send in the troops.
>
> Possibly the only successful ground action this country has taken since World War II was Grenada, or at least we perceive it as such. We got away with it by establishing special ground rules, by not letting the press in and justifying it later.[1]

In Panama, Bush Administration officials worked to make sure that the press did not witness the crucial openings scenes of the invasion, despite the institutional arrangements designed to guarantee its presence on the battlefield. And while the press was bottled up by the military in the press pool, the administration spoke in glowing terms of how well the operation was going, stressing how evil Manuel Noriega was and the need to capture him, and glossed over any real details of how the fighting was really going, especially those actions which left Americans dead or wounded. The result, as with Grenada, was that the president enjoyed a political boost in the wake of a quick military victory.

The new strategy reached its peak during the Gulf War. The Bush Administration applied both the military and the media side of the strategy on an unprecedented scale. Not only did the administration direct the largest military campaign since Vietnam with speed and great effectiveness, it also restricted the largest press corps from getting to the battlefield in history. The administration did both of these while providing a constant flow of upbeat information about the conflict, avoiding the gritty and painful aspects of war, emphasizing the positive. Again, the result of the military victory was a huge political boost for the president.

In each case, it appears that those at the White House believed that a military victory was not enough. Even a decisive military victory could be tarnished if the press were to show the public too much of the horror and confusion of war. In trying to keep the public focused on the larger goals of the operations, the White House hoped to avoid the sort of press coverage which would lead the public to judge a conflict by a single event. And, as successful in the end as recent American battles have been, each has also provided material that might easily have produced the sort of coverage that White Houses fear most. What might have happened, for example, if a television crew had accompanied the Rangers in Grenada when they discovered that they had only rescued half of the medical students, and that the other half were vulnerable on another campus miles away? How would the public have viewed the Panama invasion if television crews had shown the public the various friendly fire incidents that claimed eighteen American lives in Panama? Would support for the Gulf War have vanished if greater casualties had been sustained during the ground war with the press there to witness them or if journalists had captured firsthand the devastating impact of the U.S. air campaign on Iraqi troops? Some might argue that the public would have supported these conflicts anyway, but from their actions it is clear that presidents and their officials refused to take such a gamble. Press restrictions and public relations have therefore become as much a part of the new American way of war as military operations.

Explaining the Continuing Popularity of the Conventional Wisdom

In the face of contradictory evidence the conventional wisdom has retained its popularity for several related reasons. First, it is an obvious and convenient explanation of the government/press struggle since Vietnam. It is obvious because no one involved with the military or the media can believe that Vietnam did not have a huge impact on military/press relations and military public affairs. Understandably, most people assumed that the answer to Vietnam for the military would be to seek revenge on the press. And because this assumption seemed clearly vindicated by military/media squabbles from Grenada to the Gulf, the conventional wisdom has become a convenient shorthand to explain all such military/media tensions and government efforts to control the press.

Further, the conventional wisdom fits neatly into the media's preferred professional self-image. Journalists accept the Vietnam hypothesis with almost religious faith. They no longer question its truth and require nothing but the occasional anecdote to prove their case. Journalists love the conventional wisdom because it bolsters their cherished myths about press conduct and impact during the Vietnam War. Journalists like to believe that the press fulfilled its democratic obligation to challenge government statements and provide independent assessments of the war for the public. The press, they believe, uncovered the ugly truth about the war and revealed government deception, helping to end a war the public did not support. Journalists knew that many in the military blamed the press for the American defeat in Vietnam, and thus have since perceived government efforts to restrict the press as the military's revenge. That the military should want revenge reinforces the media's Vietnam dogma because it speaks to the powerful role that journalists believe themselves to have played in that war.

The conventional wisdom also escapes the normally critical judgment of the press because journalists have the misfortune of being too close to the action to understand the larger forces at work during war. Reporters in the press pool see the military up close and impute too much to its actions. Thus, it seems quite obvious to them that the military which tells them they cannot go here or there must be ultimately responsible for decisions regarding access to the battlefield and treatment of the press. Moreover, most journalists who cover war share similar personal experiences, and when they swap stories they reinforce their limited perspective, which goes unchallenged by other journalists who want to believe the conventional wisdom anyway. Thus the conventional wisdom emerges refreshed with each conflict, though no closer to the truth.

In view of the trends shaping the world of politics since Vietnam, however, it should not be surprising that the White House believes that the press is too important to be left to the generals. Presidents and their advisers know that if they are to shape press coverage to best advantage they, and not military leaders less knowledgeable and sophisticated in the ways of the media, must craft press policies and control what the public is told during war. Even if the military successfully curbs the press and follows the White House line in its public statements, presidents and their advisers must still be personally involved in public communications if they are to build public support, rebut their critics, and claim credit for successes. This belief has been repeatedly illustrated by the coordinated White House public relations efforts during the conflicts in Grenada, Panama, and the Persian Gulf described in preceding chapters. It should be clear to all that when it comes to media matters, presidents and their advisers are calling the shots, not military leaders.

THE ELEMENTS OF PRESIDENTIAL POWER AND THE LIMITS OF CONTROL

The growth of the media's importance in politics has made life more difficult for presidents as greater numbers of media outlets and growing audiences spur more voices, ideas, and opinions to compete with official claims and announcements. Just as this trend has driven presidents to seek increasingly stiff press controls during war, it has also made imposing control more difficult. Why, then, have presidents been so successful recently in doing so? What are the limits of their power to exert influence over wartime press coverage?

The Elements of Power

Presidents seek to keep journalists from producing coverage threatening to White House political interests while at the same time encouraging them to give administration actions positive coverage. The president's power to manage this feat depends on controlling press access to the battlefield and on influencing wartime press coverage by exploiting the inherent advantages of the presidency. Some of the variables that contribute to the president's success are subject to his control, some are not. His power emerges from the unique role presidents play in media routines and in foreign policy, from his command over the military and the physical resources necessary for press control, from the strength of public opinion on national security issues, and from less tractable factors such as the geography and lethality of the modern battlefield.

Controlling the Battlefield

In keeping the press away from the battlefield, presidents are aided by three key factors. First, presidents benefit from the very nature of the battlefield. The modern battlefield is so lethal for the ignorant and unprotected, not to mention for those carrying weapons and presumably knowing what to do, that journalists have few options but to cooperate with the government if they want to see military units in action. Even if they were all free to do so, very few journalists would venture too close to the front lines when the battle was joined, as both the invasion of Panama and the Gulf war illustrate. A large contingent of journalists already in Panama when the invasion began took refuge in the Marriott Hotel even though they could have ventured out into the thick of things. Things were too thick, evidently, and reporters wound up filing telephone reports from their hotel rooms instead of eyewitness reports from the field. In the Gulf, journalists did not break from the pool system in large numbers until it was clear that the ground war had turned into a rout and it was relatively safe to venture out into the desert without military escorts.

Another factor that often aids the official cause is the attitude towards the press of the country in which a conflict takes place. During the Gulf crisis Saudi Arabia's poisonous attitude toward freedom of the press made it very difficult for the press to get the same kind of access that they would have enjoyed somewhere else. Saudi Arabia's leaders did not allow the Western press to base themselves in their country even before the war, and were extremely reluctant to allow waves of journalists to cover the crisis. This attitude proved a great boon to the Bush Administration, helping to minimize the number of journalists covering the first weeks of the American buildup, during which time U.S. forces were quite vulnerable to Iraqi attack. Had the crisis erupted somewhere more accessible to journalists, it would have been much more difficult to keep the enemy from knowing just how little American firepower was on the ground in those first weeks.

The final and most important factor giving the president the ability to control the press is the zealous cooperation of the military. Even though the White House bears primary responsibility for restricting the press in recent conflicts, the military's eager help has been a necessary ingredient of government success. The military's professional interests have prompted military officials to believe that they, too, have much to gain by maintaining control over the press on and near the battlefield. Thus, the military has gladly implemented the restrictive policies sent down from the White House and civilian officials. The military has done a superb job of ensuring that journalists do not wander unescorted into areas the government would rather they not go. In addition, the military has kept close track of the names and locations of correspondents covering the war, enforced reporting guidelines and administered the press pool, apprehending and scolding those who broke the rules. Without such help, a president would have been forced to accept far less effective control over war correspondents.

Dominating Press Coverage

With control over press access to the battlefield, the president has taken the first big step towards his ultimate goal of dominating press coverage. With fewer journalists scouring the battlefield to report things which might contradict official statements or twist public opinion, the White House immediately gains in its efforts to be a dominant and credible voice in the public's eye. But beyond control of the battlefield itself, the power to influence press coverage of war flows from several sources.

The first and most important source of presidential influence over press coverage is the president's unique position not only in American government and the conduct of foreign policy, but also in the newsgathering routines of the media. What Teddy Roosevelt first called the "bully pulpit" now occupies a brighter spotlight than ever. Presidents in the media age accrue the lion's share of both media scrutiny and coverage, with other key government figures such as members of Congress almost invisible at times by comparison.[2] Presidents thus enjoy unmatched opportunities to use the media to advance their political interests. Moreover, what is merely a great advantage in peacetime becomes a potential source of dominance during war. Thanks to his role as Commander-in-Chief and top foreign policy maker, every presidential action and utterance during a crisis is even bigger news than usual. All eyes follow him as he charts the nation's dangerous course through wartime. The media redouble their efforts to cover the president and in turn, to cover any military forces he has deployed. Other concerns fall from the news, and those who would criticize the president find it much more difficult to make themselves heard in major media outlets. A wise president may exploit this dynamic to build public support for war, intimidate the enemy, mollify doubters, and afterwards claim victory.

The second source of presidential influence over press coverage is public opinion. When the president orders troops into battle, the public rallies to his side, his approval soars, and people focus not on the justifications for war but on the well-being of their men and women in uniform. This rally-to-the-flag phenomenon causes the acceptable range of stories in mainstream media outlets to narrow. When the president's actions are popular, journalists tend to frame their stories accordingly. Whether consciously or not, rather than adopt a critical or objective tone towards government, reporters are more likely to imply that our officials are wise, our military is strong, and our enemy is pure evil. The president's rise in popularity also adds to his credibility as a news source, and makes it more difficult for journalists to challenge his arguments or to include critical points of view in their stories.[3]

Moreover, the public's preoccupation with a military victory and with the welfare of its troops makes it unpleasant for the press to complain about government restrictions on reporting. Official arguments that operational security and the lives of troops are on the line ring loud and clear during war. Media objections about freedom of information and the First Amendment, on the other hand, most often sound hollow and self-serving. Many in the press worry about complaining so loudly that the public's already dim view of journalists will worsen. As we saw in the Gulf War, the military's national security role is far more popular than the media's information role; journalists have still not recovered from their wartime comparison to the generals. This mismatch clearly daunts some, if not many, in the press who would otherwise challenge official pronouncements, and it has given presidents the courage to continue restricting information and press access to the battlefield.

The final source of the president's impact on press coverage is the military's cooperation in administration public relations efforts. During Vietnam Lyndon Johnson successfully used a reluctant General William Westmoreland to lend credibility to his administration's "progress campaign" in 1967. Unfortunately for Johnson, however, he never enjoyed similar support from the military public affairs system in Vietnam. In fact, despite the military's generally helpful press policy its handling of public affairs in Vietnam eventually helped to destroy the government's credibility and degrade public confidence in the war effort. In the Gulf War, by contrast, Bush commanded a military whose senior officers were both willing and capable of playing a highly visible public relations role directed by the White House. Impressive and professional general officers gave polished television performances that reinforced the White House line. In fact, the daily briefings seemed to rekindle the credibility that the military had lost in Vietnam. And with the White House and military speaking with one powerful and authoritative voice, the Bush administration's public communications efforts were, by all accounts, extremely successful.

The Limits of Control

Before conceding everything to the president we must clarify that the government's efforts to control the press during war do not necessarily ensure that control will be forthcoming. The government's tremendous success in curbing the press during recent conflicts has been due to circumstance as well as to government strategy. Though presidents will always seek to control the press and dominate press coverage, they will not always succeed. In fact, every presidential power noted above has its limits, and other obstacles also await the president looking to have his way with the press during war.

Losing Control of the Battlefield

Future presidents will undoubtedly face situations in which they cannot, despite their best efforts, achieve the same level of control over the battlefield that Reagan enjoyed in Grenada or that Bush managed in Panama and the Gulf. Presidential control over media access to the battlefield will deteriorate when war breaks out in an area more easily accessible to journalists, when a war lasts long enough for journalists to make their way into military units despite press restrictions, when a war is waged at a low enough level of intensity that greater numbers of journalists are willing to risk covering the war up close, or when the enemy decides to allow the media to cover the war from his side of the battlefield.

George Bush faced a dream scenario in the Gulf War because Saudi Arabia proved a hostile and lethal environment for the free press. In other situations the government will not be so lucky, as the Clinton Administration more recently discovered. As the administration openly telegraphed the invasion of Haiti in an attempt to coerce its military rulers to submit, the press swarmed into Haiti and set up camp atop the tallest buildings in Port-au-Prince with their television cameras to film the American military landing. The Haitian military government allowed the press in, and even granted interviews to Dan Rather, among others. The prospects for control had Clinton gone through with the invasion were dismal, and the press would have once more offered combat footage to the public uncensored by government. Clinton, in turn, would have found influencing press coverage of the invasion to his advantage very difficult, especially if the press was able to focus on actual fighting or portrayed American casualties.

Threats to Presidential Dominance of Press Coverage

The most debilitating loss of influence would come if the president led the nation into a war opposed by a majority of the public or by a substantial coalition in the Congress, or if he persisted in prosecuting a war that had become widely unpopular. The negative effects on a president's ability to wield influence from the bully pulpit would be multiplied if the president was, in addition, personally unpopular at the time. An unpopular president, waging an unpopular war opposed by political elites, would find it very difficult to garner favorable press coverage. Journalists would downplay his victories and play up his mistakes and defeats. Congressional critics would make the front pages, and statements from administration officials would be harshly challenged at every press conference. If the war went poorly, the same public opinion which has served presidents so powerfully in other crises would instead become the source of a president's worst nightmares.

A milder scenario in which a president could lose some of his media dominance would be one in which the White House and the military were at odds during war. This might occur when the White House sent a military force somewhere military leaders had been reluctant to get involved. Tensions could also arise if the White House tried to micromanage the war from Washington, ignoring military pleas for control over how to employ its troops and equipment. Examples of these scenarios are readily available from U.S. experiences with Bosnia and Somalia. In 1992, in the midst of debate over whether the United States should use military force in Bosnia, General Colin Powell, then the Chairman of the Joint Chiefs of Staff, became so upset at the prospect of U.S. military involvement that he published an op-ed denouncing the idea. In Somalia, the military's outrage at Secretary of Defense Les Aspin's denial of its request for heavy armor, which had come only a short time before the clash which left seventeen U.S. troops dead, led to serious public complaints about Clinton Administration foreign policy and its top officials. The military, until then a stout ally of administration intervention in Somalia, suddenly began feeding the press material harmful to the president and his goals. Such public outbursts from the military challenging administration actions and thinking are rare, but these examples reveal that when the military feels it necessary, it will not hesitate to use the media to advance and protect its interests, even if it means clashing with the White House. And although recent history suggests that presidents and the military tend to be in sync on these issues, it also illustrates that inevitably there will be times when the White House and military are at odds. When they are, the president will face greater obstacles to creating a positive image of his activities in the news.

Finally, perhaps the most unpredictable threat to presidential control over the press and press coverage will come if an American enemy grants enough access and autonomy to Western journalists to reveal what war is like for those on the other side. From Harrison Salisbury's trip to Hanoi during Vietnam to Peter Arnett's presence in Baghdad during Desert Storm, government officials have feared the impact that reports from the other side might have on public opinion. To date, these fears have gone largely unrealized, even during the Gulf war. Saddam Hussein, despite ample opportunity to test the impact of war coverage from Iraq on American public opinion, never figured out just how to wield the media to maximum effect. Hussein's poor understanding of American psychology and politics, as well as of the routines of Western media betrayed him. Indeed, Iraq's experience shows that the risk of a backlash from using an enemy's media against him is great. Nonetheless, advances in media technology combined with the increasing sophistication of most governments in understanding and using the media make it certain that future presidents will face at least some of the fallout from enemy media management.

Several possibilities, in particular, stand out as threats to presidential dominance of the news. First, and most obvious, if an enemy were to grant the Western press free access to the battlefield from his side, the amount of graphic coverage of war could increase dramatically, laying waste to White House efforts to restrict such coverage through press controls on the American side. This access could prove troublesome if the media were to focus on the consequences of U.S. firepower and showed bombed out towns or villages or interviewed enemy troops who had been routed by an American unit. As many observers have noted, the camera does not explain the larger principles of war to the viewer; rather, it tends to promote empathy for its subjects. It might be difficult for a president to inflame war lust in a public who had to witness what war does to those caught in it, even if its victims were technically the enemy. What could be worse, however, would be if television were present to record the toll of war on American troops. In recent conflicts the United States has been fortunate not to suffer many casualties. A war in which the United States suffered thousands of dead and wounded and that was heavily covered by television crews could prove, as many fear, impossible to prosecute. Though it would undoubtedly infuriate American officials, it would not matter to the viewing public that the television crews were there only because the enemy had allowed their presence on the battlefield. The consequences would be the same as long as the newscasts were credible.

Second, press coverage from the enemy side could produce pressures on the president to act in ways that threatened the larger interest of winning the war. The Iran hostage crisis supplies an example of how the press can cover an event and thereby put almost intolerable pressures on the president to take an action which does not serve broader American foreign policy goals. If during a future war an equivalent situation arose, perhaps one in which the enemy invited journalists to film the execution of American hostages, the intense media coverage and public torment over the plight of the POWs would make it difficult for the president to focus public attention on other issues. Not only could such enemy media tactics hurt the president politically, but they would take the public relations initiative away from the White House and force it to concentrate on damage control rather than on its preferred strategy of building support and putting a favorable spin on events. It would obviously be very difficult for the president to claim that the war was going well when several hundred POWs were being abused and their pain transmitted via television to American living rooms. Further, every enemy "counter-public relations" success would steal potentially valuable press coverage away from the White House; every story on the plight of the hostages would be a story the media did not do on Administration successes.

Finally, if the American media, by enemy consent, were allowed to roam free on the battlefield and behind enemy lines, the chances that a correspondent would uncover instances of U.S. government exaggeration and deception would rise. Just as Harrison Salisbury discovered in Hanoi that U.S. bombs had indeed struck civilian structures despite official denials, future news seekers could reveal that high-tech wars waged with smart bombs are not as clean as their masters would have the public believe. With an unrestricted and uncensored press in the war zone, American presidents and military officers would have to be much more careful than they have recently been when they discuss the war's progress and the performance of U.S. troops and equipment. In Grenada, the government insisted for over a week that there had not been any civilian casualties. The press later discovered that this was not true. In Panama, a journalist discovered that the military had lied about the accuracy of the Stealth fighters' bombing run. And in the Baghdad, CNN revealed what Bush and the military did not want to talk about—the fact that civilians were in grave danger from the Allied air campaign despite the use of precision guided bombs. In each case, the lies and obfuscations were made possible by tight government control over press access to the battlefield and thus to information. Presidents enjoyed better press coverage than they deserved as a result.

In the future, however, a clever enemy might challenge this advantage by allowing American journalists free rein to check up on presidential and military claims about the war's progress. In the extreme, press coverage from the enemy side could force the government to abandon its preferred tactics for waging war. If television routinely revealed the human consequences of the use of carpet bombing, napalm, or fuel-air explosives, for example, their continued use could quickly become political suicide. And even if the public did not demand a halt to their use, no president or military leader wishes to be linked to war's horrible toll. In the future a president faced with coverage of such events might well, as George Bush did after the Amiriyah incident, decide to halt the use of such weapons before the public started believing that he personally endorsed such actions. In such cases not only would the president find it hard to create positive coverage of carpet bombing, for instance, but he would also likely spend a good deal of time trying to distance himself from war's uglier realities.

Summing Up Presidential Control and Its Limits

In the conflicts examined here, presidents have clearly succeeded in controlling press access to the battlefield and in heavily influencing press coverage to their advantage through use of the various powers under their control. The president and the military have worked in harmony, with the military keeping the press away from the action and providing its own spin on events. White House public relations strategies have been well thought out and executed, taking full advantage of the media's obsessive focus on the president and his actions. In each case, the location of the conflict and the nature of the battle have made it extremely difficult for journalists to cover the action on their own without either military assistance or interference. The press, meanwhile, proved both incapable of organizing itself to challenge government restrictions, and so unpopular with the public that the White House never felt any pressure to ease them.

Nonetheless, the prospects for a loss of presidential control are real. The White House cannot expect to be so fortunate on every occasion; there are simply too many ways in which events could work against presidents and for the press. The question, then, is what is a loss of control likely to mean in the future? For the president, being unable to manage the news could mean simply that the press had access to more information than he would prefer, perhaps frustrating his attempts to focus attention on pet issues and to create favorable coverage of his actions. It could, however, result in far more serious scenarios if an enemy were successful in using the media to derail presidential war plans or if the press were to uncover official deception about events on the battlefield, thereby turning public opinion against the president and the military.

THE IMPLICATIONS OF THE NEW MEDIA STRATEGY

The findings that presidents, not the military, are primarily responsible for recent press restrictions and that they have done so in response to fears and incentives heightened by the rise of media power should warn us that increasing government restriction of the press during war is a far more serious and far more political issue than previously believed. The new presidential media strategy for wartime may threaten the working relationship between the president and the press, causing problems for politics and policy making that last long after the guns fall silent. The conventional wisdom argues that press restrictions are fundamentally the result of a long-running feud between the military and the media. Though annoying to those who wish to see freer press coverage of combat, a feud between two institutions who only rarely have much to do with each other hardly seems a threat to the democratic process. In fact, the two institutions have fought tooth and nail over the same issues since the founding of the republic with little real consequence. On the other hand, however, the repeated and conscious attempts by presidents and their advisers to obstruct the functioning of the press during war and to replace journalists' products with their own messages and images pose the threat of poisoning the everyday working relationship between the president and the press. Especially given its already adversarial nature, there is not much room for abuse by either side. Regardless of whether one believes that the measures taken by presidents in recent conflicts have been appropriate, they have certainly incurred the wrath of the media. Moreover, this wrath has not disappeared after each conflict, but instead became a part of the media's approach to interpreting the rest of a president's tenure in office. In this age no one needs reminding how central the press is to a president's ability to govern effectively. A press corps convinced during a conflict that a president seeks too much control over the news, even for a good cause, will without doubt prove a barrier to presidential policy making and political well-being. Thus, presidents risk losing a broader "war" by restricting the press during battle. Worse, problems between the president and press may very well not remain local, but are likely spread to the rest of the political system. Anyone who needs proof of the damage a tear in the president/press relationship can cause should simply recall the deterioration of the relationship outlined in Chapter Three, the impact of which is still felt not just during conflict but every day.

My findings also encourage us to rethink the modern connections between presidents, the press, and public opinion. Whereas conventional explanations for press restrictions ignore the role of the White House, this reexamination of recent history has shown that White Houses have viewed their wartime press policies as tools with which to shape public opinion. In addition, the argument I have proposed here provides clues to the nature of the relationship between the press and government more generally, and suggests potential disfunctions in U.S. foreign policy in the future that the focus on the military has obscured.

War, Presidents, the Press, and Public Opinion

One broad but undeniable consequence of the new media strategy can be identified from the case studies: The public knew less about the conflicts than they would have if the press had been left to its own devices. Relatedly, had there been no press restrictions, the public would have seen more of what journalists think is newsworthy about war (i.e.—casualties, combat, action, soldiers) than they did. Instead, in each conflict the public clearly received a version of events very close to what White House and Pentagon officials wanted it to get. Officials were quite successful in keeping the horrible side of war out the news with the result that the public has not had to witness American casualties or the toll taken by American military might on the enemy.

But although is it clear that the public was less knowledgeable, it remains much less clear whether or not the public would have felt any differently about the conflicts or the presidents who initiated them if the press had been allowed to cover them more fully. It seems quite reasonable to assume that the nature of press coverage, being the dominant source of information for most people about a war, should have a similarly major influence on how people assess war, their civilian and military leaders, and so on, subject of course to individual beliefs and attitudes about such things. Mueller, however, has argued powerfully that media coverage of war had nothing to do with the level of public support. As long as the casualty list grows, public support will continue to decline.

These findings do not directly confront Mueller's contention that the connection between war and public opinion does not depend on media coverage. Mueller notes in his recent book on the Gulf War—and I agree—that the Gulf War was a poor test of that connection for the simple reason that there were so few American casualties and the war was so successful.[4] The Grenada and Panama invasions offer similarly weak tests of the relationship between casualties and opinion. Nonetheless, the cases studied here reveal quite clearly that Mueller's argument gives an incomplete picture of the importance of the interplay of the media, war, presidential actions, and public opinion.

Whether or not press coverage affects the level of public support for war, presidents, military leaders, and other government officials believe it does, and further, they act vigorously on that belief. This belief, in fact, is so widespread among elite circles that it has taken on a self-fulfilling momentum. If everyone in Washington, D.C. believes that the president would be wounded politically by graphic coverage of war dead, or by negative commentary concerning military performance, then, ipso facto, he will be wounded, and people in Washington will act accordingly.[5]

The result of this belief, as I have shown, has been the growth of press controls and public relations to prevent negative coverage and to frame issues and events in a positive and politically advantageous manner. What we have witnessed over the last generation has been the institutionalization of a theory of the war-press-public opinion connection. Military public affairs policy, the DoD press pools, and White House public relations tactics now play a permanent and integral role in trying to mollify the impact of war and press coverage of war on public opinion.

Mueller's argument, moreover, should not obscure another central theme of my argument: that there are many reasons for a president to want to control the press and influence press coverage of war. Presidents worry not only about the percentage of people who say they support the war, but also about opinion and attitudes concerning a number of other issues. Even if a president could do nothing to prevent a decline in public support for war as casualties increased, consider again the other critical realms of opinion he may influence.

First, as noted in each of the cases, a president has a good deal of power to use the media to justify the need to go to war in the first place. In the Panama and Gulf cases, Bush launched a public relations attack on the enemy-to-be, vilifying Noriega and Hussein and emphasizing their heinous acts in an attempt to ensure that the public would understand why using military force would eventually be necessary. In both cases, Bush successfully convinced much of the public that these evil men had to be confronted. At the very least, the White House's preparation of the public allowed Bush to avoid any unpleasant surprises on the public opinion front when crisis turned into conflict.

Second, by dominating press coverage before a conflict begins, a president may be able to frame the crisis in terms favorable to his preferred solution and which allow him to determine the criteria for successful resolution of conflict. In Panama, Bush's rhetoric made it clear that ousting Noriega was necessary and that this goal, rather than ensuring Panama's long-range well-being, was the main criterion for successful U.S. policy toward Panama. The proof of Bush's success in framing the crisis in this way became clear once U.S. forces had mopped up the PDF but Noriega remained at large. Both opinion polls and politicians in Washington refused to call the invasion a success until Noriega was captured. But as soon as Bush appeared on television to announce his arrest, victory and public support were his.

Finally, even if one agrees that the way in which the media cover events does not affect the public's interpretation of them, it still makes sense for a president to keep the press away from the battlefield. The more journalists there are on the battlefield, the more events they will cover, and the greater the chances that one of them will file a report that upsets the public, makes the U.S. military look bad, challenges official statements about the war, or raises questions about how well the president is managing the military operation. Though these episodes may not affect the level of public support for the war itself, they could very well affect public support of the president.

In sum, Mueller may be correct in asserting that the media have no impact on the decline in support for war as casualties rise. It will take the misfortune of another lengthy and costly war before this finding can be replicated. In the meantime, however, it is clear that presidents disagree wholeheartedly with Mueller, and that even if he is correct, they still have other political interests that demand the use of press restrictions and public relations during war.

The Relationship Between the Press and Government

By identifying the president/press relationship as the central dynamic behind press restrictions, we add another set of case studies to the debate that has raged over the last generation concerning the role the press plays in the American political system. Three competing theories vie to describe the relationship of the media to government: the "watchdog," the "lapdog," and the "attack dog." Watchdog theory asserts that the press works as a balance against the government, providing the public with an independent source of information with which to form opinions and make decisions concerning the political issues of the day. The press monitors the government to ensure that it does not abuse its powers, and to let the public know when policies are failing and should be reconsidered. Lapdog theory, on the other hand, argues that journalists rely so heavily on official and elite sources of information and opinion that the press does not operate as a watchdog, but instead serves to promote the interests and policy positions of those in power at the expense of others. Finally, attack dog theory complains that the press' emphasis on the negative and sensational creates press coverage that disrupts policymaking and encourages public cynicism and mistrust of government institutions and leaders.[6]

Each theory predicts a different output from the news making process during war. The watchdog theory suggests that we should see a good deal of analysis of government decisions, including the most important one about whether or not to use military force. Press coverage should be critical, not in the sense of negative, but in the sense that it should focus on problems and should not shy away from calling a government failure a failure and identifying those responsible. Lapdog theory, however, predicts that press coverage will be fundamentally uncritical of government leaders and their actions. Most news, moreover, will come directly from the government without a great deal of independent analysis from the press. Attack dog theory, finally, predicts that press coverage will be quite negative toward government officials and their policies, focusing on the sensational aspects of events at the expense of substantive elaborations of policy.

My research lends qualified support to the lapdog theory. In all three cases, the press did little analysis that raised questions about the need for moving to a military option. Once the fighting had begun, the majority of news stories and columns accepted the president's assertions that such action was necessary. In no case did criticism of an administration's actions reach a significant proportion of total press coverage, particularly on television. One study found that during the Gulf War 95% of all sources on television made positive comments about the U.S. military's performance.[7] And as lapdog theory predicted, what criticism there was focused almost entirely on the best means to achieve victory, rather than on the need to go to war in the first place.[8] During each conflict, relatively few journalists took the risks necessary to circumvent the military's restrictions to gather information independently. Most stayed close to the military briefers in Saudi Arabia and to their beats in official Washington.[9] And in the aftermath of war, when one might expect to see more calculated discussion or analysis of a conflict, instead we saw yet more positive coverage, much of it praising the boldness of the president and the effectiveness of the military. Few stories raised questions of the legality, morality, or wisdom of using military force. Those follow-up stories of a critical nature the press did produce (again, usually concerning military performance) tended to wind up buried deep in the papers, with very few making it to the evening news. As a result, neither the watchdog nor the attack dog theories find much support in the cases presented here.

The next question to ask is how generalizable these findings are for the day-to-day government/press relationship. The answer is not completely, though we have gained more than a simple analysis of military/media tensions would have offered. The combination of press restrictions, public relations, and the position of the president works to make playing any role other than lapdog very difficult. As noted in the previous section, wartime gives a president great resources for exerting control over information, the physical and logistical capabilities of the press, and for getting his views heard by the public. This power, as the cases show clearly, erodes the ability of the press to provide independently gathered news about armed conflicts. Moreover, the overwhelming importance of the president's role during war would make it difficult to maintain a balance between competing views of crisis and war, even if the press wanted to do so.

The lapdog theory thus wins support from these cases not necessarily because they make it obvious that the media is fundamentally subservient to government but because during war the media's options for newsgathering have been severely constrained. During war, more than at any other time, the press must go to government officials for information and analysis of the day's events, despite how journalists feel about this. It seems clear that most of those correspondents who went to cover the U.S. conflicts wanted to report on much more than they in fact did. Whether their intentions were to assess critically U.S. performance or the necessity of military action or simply to send back visually exciting footage of combat, the end result under a less restrictive system would have been a far less subservient press. No self-respecting news organization would have used government-provided footage of aircraft taking off or secondhand accounts of battles when eyewitness reports and on-the-scene footage were readily available. Further, it seems very likely from the few instances in which journalists did manage to gain independent access to information, such as the encounter at Khafji, that the press, if left free to roam the battlefield, would have reported poor military performance, misconduct, and noted inconsistencies and inaccuracies in government statements without hesitation. A better way to describe the press during recent wars, therefore, might be to call it an imperfect watchdog on a very short leash.

U.S. Foreign Policy in the Media Age

Finally, the rising importance of the press and increased presidential concerns with controlling press coverage in order to maintain public support also suggest important questions for foreign policy making. In particular, many have argued that television coverage of events overseas and the White House's concerns over the potential impact of that coverage on public opinion may at times dictate or heavily influence U.S. foreign policy, pushing aside more reasoned calculations of the national interest.[10] This dynamic, which has become widely known as the "CNN Effect," has achieved a good measure of popularity among foreign policy observers, in part because a good number of former officials have admitted that television news had serious impacts on their policy making efforts.

Fears of a "CNN Effect" first gained wide notice with the Iran hostage crisis, during which the constant drumbeat of media coverage affected not only the manner in which the Carter administration dealt with the crisis but Carter's entire presidency from that point onward. Lloyd Cutler, Carter's White House counsel from 1979-1980 and a witness to the media barrage, was among the first senior officials to lay out the impact of television news on foreign policy:

> But it came as a distinct surprise to me how much television news had intruded into both the timing and the substance of the policy decisions that an American president is required to make. TV news now has a much greater effect on national policy decisions—especially foreign-policy decisions—than print journalism has ever been able to achieve and more than most experienced observers realize. . . . A vivid account on TV news commands the attention and concern of most of the larger TV audience. The impact of TV news thus has major consequences for the foreign-policy agenda of any administration.[11]

Although not purporting to offer a complete explanation of the impact of television on U.S. foreign policy by any means, the argument pursued in this book, as well as commentary from former officials and other observers, suggests that with respect to foreign policy, the CNN effect may operate in at least two different ways, neither of which seems likely to be healthy for U.S. foreign policy. First, television coverage of vivid, bloody, or emotionally charged scenes from abroad may cause a president to reverse course quickly for fear of losing public support for the mission without a cool and considered analysis of the broader national interests at stake in doing so. The Clinton administration's rather sudden exit from Somalia in the wake of vivid press coverage of the deaths of fewer than twenty American soldiers, one of whom was dragged through the streets of Mogadishu, seems plausibly explained by this dynamic. I am not arguing that presidents care only about press coverage and public opinion and not at all about U.S. security interests and foreign policy goals. But if, as I have argued, the White House now cares more than ever about the connection between media coverage and public opinion, it seems reasonable to worry about the possibility that television coverage, especially if U.S. citizens are directly involved, will exert a powerful influence on White House foreign policy making. As James Hoge has argued, this sort of dynamic seems most likely to play out in cases in which the president lacks a clearly defined sense of the situation and concrete policy goals.[12] The reasonableness of this concern is supported by David Gergen's observations about television's influence on Reagan administration policy toward Lebanon:

> I worked in the Reagan White House and I can tell you that television had an enormous impact on our policy in Lebanon. We withdrew those marines from Lebanon in part because of television. We asked the Israelis to stop bombing in part because of television pictures that were coming back from Beirut.[13]

A second way in which the CNN effect might be realized, though less visibly, would be if a president became so concerned with the need to avoid press coverage of American casualties and so certain that televised and lengthy foreign policy engagements could not be supported by the public that he decided not to commit the U.S. military in some situations despite believing that there were good reasons for doing so. Though a troubling possibility, this scenario seems most likely to occur when U.S. national security interests are not directly involved, such as with humanitarian or peacekeeping missions when the geopolitical stakes are relatively low and presidents might conclude that the potential gains from action were outweighed by the potential damage from media coverage. It seems far less likely that a president would fail to act in a situation with the national interest directly at stake simply because the media might portray the results in a negative or sensational light. It seems a safe conclusion, however, other things being equal, that the increased potential for critical media scrutiny of U.S. military action will very likely act as a brake on White House willingness to use force in situations in which media coverage will be hard to manage. And though most commentators seem to feel that this effect would have primarily negative consequences for the conduct of U.S. foreign policy, it may not be a bad thing that television makes presidents think hard before acting. As Lloyd Cutler observed, "TV news can provide a useful early warning that a policy course that costs American lives or jobs will be very difficult to sustain over an extended period. It can force an administration to calculate fully the costs and benefits of such a policy before it casts the die."[14]

PROSPECTS FOR THE GOVERNMENT/PRESS STRUGGLE

Previous chapters have established both the elements and the consequences of the post-Vietnam development of a White House media strategy for wartime as well as documented the successes of that strategy in recent conflicts in restricting negative coverage of war and in amplifying positive presidential messages to the public. It is now time to consider the prospects for the government/press struggle as it heads towards the twenty-first century.

A Return to Censorship?

Most treatises on government/press wartime relations include a call to either the military or the press to mend their ways and to respect the other's unique role in society.[15] Such efforts, however well-intended, are a waste of time. Proposals voiced on behalf of the media beseeching the military to permit greater numbers of reporters on the battlefield, to give them greater access to the military's activities, or to get rid of security review and trust reporters instead, all benefit the press at the expense of the government. In addition, they wrongly tend to focus on the military instead of the principal press restrictor—the White House. Likewise, proposals offered on behalf of the military, such as asking the press to send fewer reporters to wars, to submit their reports cheerfully to commonsense security review, and to accept the need for military escorts, all benefit the government while doing nothing but make covering war more difficult for the press and ignoring the fact that the press has no way to organize itself to agree to such conditions anyway. Since neither side will give the other something for nothing, simply listing all the things everyone ought to do in a perfect world does no good. And worse, almost all advice given to the combatants ignores what I have argued here, which is that several fundamental trends underlying the government/press relationship are driving the White House to restrict the press. Proposals that focus on symptoms rather than root causes will offer little in the way of results.

The only proposals worth making, then, are those that would make both sides better off and have some likelihood of adoption. After over 200 years of government/press struggle during war without resolving these issues, many observers find it unlikely that such a proposal exists. And in fact only one existing proposal merits a close look given today's circumstances—a return to full-scale military censorship. On the face of it, arguing that military censorship would represent an improvement for everyone might sound facetious. Surely the press would not benefit, people would argue. But no less giant a journalistic icon than Walter Cronkite has endorsed such a proposal.[16] And an analysis of the censorship option does suggest that it has the potential to resolve many of the tensions raised by recent struggles over wartime press coverage.

A return to official military censorship would probably involve much the same set-up as seen in Desert Storm with a few key changes. Qualified military intelligence officers in the rear, as opposed to public affairs escorts at the scene, would censor, not just review, all press materials before releasing them for transmission to news organizations. As in the past, there would be guidelines detailing what information could be published and what could not. The list would look very similar to that drawn up in the Gulf, which in turn had been culled from World War II and Korea censorship rules, among others. There would probably be an appeal process for journalists to challenge the censors, but unlike in Desert Storm the government, not the press, would make the final decision whether or not to allow a story to be published.

From the military's perspective the benefits are clear and in fact many military officers have argued for a return to such a system. Only with censorship, they argue, can the military be totally secure in its knowledge that the press will not provide useful information to the enemy. And from a more professionally interested perspective, the military would likely view a censorship system as far less likely to reveal its warts and failures, even though technically these issues would not be subject to censorship.

The White House would also be very likely to endorse such a system, having over successive administrations attempted to move closer to that model surreptitiously anyway. To presidents, any system that provides for a greater level of control over journalists' reports, the better. And censorship, regardless of what the details of the system might be, stands for the ultimate possible control over the press.

Why might the media benefit from such a system? Recall that a journalist's wartime dilemma is resolving the trade-off between autonomy and access with access to the story their number one concern. Though war correspondents obviously would prefer to operate autonomously and without restraints, their highest priority is to get close to the action first and worry about what they can report later.

Journalists during World War II accepted the censorship system fairly willingly not only because they believed in the cause, but because the system allowed them great access to the battlefield and to secret information concerning battle plans. Knowing that journalists could not broadcast their eyewitness knowledge of military information to the enemy, the government was far more willing to allow them to travel throughout the war zone for news. Censorship also allowed military officers to speak much more candidly and openly about their actions and decisions. Reporters who covered World War II remember sitting in military field tents going over battle plans, sometimes even being asked for their advice. Even before D-Day, Eisenhower went over the attack with journalists; the secret did not leak. And although journalists would prefer to report such information as they received it, it remains valuable for postwar articles and histories nonetheless. Their presence also allows journalists the possibility of telling all later and the knowledge of this fact must certainly encourage honesty and openness on the part of government and military officials. In the eyes of a journalist it is far better to reveal this information eventually rather than let it remain undisclosed forever.

During the Gulf War, in stark contrast to World War II, journalists got nowhere near the battlefield as a rule, in large part because there were no security guarantees, and because television technology had intensified the dangers of reporting from the front. In addition, candid conversation about battle plans between officers and correspondents was rare during the Gulf War. For the most part during the Gulf War military leaders felt that they had to be wary of talking with journalists capable of releasing the details of their conversation in capitals around the world minutes later. As a result, military officers often did not feel comfortable revealing much information to the press, causing tension with reporters trying to piece together a very complicated story. Perhaps the ultimate example of the untrusting military/media interaction was General Schwarzkopf's successful effort to trick the press into thinking the main assault against Iraq would be the Marine amphibious attack instead of the Hail Mary in the west.

A return to censorship, then, might benefit journalists because it could reestablish trust between a nervous military and a skeptical press. If the press in the future could count on getting enough access to military operations and leaders, censorship might conceivably be worth the resulting lack of autonomy. Journalists might also escape the public wrath they have incurred as a consequence of their visible complaining about government restrictions.

A brief analysis thus indicates that a return to censorship might resolve many of the tensions between the government and the press. Nevertheless, two questions remain. First, is the system likely to work in the idealized manner suggested here? Second, would such a system benefit the public and democracy?

The answer to both questions is probably "No." Recent history should prompt serious doubts about whether censorship would either resolve the government/press struggle or operate in a manner acceptable to a democracy. Official fear and loathing of the press' power to disrupt their policies, heightened by the media age trends noted above, make it seem unlikely that the government can be trusted to employ censorship today in an evenhanded manner guided by the principle of freedom of information. It seems more likely that the government would use the system to increase its control over the press, the news, and public opinion. Although some might approve of this from a "national interest" perspective, many more would probably disapprove of such a system if used to enhance the president's own political situation.

Three potential problems in particular seem likely should such a system be implemented. First, the access the press expected by acceding to censorship would be unlikely to be forthcoming. The experience of the last decade, but especially in the Gulf, indicates that the last thing presidents and militaries want to do is to let journalists film combat or witness combat firsthand. Although censorship would make moot issues of operational security, nominally the reason for limits on access, it would not reduce White House political interests or military institutional interests in keeping the press away from the blood, the confusion, and the horror of warfare.

Second, a censorship system would not necessarily improve the military's public affairs shortcomings that proved so disastrous in recent conflicts. A system that provided even more control over the press to the military would in fact curb, not encourage, incentives for improvement. It is worth noting that the information center in Vietnam was the most organized of recent wars, when the press was most free. JIBs were far less well organized in more recent conflicts when the press was shut out and kept away from the action. Under censorship, press reports would continue to be delayed for days while they worked their way through the military's bureaucratic system, made even slower by the need to censor reports rather than wave them through after a quick perusal. Nor would there be any reason to improve logistics, communications, or any of the other public affairs problems that have plagued reporters' news gathering efforts.

Third, and most worrisome, would be the temptation for officials to use the censorship system for political reasons rather than for strictly military reasons. This problem revealed itself in the Gulf War with the security review system, even though the military had no authority to censor press reports. Many journalists found that their copy had been reviewed by several different officers interested in limiting what was reported, and in at least a few cases officers made changes in violation of public affairs policy. Under a censorship system, there would be little immediate pressure to prevent military censors from operating out of professional self-interest, rather than from operational security guidelines. Journalists, busy trying to put together stories for deadlines in a chaotic wartime environment, would have difficulty challenging such censorship at the time. And the White House would have little incentive not to instruct the military to censor particular items of political importance, knowing that all the press could do would be to complain, and that it could not publish the material until after the war when it would carry less impact. Even if in general the White House respected the guidelines for censorship, the political incentives that would exist at critical moments, such as in the wake of a disastrous defeat that could cause panic among the public or among allies, or before a presidential election, would encourage presidents to censor for political security first and justify their actions later when the danger had passed.

In a worst case, the censorship guidelines would foster such behavior. In World War II valid areas for censorship included unauthenticated reports and rumors, and anything that would harm the morale of Allied Forces. Such guidelines today, as in fact was the case even then, could and would be used to justify much censorship of a political, rather than military, nature.[17] Would details of a horrible defeat harm morale? A White House could easily argue that it would. And in light of official concerns that journalists actually seek to derail presidential policies, the opportunity to stop critical reports before they did their damage would be too great for officials to pass up.

Regardless of its consequences, however, a system of military censorship is not a live option in the current "negotiations" between the government and press on future public affairs policies. The most basic reason for this is that in order to declare censorship, Congress must have first declared war. Quite obviously, the majority of future conflicts will not meet this essential criterion. If the president wishes to launch war entirely on his own authority, as Reagan and Bush did in Grenada and Panama, censorship will not be an option. And second, censorship may have much to recommend it, at least on the surface, and especially to officials, but it lacks wider political acceptability. The military dropped its field censorship reserve units because it realized that the age of censorship was long over. In large part this reflects an understanding of the central role of the press in politics and the journalists' changed attitudes and stance toward government. Today's journalists would be far less willing than their counterparts fifty years ago to accept the level of control over their work that outright censorship implies, despite the promise of greater access. The press is now accustomed to the power to tell all, including those things which will damage morale or disrupt policy, as long as they consider the information to be newsworthy. Journalists, in fact, disavow any need to consider what consequences their reporting will have, short of causing injury to American soldiers. In light of Vietnam, Watergate, and the credibility gap, it does not seem likely that censorship could ever be declared during a limited war. As the media age has matured, censorship has become an increasingly less appealing option to presidents, at least in any situation short of another world war. Limited restrictions carried out for reasons of operational security are easy to sell to the public, but censorship of press dispatches from Grenada, for example, a tiny nation of no possible threat, would look too heavy-handed. No president wants to deal with the media firestorm and political backlash that would accompany such a misguided effort at control. In today's world where sophistication in public relations is the standard, presidents look to more subtle methods of control. This helps explains, in fact, why recent restrictions have taken the form they did.

If we will not return to censorship any time soon, we must ask about what the players involved are doing instead to improve their lot for the next conflict. As noted in Chapter Five, representatives from fifteen major news organizations wrote a letter of protest to Secretary of Defense Richard Cheney, setting forth both their concerns about Gulf War press policy and their proposed guidelines for the next conflict. Once again, officials have made noises about making press policies more friendly, and some rethinking of public affairs policy has cropped up in military journals.[18] But after several years public affairs policies look much the same as they did at the end of the Gulf War.[19] And as Grenada, Panama, and the Gulf illustrate, it would be foolish to pay much attention to what the military says press policy will be next time. The promises the military makes will almost certainly vanish in the wake of presidential political interests and White House control over press policy once crisis strikes. In addition, as we will see below in a brief analysis of the near invasion of Haiti, it would be foolish to assume that the press would rely in the future on negotiating with the very institutions that have restricted journalists in the recent past.

The Government/Press Struggle Continues...

The fundamental nature of the trends that have brought us to our current situation invites an obvious prediction: As long as we live in this media age, presidents will continue to seek to impose restrictions on the press and to shape the news through public relations during war. We should expect, therefore, to see press restrictions for the foreseeable future as media technology continues to advance, officials and reporters continue to view each other as adversaries, the United States continues to lack consensus in foreign policy, and the White House continues to view public relations as a key tool of governance.

Some might question this prediction despite the evidence presented here. Opponents of America's recent conflicts may be inclined to point out that two conservative presidents with little love for the press were responsible for initiating the growth of controls on reporters. They might argue that the need for press restrictions arose because the conflicts were either unjust or unnecessary. Without such curbs on the press and without heavy doses of public relations, the public likely would not have supported these wars. Had the wars been just and the presidents more liberal, the argument concludes, there would have been neither the need nor the inclination to impose severe restrictions on the press.

Enticing though this argument may be for some, it is faulty, based on a poor understanding of the forces at work in the White House. All presidents, liberal and conservative, fall into what I labeled earlier the "national interest" camp. Their role as commander-in-chief demands that they worry far more about the outcome of their war policies than about whether journalists are happy with their experiences as war correspondents. And just as importantly, presidents also belong to the self-interest camp. In today's media-dominated political environment, their political interests force them to seek ways to control the news, to influence what the public sees and hears about war. If they cannot, presidents know that the media have the power to turn even a military victory into political defeat. No matter whether presidents presiding over future conflicts are liberal or conservative, they will find themselves looking for ways to reduce the risk posed by journalists on the battlefield. As I will discuss below, the Clinton Administration's instincts during the build-up to the aborted invasion of Haiti illustrate that even Democratic presidents are certain to disappoint those who believe that Reagan and Bush were themselves the primary cause of press restrictions in America's last three conflicts.

. . . As Haiti Goes Prime Time

The near-invasion of Haiti displayed all the traits of war in the media age, including White House efforts to control the press and manage the news to its advantage. The press was a pervasive presence throughout the crisis. The intense press coverage of the Haiti dilemma raised the political stakes for Clinton, not only by creating popular awareness of violence and abuse in Haiti, but by providing an outlet for the harsh criticisms aimed at Clinton by congressional Republicans and other opponents of Clinton foreign policy. The scathing media commentary over Clinton's perceived waffling on Haiti policy created tension between the White House and the press, and made conceiving and implementing policy more difficult for the troubled president, especially as pressure mounted in the summer of 1994 for him to take decisive action.

Haiti illustrates that even liberal presidents will seek to spare themselves the potential consequences of televised military action and deploy their officials in public relations blitzes to secure public support. Like all White Houses in the media age, the Clinton White House attempted to use public relations to create a favorable climate of opinion for its Haiti policy. Unfortunately, it did so in a highly charged political environment with a distinct anti-military intervention bent. Republicans in Congress—particularly minority leader Robert Dole—and several prominent Democrats, including Sam Nunn, opposed an invasion, and pressed Clinton to seek congressional approval for any use of force in Haiti. In addition, two-thirds of the public opposed an invasion.

Knowing that congressional approval would not be forthcoming, however, the Clinton Administration opted instead to "go public" in a major last-ditch effort to sway public opinion before committing military forces. The big gun was Clinton's prime-time television address on September 15, during which he told Haitian military leaders that it was "time to go" and outlined the justification for his decision to invade if they did not step down immediately.[20] Unfortunately for Clinton, his speech was made into what one commentator called a "howling political gale;" Clinton's speech changed few minds, and fell on deaf ears in Congress. In fact, as preparations for an invasion moved forward, the House began its preparations to vote to cut off funds for the invasion should it take place, a belated attempt at last by Congress to curb the imperial presidency.[21] To his good fortune, Clinton was spared the need to invade Haiti at the last moment when his all-star negotiating team—Jimmy Carter, Sam Nunn, and General Colin Powell—managed to convince Haiti's military leaders to step down just as American planes were heading towards Port-au-Prince.[22] Like any president, Clinton immediately went back on television to claim credit for the entire operation.[23]

In preparing to wage war in the media age, however, the Clinton Administration had run into several difficulties. Haiti represented the limits of presidential powers to curb media impact. When the press can get to the war zone and report on its own without military assistance, presidents have little opportunity to restrict press coverage. And since the White House had been trying for weeks to coerce Haiti's military to leave power by threatening a U.S. invasion, the press had had plenty of time to set up camp in Haiti. By the scheduled day of the invasion, the press corps in Haiti was hundreds strong, armed with even more advanced technologies than had been available in the Persian Gulf. Television crews, in particular, were prepared to film and transmit the sound and fury of combat in living color, with the potential for live coverage of the invasion as it unfolded.[24] Journalists were camped out anywhere the U.S. military might land. The quintessential evidence of how close the press was to the story was Dan Rather's extended interview with General Raoul Cedras, Haiti's top military leader, which took place the same night that Clinton issued his ultimatum on national television. And when U.S. military units arrived as peacekeepers rather than invaders, they were met by scores of television cameras and reporters. As one officer noted, "Then, when we landed over here, I saw a bunch of press, which was good. I assumed if the press was here, then the enemy probably wasn't."[25]

Facing such a media onslaught, the Clinton White House was unable to take advantage of press restrictions in the way that Reagan and Bush had done. This did not stop the White House from trying to limit what the public saw of the invasion, however. First, the Pentagon called up the press pool, despite its redundancy in light of the media hordes in Haiti already.[26] The most likely use of the press pool would have been to justify not giving any assistance or access to U.S. military units to journalists operating unilaterally in Haiti, as was the case during the Panama invasion. Second, the White House, finding itself unable but clearly desiring to restrict television coverage of the opening scenes from the invasion, called the major networks to implore them to observe a television blackout for the first six to eight hours of the operation. In addition, the White House sought to get an agreement from the networks to abide by a set of reporting guidelines that would prohibit broadcasts showing troops movements or revealing their locations as they landed in Haiti. The networks, although agreeing not to report anything that would endanger the lives of soldiers, refused to blackout coverage. The Pentagon, perhaps in a fit of pique, told news organizations that the military could not be responsible for the danger to camera crews perched atop hotels and other tall buildings if they were mistaken for enemy troops with guns.[27]

Haiti illustrates the circumstances under which a president may lose control over press access to the battlefield and his influence over press coverage. In fact, Haiti probably lies near the extreme end of scenarios in which control is beyond the White House. Clinton had almost nothing going for him. The media had no trouble gaining access to Haiti or setting themselves up to cover the invasion from advantageous locations. The long forewarning gave the media time to send in its troops and, just as importantly, the equipment that would allow it to send back reports from the invasion without military assistance or interference. In addition, the long lead time to the invasion allowed plenty of time for critics of Clinton foreign policy to make themselves heard. Because Clinton did not enjoy the rally effect of public opinion that others had done after launching invasions, he did not enjoy the patriotic and White House-dominated press coverage featured in Grenada or Panama. Whether Clinton might have regained some measure of control once an invasion had actually begun is another matter. Certainly the press would have had to turn to the Pentagon and White House for some information and for comment, but with so many journalists already in Haiti, Clinton's ability to set the tone for wartime coverage would have been very slight at best.

Finally, the Haiti case illustrates that despite the almost routine success of the White House in the cases studied in previous chapters, predicting the outcome of the government/press struggle is a dangerous and foolish game. The best that can be done is to outline the conditions under which presidents will have an easier or harder time plying their media strategies. Without knowing where future conflicts will take place and under what circumstances, we must conclude assured only that the White House will make every effort to employ press restrictions and complement them with heavy doses of public relations. We must then wait to see whether in the future the press will succeed in evading its restrictions and providing an independent view of events, and whether presidents will be able to maintain control if America's opponents develop equally sophisticated media strategies.

ENDNOTES

1. Michael Deaver, with Mickey Herskowitz, *Behind the Scenes* (New York: William and Morrow, 1987), p. 147.
2. See, for example, Robert E. Gilbert, "President versus Congress: The Struggle for Public Attention," *Congress and the Presidency*, Vol. 16, No. 2, Autumn 1989, pp. 83-102; Michael Grossman and Martha Kumar, *Portraying the President* (Baltimore: Johns Hopkins University Press, 1982).
3. On the "rally effect" and its consequences, see Mueller, *War, Presidents, and Public Opinion*; Brody, from *Taken by Storm.*
4. John Mueller, *Policy and Opinion in the Gulf War* (Chicago: University of Chicago Press, 1994).
5. This argument follows Richard Neustadt's line of argument in *Presidential Power and the Modern Presidents: The Politics of Leadership from Roosevelt to Reagan* (New York: Free Press, 1990).
6. For a more detailed description and review of the three theories see A. Trevor Thrall, "Competing Images of the Press," delivered at the 1995 Annual Meeting of the American Political Science Association.
7. Robert S. Lichter, "The Instant Reply War," pp. 224-230 in Hedrick Smith, ed., *The Media and the Gulf War: The Press and Democracy in Wartime* (Washington, DC: Seven Locks Press, 1992).
8. This can be seen most clearly in the Grenada case, when follow up reports found a great deal to be desired in the military's performance, but commented little on the highly debatable question of whether the Americans on Grenada were ever in any real danger.
9. On the dominance of beats in providing information for news see Timothy Cook, "Domesticating a Crisis: Washington Newsbeats and Network News after the Iraq Invasion of Kuwait," in Bennett and Paletz, eds., *Taken by Storm* (Chicago: University of Chicago Press, 1994).
10. Cutler, "Foreign Policy on Deadline," *Foreign Policy*, Fall 1984; James F. Hoge, "Media Pervasiveness," *Foreign Affairs*, July/August 1994; for a skeptical academic analysis see Steven Livingston and Todd Eachus, "Humanitarian Crises and Foreign Policy: Somalia and the CNN Effect Reconsidered," *Political Communication*, Vol. 12, 1995.
11. Cutler, "Foreign Policy on Deadline."
12. Hoge, "Media Pervasiveness."

13. Interview with David Gergen by Richard Valeriani in "Talking Back to the Tube," *Columbia Journalism Review*, March/April 1991.
14. Cutler, "Foreign Policy on Deadline."
15. Aukofer and Lawrence, *America's Team, The Odd Couple*; Janet Sharkey, *Under Fire: US Military Restrictions on the Media from Grenada to the Persian Gulf* (Washington, DC: Center for Public Integrity, 1991); Richard Halloran, "Soldiers and Scribblers Revisited: Working with the Media," *Parameters*, Spring 1991, pp. 10-20.
16. Walter Cronkite, "What Is There to Hide?" in Micah L. Sifry and Christopher Cerf, eds., *The Gulf War Reader* (New York: Times Books, 1991), pp. 381-384.
17. Peter Braestrup, "Background Paper," in *Battle Lines: Report of the Twentieth Century Fund Task Force on the Military and the Media* (New York: Priority Press Publications, 1985), pp. 27-46; Philip Knightley, *The First Casualty* (New York: Harvest, 1975), pp. 270-302.
18. Major General Charles W. McClain, Jr. and Major Garry D. Levin, "Public Affairs in America's 21st Century Army," *Military Review*, November 1994, pp. 6-15.
19. The vanishing likelihood of any real change became evident with the adoption eight months after Desert Storm of "new" principles of wartime press coverage. In fact the new principles looked a lot like the old principles that had been routinely ignored by the White House over the last decade. See "DoD Adopts Rules for Combat Coverage," *Marine Corps Gazette*, July 1992, p. 6; also Lt. Colonel Richard F. Machamer, Jr., "Avoiding a Military-Media War in the Next Armed Conflict," *Military Review*, April 1993, pp. 43-54.
20. Douglas Jehl, "Clinton Addresses Nation on Threat to Invade Haiti; Tells Dictators to Get Out," *New York Times*, September 16, 1994.
21. R. W. Apple, Jr., "Preaching to Skeptics," *New York Times*, September 16, 1994; Katharine Q. Seelye, "Few Opinions, Pro or Con, Seem to Change in Congress," *New York Times*, September 16, 1994.
22. Douglas Jehl, "Haiti's Military Leaders Agree to Resign; Clinton Halts Assault, Recalls 61 Planes," *New York Times*, September 19, 1994.
23. "Transcript of Clinton Television Address," *New York Times*, September 19, 1994.
24. Bill Carter, "TV Ready for Battle, with High-Tech Access," *New York Times*, September 18, 1994.
25. John Tierney, "'The Press Was Here,' But Not The Enemy," *New York Times*, September 20, 1994.
26. Debra Gersh, "Press Pool Ready to Go," *Editor and Publisher*, September 26, 1994. A small improvement was that it appeared that this time the pool might actually make it to the opening skirmishes in a conflict in Haiti.

27. (AP) "TV Networks Say Coverage Would Not Endanger Troops," *New York Times*, September 19, 1994; the networks did in fact manage not to report the fact that the invasion had begun when planes took off from Fort Bragg; Bill Carter, "Networks Held Back News That Invasion Had Begun," *New York Times*, September 20, 1994.

Author Index

C

D

Subject Index

Printed in the United States
56532LVS00003B/160-237

9 781572 732476